Soldier Boy takes you into the world of the new recruit and allows you to experience first hand – in authentic, often coarse, GI language – what soldiers think about ... Feel the loneliness and the camaraderie, the frustration and the exhilaration of being a soldier ... A journey of self-discovery, which takes a boy along a treacherous, fearful, often painful path – and spits out a man at the other end. ... Bazzett has done a marvelous job of resurrecting the ASA. Waves of memories came flooding back to me – of Devens, barracks life, the bars, the pranks and the practical jokes, but most of all of the eclectic hard-working group of dedicated people who truly loved the mission ... I will highly recommend this book to any and every old ASA buddy I can track down, as well as to anyone who simply wants to know how a boy turns into a man. If you served, you will live it all over again. If you didn't, here's what it was like. A great read!

– *LTC Chuck Squires, US Army (ret.),*
   former Defense Attache, US Embassy Bishkek, Kyrgyzstan
   – and former ASA ditty-bopper.

SoldierBoy

SoldierBoy

At Play in the ASA

Timothy James Bazzett

RATHOLE BOOKS

SOLDIER BOY

Published by Rathole Books
Reed City, Michigan
www.ratholebooks.com

Publisher's Cataloging-in-Publication Data

    Bazzett, Timothy James.

        SoldierBoy : at play in the ASA / Timothy James Bazzett. – 2nd ed. –
        Reed City, MI : Rathole Books, 2008.

        p. ; cm.
        ISBN: 0-9771119-1-1
        ISBN-13: 978-0-9771119-1-6

            1. Bazzett, Timothy James. 2. United States. Army – Military life –
            Anecdotes. 3. United States – Armed Forces – Anecdotes.
            4. Soldiers – United States – Anecdotes. 5. Veterans – United States –
            Biography. I. Title. II. Soldier boy.

            U766 .B39 2005   2005930346
            355.1/00973--dc22   0508

Printed in the United States of America
10 9 8 7 6 5 4 3

Cover and interior design by Scott Bazzett
Second Edition: March 2008
Second Paperback Edition: March 2008

To order additional copies send check or money order for $16.00 made payable to TJ Bazzett to:

TJ Bazzett
330 West Todd Avenue
Reed City, MI 49677

(Michigan residents add 6% sales tax)

For more information, visit us online at:
www.ratholebooks.com

Blessed are the peacemakers,
for they shall be called sons of God.

– Matthew, 5:9

Dearest comrades, all is over and long gone,
But love is not over – and what love, O comrades!

– Walt Whitman, "Ashes of Soldiers"

In loving memory of
Richard Ellis Bazzett
1938 - 2001
(Spec 5, USASA, 1961-1965)

And for all my old army buddies,
especially Joe,
who was with me through it all.

INTRODUCTION

Tim asked me if I would write an introduction to this, his second book. He and his son, Scott, thought it might "soften" the "rawness" of what he has so honestly written. Soften it possibly for older readers – like me? – who might be shocked by the four-letter words he employs so lavishly, and the startlingly frank accounts of sexual experience.

I am his 88 year-old mother. I have read the advance proof copy of *Soldier Boy*. If anyone should be shocked or turned off by it, I would be the one. But I wasn't. I recognize it as a painfully honest account of what happened to one young soldier during his three years in the army. And I think it may very well be typical of many, many soldier boys who were suddenly thrust from a comfortable home life into a completely different and altogether alien environment. Since Tim was the fourth of five boys, it was no doubt easier for him to adjust to strictly regimented routines than for "only" sons. But even so, he seemed to go off with such a jaunty air: "I'll show Dad. I won't go to college and I won't get a job either. I'll join the army!" I remember him telling us much later, "After a week at Fort Leonard Wood, I thought, 'What the hell am I DOing here?'"

His dad and I knew of course where he was. He did write home. But most of his experiences I just now learned from reading the book. They were not things a boy or young man talks about to his mother – "Don't tell Mom" things.

Concerning the four-letter words he uses the most, it's not

i

pleasant to hear. But I understand that he is using the language to show the way boys learn to talk among themselves to show (they think) how grown-up they are. It's a bit like their smoking to try to appear like "the Marlboro man" or other similar TV role models.

I was saddened when I read in *Reed City Boy* about Tim's difficulty with coming of age sexually. I wished that he could have been enlightened about what was happening to him, by his dad, or someone – anyone. That would have made his growing up easier. But he didn't even ask anyone, and was so alone in that. ... For my daughter there was at least *Marjorie May's Twelfth Birthday*, a small pamphlet published by Kotex, although I'm not sure even that did much for girls in the way of real information. I know of no such coming-of-age book for boys.

With sex such an open subject now, it may be hard to believe how innocent, or ignorant, many people were forty years ago. No wonder Dr. David Reuben's book, *Everything You Always Wanted to Know about Sex * but were afraid to ask*, was such a hot seller. Originally published in 1969, our copy was from the July 1970 seventeenth printing. I'm not sure whether Dad and I bought it, and later Tim borrowed it, or Tim bought it and loaned it to us. Written in the flyleaf is:

Ellis E. Bazzett
Reed City
T.J. Bazzett.

It's a bit dog-eared, so I doubt if our two youngest were quite so ignorant or innocent at 18.

But still, sex was something you just didn't talk about back then. Who would believe that Tim's dad and I "went together" for four years – my last three years of college and one year of teaching – and were still virgins when we married? But it was so – and well worth the waiting for such a truly wondrous and loving experience that endured for us for all of our 52 years together. Granted, there weren't so many opportunities or situations then in ordinary dating for more than "petting". For instance, the car Ellis had some of those years was a cute little 1930s Ford Roadster with a rumble seat. In double dating, there certainly wasn't much room to maneuver in the open-air rumble seat, or in the slightly more comfy front seat. And, except for the first few months of our dating, there was a distance of over a hundred miles between us. And a hundred miles seemed a lot longer back then than it does now.

Why do I dwell on the accounts of sex in this book? When Tim had a "Meet the Author" and book-signing at the local library for *Reed City Boy* earlier this month, after his presentation and reading, he took questions from the audience. One question by an obviously flustered lady dwelt on hints and innuendoes and was not coming to any obvious point. Tim finally interrupted her and asked, "Are you asking about the sex?" Of course, it turned out she was – and this broke the ice and it became plain that everyone was very interested in that part of the book. And so I expect it will be with *Soldier Boy*.

Tim has been very pleased to re-connect with many of the very real people in this book, by e-mail and by phone. Many people from all over Michigan and also from dozens of other states contacted him after reading *Reed City Boy*. And I believe this new book will appeal to an even wider reading audience – to anyone who went through the military experience and, in the process, established lifelong friendships.

Unlike his oldest brother, Richard, who went into the army at age 23, served three and a half years, then was discharged in Germany and never really came home again, Tim did come back home. He used the GI Bill to go to Ferris (and later CMU) and fit in very well again in our family life for a couple more years before striking off on his own. I don't think he was scarred at all by army life. Like many in his age group, he saw no combat. But he did learn, while he was in Turkey, how frightening it is to be hated, not because of who he was, but because of what he represented – a soldier of a wealthier foreign country, a U.S. soldier. I would guess that in the same way his year in the seminary instilled in him good study habits and sound moral values, so did his army years, in spite of all the drinking and carousing, give him a more mature outlook on life. Tim was always a good son, and he became a good husband and father, and today, as he always did, he still gets "fun out of life."

Daisy C. Bazzett
November 29, 2004
Reed City, Michigan

FOREWORD

I didn't serve in Viet Nam and I never saw combat, so this is not a "war story" in a literal sense. But anyone who has ever served in the military has his own "war stories" to tell. Every time a few old army buddies get together, for whatever reason, these "war stories" get dusted off, polished up and trotted out again for re-telling. We never get tired of hearing them – or telling them. Our wives probably get sick of hearing them, and maybe so do our kids. But to us these stories are special, and as we grow older, they become even more precious.

The stories and memories I've put down here are from forty years ago. There are some pictures too. As *Soldier Boy* was taking shape I probably spent hours studying these old photos. My *God!* We were so *young!* Is it really possible that boys like these were entrusted with the mission of protecting our country and preserving the American way of life? What an awesome and terrible responsibility to lay across such young shoulders!

That is what I think now as I look again at those faces from forty years ago. But at the time, in those turbulent years that were the sixties, we seldom felt the weight of that responsibility, because we were not alone. We were with friends. We were together. We probably didn't realize it at the time, but the bonds of friendship forged during those few brief years would be the strongest we would ever know in our lifetimes.

"Old army buddy" is a phrase that has received more than its share of derision and ridicule. But those of us who have been there know that there really is no friend like that "old army buddy." I've had my share of good friends in my life, but when pressed to name *best* friends, the names that immediately and spontaneously pop into my grey-haired head are *Joe, Al, Norm, Tom.* Most of these guys I have seen only rarely or not at all in the last forty years. Yet I still think of them as my best friends.

Why do you suppose that is?

I think it's because of all the stuff we went through together. We shared rooms. We smelled each other's farts and feet and B.O. We stood inspections together. We sat rack together. We got drunk and were hung over together. We swapped stories and told lies and laughed a lot. We were scared together in late November 1963. We got pissed off at each other and then got over it. We talked about girls and women and sex – a *lot.* But we didn't really know much about anything. We were too *new.* We were still learning, still *becoming.* We grew up together.

One of the things that most united us and cemented our friendship was the army itself. We hated it. And we loved it. Well, maybe we didn't *love* the *army,* but we shared a common pride in the work that we did. We joked about it a lot, but we all knew that what we were doing was important, and we never shirked that responsibility.

I may be wrong, but I don't think there have been many memoirs written about the Army Security Agency. That's because ASA personnel are prohibited from talking or writing about the specifics of their jobs. Our work was mostly classified. We respected that rule then and I still respect it today. So there is almost nothing recorded here about our work, about our mission. Instead this book is about the guys who worked that mission, and how they played just as hard as they worked.

I've often wished I could write a great novel about those days, but I don't know if my writing skills would be adequate to the task. But if you want to read a really ripping good work of fiction about the ASA, then pick up a copy of James Crumley's *One to Count Cadence* (Random House, 1969). It's one hell of a great book, and a "war story" to boot, since the narrative includes a bloody clandestine ASA operation in Viet Nam in 1962, before most Americans even knew where Viet Nam was. I don't know if the book was ever a best seller, but it does have a devoted cult following, and I suspect that many of its readers are ex-ASA-ers.

My three years in the ASA were probably like a lot of guys' experiences. They were fun, frustrating, frightening, exhilarating, exciting, boring, exasperating – educational even. While I was writing this book I re-connected with a lot of the guys you'll meet in these pages, most of them gone grey or balding by now. Our memories aren't all the same, but for the most part, in one way or another, almost all of these men agree that those years were indeed some of the best years of their lives.

As I was writing *Soldier Boy*, which is a sequel to my first book of memoirs, I was casting about for a suitable title. I tried on and discarded several possibilities, including *Army Daze*, *Prodigal Soldier* and *Cold War Warrior*. I almost settled on *Reed City Boy II: The Lost Years*, but as the memories continued to flow from my pen I realized that that title wouldn't work either, because those years were never lost at all. They've been with me all along and are an important part of who I am – of who I *became*.

My mother, who at 88 is still a voracious and discerning reader and perhaps my staunchest supporter, finally suggested the title you are holding now. At first I rejected it, probably because I was unable to separate it in my mind from the song of the same name by the Shirelles, with all its sappy intimations of first love and teenage promises of constancy and fidelity. (But it *is* a great song, nevertheless.) However, as I wrote about our youthful escapades and recalled our dreams and aspirations and our fears and frustrations, and as I continued to to study the old pictures, I realized what *boys* we had still been back then. And we were soldiers too. We began as boys, and somehow the army managed to make us into men. But for one all-too-brief and shining moment in time we were, all of us, Soldier Boys.

Thanks, Mom.

Timothy James Bazzett
July 10, 2004
Reed City, Michigan

PART I

BCT: FORT LEONARD WOOD, MO

"Turn around, bend over, and spread your cheeks," intoned the anonymous white-coated doctor as he walked slowly down the line of naked potential recruits representing every body type from endo- to ectomorph. Being rather tall and skinny, I fell somewhere toward the ecto end of the body-type spectrum. I was eighteen years old, about 170 pounds and stood somewhere around six feet four, and I was nervous as hell about all this, but I assumed the position remembered from a few previous high school sports physicals. Only this time there was no wise-ass locker room wag around who was spreading the cheeks of his face to get a laugh.

Fort Leonard Wood front gate.

No, there's something about being naked in a roomful of strangers that makes you a little nervous. It's not that a row of bare naked men doesn't offer ample opportunity for laughs, because there were plenty of funny-looking bodies there. The fact was, I was just beginning to grasp the enormity of what I was embarking on.

It was late September, 1962. I had joined the Army on a delayed entry program a few months previously on a capricious whim. I had graduated from Reed City High School with a respectable academic record, but I had never quite gotten around to filling out any college applications, even though my parents kept reminding me I'd better get cracking on college plans or else I'd better find a full-time job. But I was just too full of myself that last year of high school, and having too much fun to think seriously about my future. So, much to my parents' dismay, I had joined the Army.

It hadn't seemed like such a bad idea at the time. I just didn't feel I could endure any more formal education right then. I'd had enough of that, slogging through the last few years of high school, sitting through hour after hour of boring and seemingly pointless lectures and lessons in algebra, geometry, civics, chemistry, physics, and all the other required courses of the college prep curriculum. And the local employment opportunities seemed pretty limited too in a town of only 2,500 where the major employers were Miller Industries, Kel-Reed, or the Reed City Tool and Die, where my best friend, Keith Eichenberg, had already begun punching the clock as soon as he graduated. There were other manufacturing or assembly line jobs in nearby Big Rapids, but none of them seemed very attractive to me. So the other logical option was the military. Plenty of other Reed City graduates had opted for enlistment in the past, and it hadn't hurt them. The military offered its usual attraction of travel, training, new faces and places. At the time I enlisted, the irreverent parody of the Army Recruitment spiel had yet to come into vogue:

JOIN THE ARMY. TRAVEL TO FOREIGN COUNTRIES,
MEET INTERESTING NEW PEOPLE, AND KILL THEM.

No, that came after Viet Nam took over the headlines. I think it was probably coined by the war protesters. This was before all that. Viet Nam was still only a brief occasional blurb in the back pages of the international news section. The Camelot of John F.

Kennedy's new administration was still taking shape and there was a wind of exhilarating optimism blowing.

The military draft was still a fact of life in 1962. Every male citizen was required to register for the draft upon reaching the age of 18. About a year previously, my oldest brother, Rich, had enlisted rather than be drafted. He had already been notified to report for his induction physical, so he knew it was coming. And once you were drafted, you had no say in what the military did with you; you were cannon fodder. Rich knew this, so he promptly enlisted in the Army Security Agency with a guarantee of training in electronics repair. At the time, it seemed to him like a better idea than digging foxholes or lugging a mortar base plate around in the mud. He had been an avid reader of *Popular Mechanics* and *Popular Science* througout his youth, so he seemed reasonably happy with the deal the Army had made him – as happy as Rich *could* seem, given his generally dour and pessimistic outlook on life.

So there was my big brother, the same one who used to play army with my brothers and me in the Holdenville sandpits – a shining example. I had no set goals or immediate aspirations other than avoiding college and the world of work. It wasn't patriotism or a burning desire to make the world a better or safer place to live. It was boredom. It was a temporary diversion. It was a smart-ass answer to my dad's constant refrain: "If you don't go to college, you'll have to get a job." I'd show him. I wouldn't do either. I'd join the Army.

So here I was, shivering and scared, bent over, ass in the air, cheeks spread for inspection by this guy in a white coat that I'd never seen before in my life and who couldn't have cared less if I already had incipient "lapelial hemorrhoids". He just wrote it down. "Lapel-ial"– is that really a word? Years later, I saw it there in my medical records, but I can't find that form of the word in a dictionary. Is it some esoteric or obscure medical term, or was this white-coat just feeling bored that day. so he decided to fancy up my asshole with "lapels," put my anus in a white sport coat and tie, with perhaps even a pink carnation? (Would Marty Robbins have approved?) I suppose if I had to spend all day looking up stranger's asses, I might get a bit fanciful in my notes as well. "La-peel-i-al..." Hmm ...

3

A little further down the line, another Reed City boy, Lynn Pontz, was suffering the same indignities (although I don't know if *his* asshole was as dressed up as mine was). We had ended up here at the Fort Wayne Recruiting Center in Detroit as an unofficial part of what the Army called the "buddy system." Under this agreement two or more friends could enlist at the same time and receive a guarantee that they would stay together through basic training, and sometimes even subsequent advanced individual training (AIT). Of course, this guarantee could easily be voided if one or more party was unable to successfully complete their training in the alotted time. Our buddy system arrangement was more coincidence than by plan. We just happened to have enlisted about the same time, so I'm calling it unofficial. Lynn and I had gone to RCHS together, and even played on the same basketball team for a few years, but we'd never really been "buddies". But group nakedness *does* breed a certain familiarity, so although I won't say our friendship exactly blossomed, since misery loves company, we did become considerably more civil to each other over the next few months than we had ever been before.

That induction physical was the first of many group indignities visited on new recruits that I suspect are specifically designed to humiliate and to destroy individuality. Anyone who has ever gone through the process remembers the "bend over and spread'em" and the "turn your head and cough" embarrassments, but I also remember having an embarrassing experience with the hearing test portion of the physical.

I was directed into a long narrow room where a medic corporal was seated on a stool by the door with a clipboard. Snatching my forms from me, he motioned me toward a stool at the far end of the room. On the stool was a set of headphones that were jacked into a plug on the wall. Fitting the headsets over my ear, I sat down on the stool and waited while the corporal scribbled something on my physical forms. Then he looked up at me with a bemused expression on his face, and said something to me, which I couldn't hear because of the headsets over my ears. Thinking the test was beginning, I looked down in concentration and pressed the phones tighter on my ears and strained to hear whatever I was supposed to hear. Nothing. I heard nothing. Beginning to perspire, I looked up again and saw the corporal shaking his head disgustedly. I said, "I

4

don't hear anything." The corporal looked at the floor, shook his head again, and then suddenly screamed at me, "You stupid fucking *moron!* Take off the headset!" Utterly confused, I quickly complied. Now looking completely disgusted, the corporal considered me carefully, then said in a very soft voice, "Can you hear me?" I managed to stutter out a "Y-yes," to which he yelled, "Then get the fuck outa here!" I had passed the hearing test.

Somehow I managed to get through that day – one of the longest days of my short life. I survived the physical and was proclaimed fit. I got through a battery of written aptitude and intelligence tests. I also underwent a rigorous psychological screening which went something like this.

Psychologist: "Do you like girls?"

I replied, "Umm, yeah?"

"OK, get out. NEXT!"

Obviously standards for military service were extremely rigorous and exacting in those days.

Everyone in our group of probably close to a hundred that were being processed that day had been led to believe that we would be shipped to Fort Knox, Kentucky, for our basic training. Once all the prodding, poking, testing and other humiliations had been completed, we all spent an inordinate amount of time being shuffled from one area to another within the vast drafty confines of the center as we were gradually introduced to one of the army's constants: "Hurry up and wait." Finally names began to be called and recruits were presented with official printed orders for travel and assignment to Fort Knox. There didn't seem to be any obvious method as to whose names were called out first or last. But gradually the vast room where we had all ended up began to empty out until it was quite late in the day and there were just six of us left without orders, including Lynn and me. Lynn and I had both enlisted for the Army Security Agency, like my brother Rich had earlier. When we started talking with the other four guys, we learned they were ASA too. We were all finally told by another bored-looking corporal that we weren't going to Fort Knox. ASA recruits went to Fort Leonard Wood, Missouri, for their basic training, and it was too late in the day to arrange transport for us. Furthermore, it was a Friday night, and all the processing personnel at the center were already starting their weekend. They'd take care of us on Monday. We were told we could have vouchers for a hotel there in Detroit or we could have travel vouchers to return home and come back Monday morning.

It seemed like a kind of reprieve at the time. After being yelled at, humiliated, bullied, and demoralized all day, we were being given an unexpected opportunity to return to the loving bosoms of our family. I found out I couldn't get a bus home until early the next morning. When I came back and explained this to a sergeant, he showed me into another building, which was used as a transient barracks for recruits and showed me into a large open bay room filled with double-tiered steel bunk beds. It was too late in the day to get any linens, but the sergeant found me a couple of brown wool army blankets and a blue and white striped pillow and told me to pick a bunk, then left me to my own devices. There were a few other stranded recruits who had already claimed bunks here and there throughout the room, but it was late, and I was too exhausted to be sociable. I found an empty lower bunk near a window that wouldn't open; it was painted shut. Nevertheless, I unrolled the mattress, which was filthy and spotted with numerous stains of piss, semen, vomit and other things I preferred not to think about. I spread one blanket over the mattress, took off my shoes and lay down and pulled the other blanket over myself. There was a light still on at the far end of the room where a couple of guys were playing cards, but I didn't care. I was pooped. It had been a long, traumatic day, but tomorrow I would get back home again and see my family, at least for a short visit. I slept.

My unscheduled last visit home wasn't that simple. I caught an early bus out of Detroit and was back in Reed City just before noon, and walked home up Church Street. That part was easy. But when I got to our house, it was all locked up tight and no one was around. Of course. It was Saturday, and the family had gone to our cottage out on Indian Lake, about twelve miles northeast of town. There was no phone at the cabin, so I couldn't call them. Deflated, I dispiritedly circled the house and found an unlocked window in a downstairs bedroom of our walkout basement, took off the screen and crawled through. I went upstairs to the kitchen and fixed myself a sandwich with a glass of milk, and sat down at the table and considered my situation. I'd slept poorly the night before, being in a strange bed in an unfamiliar setting, surrounded by the city noises of downtown Detroit. I'd spent four or five hours on a bus to get home to see my folks again, and now no one was here. Back then, I don't think anyone said things like, *Bummer,* or *This really SUCKS*, but if they had, I would have freely employed both expressions. I did utter a few dispirited *shits*, and even a couple *fuck*s, a word I had never used before, but that I had heard so many times the previous day, I figured maybe I'd better practice using it myself or I'd never fit in. It didn't taste very good coming out of my mouth. I was more comfortable with shit. There had always been plenty of shit around Grandpa Bazzett's farm next door. I'd done my share of shoveling it, hauling it, and spreading it. But fuck was a kind of novelty, so I tried shouting it, right there in Mom's new dining room. *FUCK!!!* It felt a bit sacrilegious, but I felt a little better, too. Finally, I said to myself, *What the hell*, went and washed up a bit, and walked back downtown to look around. I stopped in at the A&P store where I'd stocked shelves and bagged groceries part time for the past year. I shot the shit briefly with Floss Earnest and Brandy Mellberg, who were surprised to see me, as they knew I'd left for the Army. I explained the foul-up and they were politely interested, but I learned something that day visiting with them and a few other friends I ran into. Once you've announced to people that you're leaving and publicized your departure date, don't come back again, because they've already written you off – you're no longer relevant. You're already gone, even if you suddenly turn up again. You've already been tuned out, so you might as well stay gone.

Suffice it to say that it was a very unsatisfying and ultimately an extremely depressing re-visit home. Even though I did manage to get word to Mom and Dad out at the lake that I was back and they came home to be with me, the next day I took a last look at Reed City and was back on the bus to Detroit again.

I got back to Detroit on Sunday evening and met up with the other ASA recruits, some of whom had spent the weekend at a hotel there and had a fine time. There were six of us. Dick Kuhn and Doug Hura were high school buddies from Grosse Ile, an affluent Detroit suburb. Rick Smeltzer was from Beulah, a town in northern Michigan, just southwest of Traverse City. One other fellow whose name I can't remember was from Three Rivers in the southwestern part of the state. Lynn Pontz, the other Reed City boy, had formed an alliance over the weekend with Rick. All in all, it was a pretty friendly group, and we spent the evening swapping stories and lies, as guys will do when thrust together in an unfamiliar setting.

Doug and Dick were already a pretty solid unit, so to speak, having been friends for years. They formed a kind of Laurel and Hardy team. Dick was the more serious, level-headed of the two, and, like Oliver Hardy, slightly rotund. He wore horn-rimmed glasses and was quite well-read and very articulate. Doug was more the "let's-do-something-crazy" type, with a crew-cut and an infectious beavery sort of grin that was pretty hard to resist. Without Dick's steadying influence, he would undoubtedly have been embroiled in one fine mess after another. Both had already attended at least a year of college. Doug had been a student at Ferris Institute in Big Rapids, which is just south of Reed City. I can't remember what college Dick had attended, but it was either there or in high school that he had received some ROTC or Junior ROTC training, so he became the logical choice for group leader of our small band of new brothers-in-arms.

Monday morning, after waiting around for the requisite three to four hours, we were finally issued our travel vouchers and assignment orders to Ft. Leonard Wood. Dick Kuhn was charged with the responsibility of getting the six of us there. We were loaded into an army olive drab van and taken to the railroad station where we boarded a pullman car bound for St. Louis.

I don't remember much about the train ride, except that it seemed like it would never end, as it made numerous stops along the way in towns and cities we were hard-pressed to identify most of the time. Railroad yards look pretty much the same no matter what state or city you're in, so if we didn't happen to see the city limits or depot sign when we slowed down or pulled into a station, it was anybody's guess where we were. The only other time I had ever been on a train was in seventh grade at St. Philip's school when we rode a train from Baldwin to Grand Rapids to attend the Shrine Circus. So although this long trip *should* have been a novelty, it wore off quickly. Boredom took over after the first few hours. I think one of the guys may have brought along a bottle of whiskey to nip on and passed it around to all of us, but even that didn't help much. I remember that I read and dozed a lot during the day, and spent a restless, mostly wakeful night in my berth. We all smoked and shared our cigarettes during the long day's journey into night... and back into the day, etc. Shit, it was a very *long* trip, OK? And we were all probably a bit nervous about what this whole army thing was going to be like, so we spent a lot of time just thinking our own thoughts.

When we got to St. Louis, we boarded an army bus that was waiting for us. There were recruits from other states on the bus, too, mainly from Illinois and Missouri. The bus was just about full for the trip to Leonard Wood, a few hours southwest of St. Louis.

Fort Leonard Wood, Missouri – aka "Fort Lost-in-the-Woods, Misery" – is mostly surrounded by a portion of the Mark Twain National Forest. A few nearby towns have names like Big Piney, Duke, Flat and Devil's Elbow. That probably should have told us something about the cultural heritage of the area, if we'd known any of this information. The truth was, we felt lost in the woods, indeed.

From the moment we raw recruits disembarked from that bus, life as we had known it– our comfortable, pampered, civilian life – was over. There was always someone screaming or cursing (or both) at us to get in line, form up or to *SHUT THE FUCK UP*!

Army life. Where to begin. I should probably state for the record that from the very outset, as soon as I set foot on the soil of Fort Leonard Wood, I spent most of my waking hours in a state of quaking absolute terror of fucking up. There's that word again, and there's no point in apologizing for it, or I'd be spending all my time apologizing. I know that today's army is a kinder, gentler, and eminently more civil organization and profanity is actively discouraged. But this was 1962. Political correctness had not yet been invented and civility had no place in the world of BCT, or Basic Combat Training. If you didn't quickly learn to understand and speak profanities, then you might as well have been a deaf-mute. So, yeah, the f-word will crop up occasionally, and it is surprising how quickly this good Catholic boy from Reed City picked up on the lingua franca of his new home.

My first home at FLW was a reception camp. This was a kind of processing pen for new arrivals. We were assigned to a barracks where we all found ourselves bunks and tried to establish small islands of peace and sanity. But first we were all herded into a large lecture hall where we filled out endless reams of paperwork,

9

enough that we soon knew our newly-assigned service numbers by heart, since they had to be affixed to every piece of paper we completed. I was an "RA" and I can still remember my number over forty years later. The RA stood for Regular Army, signifying an enlistee. Some of the guys were US's, meaning they were draftees, and only had a two-year service obligation. (We RA's liked to tell them that US stood for Unbelievably Simple or Ugly Shit.) RA's were three- or four-year men. The modern military simply uses social security numbers as service numbers, simplifying matters somewhat, I suppose, although with the current problems with identity theft, I'm not sure if it's entirely wise.

For the first few days at reception camp, we were still in the same civilian clothing we had been in since we left Detroit, or whatever recruiting centers the other men came from. Only a few guys had had enough sense or foresight to bring changes of clothing, or at least some extra underwear. Most of the men were looking pretty rumpled and seedy after four or five days in the same outfits, and quite a few were smelling pretty rank, too. There weren't any washing machines in the barracks, so even after taking showers, there were no clean clothes to put on, although a few guys washed out their shorts in the sinks. but I remember a few guys who had some really serious racing stripes in their shorts that got really rank. Part of this was just unavoidable, as the sudden change from a civilian to a a military diet could really play havoc with your bowels. People reacted differently to this. Some of the guys complained they hadn't shit in days. Others were afflicted with galloping diarrhea – hence the aforementioned skid-marks in their shorts.

You might ask how was it that I noticed the condition of other guys' shorts. Was I some kind of twisted pervert peeping Tom, or what? It's a fair question.

Let me tell you about the toilet facilities at the reception camp– and later in our barracks, too. The bathrooms, or "latrines," in army parlance, offered absolutely NO privacy. Not even for that most private of bodily functions. It was a community type bathroom situated on one end of the barracks. You stepped down a couple of steps into the latrine and were facing a row of eight or ten sinks and mirrors on the opposite wall. On the other wall, facing the sinks was a long trough-like urinal, probably several feet long. Along a third wall was the entrance to the showers, which was also pretty public– just a dozen or so shower heads, projecting out of the walls on both sides with floor drains in the middle. Along the same wall as the shower entrance was a row of seven or eight toilets, or "commodes," as our platoon sergeant later so genteelly referred to them. Just toilets. No stalls, walls, or partitions. No doors, partial, swinging, or otherwise. Just a row of white crappers with black enamel open-ended seats. There was nothing accommodating about these commodes. They were purely functional, and stood right out in the open in a row with no more than a foot separating them.

So, yeah, anyone could see if you had racing stripes in your undershorts. There they were crumpled around your ankles in plain sight, and in some cases, "stinking to high heav-en," just like that "Dead Skunk in the Middle of the Road." (Remember London Wainwright III and his highway anthem?)

Like I said, some of the guys, the ones with shy bowels, didn't shit for a week or more. Boy, were they stopped up, gassy, and uncomfortable. Luckily, I wasn't one of them.

I came from a big family of five boys and one girl and I'd shared a two-holer outhouse with my brothers and occasionally even my Dad. This outhouse was situated on a rise out behind our Indian Lake cabin. My brothers and I all tried *not* to share the outhouse with Dad at night. One, because his shit *really* stank! And two, because Dad liked to sit on balmy summer evenings with the privy door wide open so he could look out at the moonlight on the lake in front of the cottage. And he wasn't above greeting a neighbor from this indelicate vantage point if one happened to pass by walking along the lake shore. This actually happened more than once when I was sitting next to him trying to take care of my business as quickly as possible.

"Evenin' Harold (or Elmer or Clarence)," Dad would say, just exuding neighborliness (along with a *ghastly* smell).

"Why, hi there, Ellis. Didn't see you in there," would come the startled reply from the lakeshore. I just wanted to disappear down the hole, I was so mortified.

So having to take a shit in front of a roomful of strangers wasn't the worst thing that could happen as far as I was concerned. I managed. Truth be told, you got used to it to the point where you would strike up conversations with the guy sitting (shitting) next to you, or down at the end of the row, or exchange sections of old newspapers or magazines to peruse while sitting (shitting).

Of course, there was an unwritten bathroom etiquette, even under these very *un*-private conditions. you *always* left a vacant toilet between shitters if possible. Likewise, while using the urinal you left a decent interval between pissers. Of course, sometimes there was a full house and even these niceties had to be dropped. But we tried to allow some modicum of privacy, especially since so much of our dignity had already been effectively stripped away by these group living conditions.

Even today, I tend to do a slow burn whenever in a public restroom, some stranger shoulders his way right up to the next urinal to me when there is a whole row of several perfectly good, unused urinals extending on down the wall. Doesn't this jerk have any *manners*? Don't they teach bathroom etiquette anywhere anymore? Anyone who has ever done time in the service will understand what I'm talking about.

Fortunately, about three days after our arrival in reception camp, we were marched over to a quartermaster clothing warehouse where we were lined up and issued our clothing and uniforms. This in itself is worth describing, but I wasn't quite sure how to do this until I talked with my oldest son, Jeff, a couple of nights ago on the phone and he was remembering his own experience with clothing issue in the Army. They issued him BDU's (basic duty uniforms) that were obviously too small and not long enough for him (Jeff was a skinny six foot six, and not an easy fit under the best of circumstances). At any rate, he ventured a timid, "Er, I think these are too small," to the clerk who had issued the uniforms. Accommodatingly, the clerk looked at him, then shouted, "NEXT!"

Thanks, Jeff, that was it *exactly*. What happened to you in 1988 was pretty much my own experience in 1962. For the whole three years I was in the army, my wrists and ankles were always cold – sleeves and inseams too short.

In '62, the everyday work uniforms were called "fatigues," a term I always found a bit puzzling. I knew fatigue meant weariness or exhaustion, but why tack the label on a type of clothing? It was the person *wearing* the clothes who was exhausted after a day spent in fatigues. However, Webster's also defines fatigue as "the cause of weariness; labor; toil." So – work clothes.

Our fatigues were plain olive drab green cotton clothes, which did, unfortunately for me, tend to shrink some when laundered. Today's BDUs are mostly camouflage-patterned ("cammies"), either in jungle green or desert tan. But plain army green was the standard color in my day and fatigues were the uniform of the day for most of our time in basic training. The "uniform of the day" was either announced or posted on the barracks bulletin board each day. There was a lesson to be learned in properly observing this UOD to the letter.

MY BCT officially began in early October and lasted through November – a time of year when things could get a little nippy at night, even in south central Missouri. Sometimes the temperatures would drop precipitously into the twenties and thirties overnight and we would awake to frost-covered windows in our barracks – even on the *inside* of the windows. These were old WWII era wooden barracks (more on that later).

The temptation was great – often irresistible – to disregard the posted UOD on frigid mornings like these and put on our (also army-issued) woolen long johns under our fatigues when we got dressed. Those long-handled underwear were so cozy and felt *soooo* good on those cold mornings when we would fall out for morning formation. They still felt pretty good while we would take on our pre-breakfast run through the battalion area. However, as the day wore on and the temperatures rose, these woolies would become distinctly prickly and most uncomfortable. For not only could the fall nights at FLW get chillingly cold, but the days could yield unseasonably hot mercury readings, with temperatures often hitting the high seventies or even the eighties. So later in the training day, those people who had ignored the posted UOD could, and often did, become victims of prickly heat rash and heat exhaustion. And on top of this discomfort they were then also subject to disciplinary action for ignoring the UOD and endangering or damaging government property, namely their own bodies.

Another major problem I had with the army-issue clothing were the boxer shorts. You weren't given a choice in those days of boxers or briefs. (Present day recruits *do* get a choice.) Boxers were standard. I had always been a briefs kind of guy. I had never worn boxers before. Never. *A major problem*? you might ask. *Come ON*, you might say. *It's not THAT big a deal.* Oh, yes it *is*, if you've always worn briefs or jockey shorts. Jockeys support. Jockeys cradle and protect. You and your boys feel a sense of security in jockeys. Not so with boxers. There's no support. None. No cradling or protection, either. As for a sense of security – forget it. Nope, with boxers your boys are left out there to twist in the wind. To bobble, to bounce, to beedle-e-um-bum-bum like the organ grinder swing.

And speaking of organs, that most important of organs of the human body had to be pretty confused too, by the sudden switch from briefs to boxers. After spending virtually his whole life in a snug weather-tight little downstairs room, the poor guy had suddenly been re-assigned to a drafty, poorly-screened side porch. And he kept getting moved from one side porch to the other as I marched or double-timed in formation throughout the long training day.

Those damned boxers were a terrible nuisance. All that marching and running created unavoidable friction, which in turn, caused a most uncomfortable and inconvenient, constant semi-tumescence. And who the hell wants to deal with a bouncing half-hardon while trying to learn close order drill, or the manual of arms, or double timing or route-stepping down a dirt trail with a fifty-pound pack on your back?

I could say more, but you get the picture, I trust (whether you wanted it or not). Yes, those boxers really were a pain in the ass, er, privates. Eventually, after a week or two, I got sort of accustomed to the inconvenience and became resigned to it. But you can bet your ass one of my first purchases after completing BCT was a package of jockey shorts so my boys and their boss could finally "relax" again.

In spite of some of the aforementioned problems of fit and comfort, it was a relief to have a full complement of clothing again, clean and new. After having spent a week or so wearing the same civvies, many of the guys simply threw those clothes away. I think I was one of them.

But there were other trials to endure on clothing issue day in Reception Camp. Not the least of these was just trying to cram your whole issue into an olive drab canvas duffel bag, which was the first item issued to you as you moved down the line going from one counter to another. First the duffel bag, then underwear, socks, outerwear (fatigues, khakis, dress greens, field jacket, overcoat), boots, belts, brass and insignia, towels, etc. The idea was to outfit you from the skin outward, and they did. But they rushed you through so quickly that you really didn't have time to carefully pack your duffel bag, which was still stiff and new, as were many of the clothing items, so you just crammed everything into the bag as you received it. Most of us still had an armful or two of stuff left over after the bag was full.

A complete issue of clothing, boots, and other miscellaneous stuff weighs something in excess of sixty pounds. The sergeants and other permanent cadre kept screaming and prodding us along through the whole process. So we emerged from the clothing station staggering under this new load and trying not to drop the stuff we couldn't manage to stuff into the bag. They hustled us all into a formation of four ranks and gave us about ten minutes to try to re-pack everything into the duffel. We quickly learned through trial and error and by helping each other and pushing the lot down into the bag with a well-placed foot or knee how to get it all in. Even then, the heels of the shoes and combat boots tended to jut out the canvas sides of the bag and dig into your side or shoulder or bang against your leg as you toted the load however you could

Tim in P.X photo from FLW, October, 1962 in fatigues, wearing my helmet liner and a bewildered expression.

manage it. Just to inflict a little more torture to the whole proceedings, our barracks sergeant then forced us to double time the several blocks back to our company area. It wasn't a very pretty formation, however, as guys were falling down and bumping into each other and lagging behind all the way there, giving the sergeant still another reason to scream and curse at us and thoroughly impress upon us what sorry excuses we were for soldiers. But eventually we all made it back to our transient barracks. We were then told we had ten minutes to get into uniform and fall out to await further orders.

In case you haven't guessed it yet, things always seemed a bit rushed. Har-har-har! The cadre absolutely delighted in running our asses into the ground at every opportunity. The running and hurrying everywhere was actually an integral part of the training. It was meant to help get us into shape, and, cruel and uncivilized as it might sound, it worked.

Haircuts. A GI haircut is simple to describe. They cut off all your hair, *all* of it. The barber simply runs his clippers from front to back over the top and sides of your head until your hair is reduced to a field of barely noticeable stubble with pink or brown or black scalp showing through all around. It takes about ten to twenty seconds, I swear. You barely get yourself settled in the chair and they're pushing you back out already.

That first military haircut is a very equalizing experience. It absolutely levels the personality playing field. You've been herded and hustled around for three or four days with a group of forty or fifty guys and have come to recognize a number of them by their clothes or hairstyle or hair color, and then suddenly you're all wearing the same clothes and have the same brand-new scalped look and chastened expression. All the usual outward signs of individuality have been removed and it's back to square one in establishing an identity within the group.

The fact is, the military means to remove that identity. They want you to be nothing more than an interchangeable cog in an impersonal machine – a well-oiled, finely-tuned efficient machine. A killing machine. A *killing* machine? Isn't that a bit melodramatic? Am I overstating the case? I don't' think so. This is BCT – Basic *COMBAT* Training. More on the killing machine later.

Let's see. Uniforms, haircuts. What else? Oh, yes, shots. One other major reason for the reception camp rigamarole and all the sleepover fun there is to allow time to vaccinate all the new recruits against practically every disease known to man. Got to keep all those government issue bodies healthy after all. They will become a major investment as they progress through the various phases of training.

Rumors, of course, are a powerful means of communicating information (or misinformation). And there may be no other environment in the world as rife and rich with rumors as a BCT camp.

We first heard about the VD vaccination almost immediately upon our arrival at the Reception Camp. Everyone knew we'd be getting shots soon. It was all part of the processing. Almost as soon as shots or immunizations were mentioned, the "VD shot" came up. The vaccination supposedly was administered with a hypodermic needle at least several inches in length and what's more the needle was *square*, and in some versions none too sharp. The site of the vaccination was in some dispute. In one version, the vaccine was injected (using that long, square, and perhaps dull instrument) into the left testicle. Ouch! OWWWWW, even! In another version, it was definitely the right testicle. Well, shit, *still* OWWWWW! The most readily accepted version of this rumor, however, was that the vaccine was injected into whichever testicle hung lower. When this variant of the VD vaccination myth came up in discussion, you could actually see the eyes widen and the hands swoop surreptitiously south as the more fearful and gullible recruits checked the orientation of their family jewels. Which one of their boys would get that wicked-sounding needle?

Well, of course, there was no VD vaccination, but that "square-needle-in-the-left-nut" story became a permanent part of every recruit's military memory nevertheless, and will always bring a smile to any veteran's lips.

What I did get immunized against that first week of October 1962 were smallpox, typhoid, tetanus, yellow fever, and cholera. I also received multiple doses of polio and influenza vaccines. The worst of these, from a pain standpoint, was probably the tetanus shot, which left you with a very sore arm for a couple of days.

One final note about shots. Many of them were not administered with a needle, but with a compressed air- powered device that looked not unlike one of today's power tools. It looked kind of like a Black and Decker power drill, but without any blade or drill bit attached. This tool was connected by a small hose to a bottle of serum or vaccine, which was then delivered directly through the pores of the skin into the bloodstream by means of a powerful burst of air. The urban myth or ugly rumor that surrounded this rather new means of vaccine delivery was that if you should move the slightest bit while receiving this air-powered injection, your arm could be split wide open from shoulder to elbow. Well, I saw no evidence that this could actually happen, but I did watch one frightened recruit who had apparently taken this warning too much to heart faint dead away as he stood next in line. He was carried away and I later learned that he was given the rest of his shots with a standard hypodermic needle, for which he was immensely grateful.

Finally, after enduring close to a week in the reception camp, our orders came through. Everyone was assigned to a specific training unit. All six of us Michiganders were sent to the same company, although not necessarily the same platoon. I was assigned to the 4th Platoon, Company D, 3rd Battalion, 2nd Training Regiment Basic, or D-3-2. For the next eight weeks, I would be a "Delta Devil" of Company D.

Fragmented memories of more than forty years ago. I'll start with our quarters – the barracks of D Company were wooden buildings. They had been built hastily to provide very basic shelter with few creature comforts either before or during WWII. As I remember it, our barracks were probably about 60 feet long by perhaps 25 feet wide, and two stories. I'm guessing here, and since there aren't any of these old barracks around here for me to go eyeball or measure, I just can't be sure, but they were the typical , long, narrow, WWII era wooden style barracks. When you came in the main door the latrine was two steps down from the landing on one side, the stairs to the second floor were directly in front of you and on the other side of the landing was the open rectangular squad bay where the recruits' bunks and lockers were located. An identical open bay bunk area was located upstairs, along with a couple of small private rooms for the platoon sergeant and other cadre or permanent party staff.

Old World War II era barracks at FLW

I've already given you a description of the latrine, so let's look at the squad bays, as the large open dormitory areas were called. On each side of a center aisle there were eight to ten double tier steel bunk beds. Each of these bunks had a corresponding wall locker and foot locker to go with it. For the eight weeks of basic training, everything you owned had to fit into those two lockers. Of course, just about the only things you were allowed to keep during that time were standard government-issued clothing and equipment. And early on, in the first day or two of our life in this barracks, we were given a detailed lesson on how to hang and arrange our uniforms in the wall locker. We were taught how to tightly roll our underwear and socks and how to correctly display these and our shaving gear and toiletries in our foot lockers. We were given a demonstration on how to properly make-up a bunk with exact 45 degree angle hospital corners and blanket and dustcover (the second blanket halved and folded over the pillow) stretched tight enough across the mattress so that you could bounce a quarter off it. (Yes, *really*! Just like in all those old GI movies we had all seen as kids.)

Who showed us all these things and demonstrated these precise methods? His name was Sergeant McKinnis. I don't know if he ever told us his first name or if I ever knew it. He was our platoon sergeant. He was black– very black. Or as I described in him a postcard home in what was still the accepted parlance of the era, a colored man – "a real nice colored guy," I wrote, as a matter of fact.

Now, I'm not sure how many guys remember their BCT platoon sergeant as being a "nice guy," since it seemed to be part of the job of the BCT cadre members to be really nasty, mean hardasses. Nope, not our Sergeant Mac. In spite of our many lapses, thick-headedness, and various stupidities, he remained unfailingly patient, civilized and soft-spoken. A slender, extremely fit, young gentleman (and he WAS a gentleman) of indeterminate age, Sergeant Mac was an anachronism in a cadre of screaming, short-tempered, foul-mouthed bullies. He probably wasn't that much older than most of his recruits, since he was only a buck sergeant, or an E-5, but he had an air of maturity about him that many young men never achieve. He did tell us at some point that he was from Cleveland, Mississippi. Other than that, we knew very little of a personal nature about Sergeant Mac. We quickly learned to respect him though, and to thank our lucky stars that we'd drawn him as our leader instead of one of the loud-mouthed assholes and jerks we had occasion to observe who were piloting some of the other platoons.

But I was talking about the barracks. They were pretty old and pretty crude. The outer walls were just the studs and the board siding nailed across them on the outside. There were no inside walls – no insulation, no sheetrock or wallboard. There were places you could see through cracks between studs to the outside. They weren't very warm when the temperatures started dropping. They were heated by coal furnaces. Since it was already October when our BCT began, nights did get pretty cold, so the furnaces were operating. We were very glad to have two army blankets and some guys slept in their long johns too. Those old coal-fired furnaces worked mightily to heat those crude drafty structures, and did a reasonably adequate job, all things considered. There was one obvious drawback to the coal heat that we all noticed right away. You would usually awaken in the mornings with a fine layer of coal-soot in your nostrils, or if you were a mouth breather, in your mouth on your tongue. Your first nose blow of the day (and you always needed one) would produce black snot. And the mouth breathers were quick to put mouthwash at the top of their first PX shopping lists. But, as far as I knew, we all survived this primitive heating system and I don't think there were any reported cases of black lung.

The floors in the barracks were plain bare plank floors – not hardwood, just bare, cheap pine boards turned dark and warped from countless scrubbings with soap and water in GI parties past. Down the center aisle of the bay, both upstairs and down ran a strip of red linoleum.

Maybe I should explain "GI party," for the non-military readers. A Gi Party is a cleaning detail, which in the case of a barracks-wide party, involves all four squads of the platoon or "every swingin' dick," as one of our squad leaders so quaintly used to put it. It involves buckets of soapy water, mops, scrub brushes and rags, vinegar water and newspaper (for the windows), cleanser, sponges, and toilet brushes, and any other implements, oils, or powders necessary to clean the inside of a barrack from top to bottom.

"Top to bottom" is a key operative phrase here. In the case of my old drafty barracks with its numerous cracks and crevices, it was necessary to scrub the upstairs floor first, because when the initial soapy water was sloshed down onto the floor for mopping, some of this water inevitably leaked and dripped through the cracks down onto the bunks and lockers and floor below. All of this of course had to be sopped up and cleaned off, so those of us on the first floor quickly learned to wait until the upstairs mopping was done before we started our GI efforts below.

Cleaning, waxing, and polishing that pristine strip of red linoleum was usually the final process of a GI party. Paste wax was painstakingly rubbed into the surface by hand and left to dry. Then it was buffed down with an electric buffer (if one was available). The linoleum was then buffed by hand with towels or rags to an even glossier sheen. Sometimes we fastened towels or rags on over our socks and skated up and down this strip to shine it even more. Once we had achieved the desired sheen, the center strip was declared off-limits until after the inspection. We tiptoed and skittered carefully along the edges of the center aisle or would make our way along the outer walls behind the bunks.

This might sound like a lot of trouble for a measly three foot wide strip of linoleum, but we actually thought we were lucky to be living in those crude old barracks, *especially* when it came to cleaning and inspections. There were newer blocks of buildings in other BCT regiments on Fort Leonard Wood where the barracks were brick structures that were warmer and more modern and comfortable in numerous ways, but the floors were all completely covered with gleaming new tile, and every square inch of those floors had to be scrubbed, waxed, and polished. We were happy with our pampered, narrow strip of old linoleum, especially since GI parties were practically a weekly event during basic.

One other common feature of these old barracks were the butt cans. Down each side of the center aisle of the squad bays there were 4x4 support pillars spaced at regular intervals. Attached by a nail to every pillar was a large coffee can painted bright red with the bottom third filled with water. These were the ubiquitous butt cans found in practically every building on base.

Practically everyone in the military ranks of the sixties smoked. Cigarettes were available for about twenty cents a pack in every PX and commissary. Throughout this period of basic training, any time the troops were given permission to stand down or take a break it was with the phrase, "Smoke 'em if you got 'em." Hence, the butt cans in every building. The cans in the barracks were emptied, washed and resupplied with clean water every day and kept scrupulously clean– or as clean as a butt can *could* be kept.

You might ask, what about outside smoking? Who cleaned up after that? There were two common practices that kept outside areas clean and free of cigarette butts. Field stripping and police call. Field stripping a cigarette butt is simply the practice of tearing open the butt and letting the remaining tobacco and ash fly away. Then you crumple any paper that is left and put in your pocket (with the filter if there is one), until you can deposit it in a butt can or trash receptacle. Voila! No appreciable ground litter from cigarettes. However, whatever butts or other trash which might somehow end up on the ground are eliminated by daily police call of the area. Police call is accomplished by spacing out a line of recruits and sending them across a given area to gather or "police up" any trash or foreign objects they find on the ground. In this manner, all outside areas of a BCT company, whether pavement, dirt, gravel, or grass, is kept immaculately clean and free of litter.

There you have a brief description of the living conditions of the Delta Devils. Unattractive and primitive as these barracks may sound, they became home to us over the next two months, especially on Sundays, when we would usually get several blessed hours of leisure time to attend church service, read, write letters, do laundry, shine boots or brass, or whatever else we needed to catch up on– like sleep. Naps were popular on Sunday afternoons since you never seemed to get enough sleep. Our bunks were welcome havens when we could finally actually lie down on them and rest. During the week, while we were training, our bunks were strictly off-limits. We were not allowed to sit or lie on them until the training day was over, usually around 10 p.m. or later. And the training day began at 5 a.m., although most of us were up by 4:30 to try to get some latrine time in, to shit, shave, and shower – the three essential "Sh"'s (which later in our Army tours would increase to the five "Sh"'s, as we made more elaborate preparations to go out and have some fun: shit, shine, shave, shower, and shampoo). So, yes, we loved our bunks, and got in sack time whenever we could. My Sunday feelings on my bunk could probably best be described by a little radio ditty I remember from my childhood:

> *"I LOVE my bed.*
> *I'm so happy when I'm IN it.*
> *I cherish every MINute*
> *In my bed.*
> *In my own SWEET bed.*
> *I shouldn't LOVE my bed.*
> *I should go to work at SEVen.*
> *But I'm cuddled up in HEAVen*
> *In my bed.*
> *In my own SWEET bed."*

Now let's talk about food. Army chow. Food in a BCT unit is probably not a fair representation of army chow in general, but let me tell you what I remember about my meals as a Delta Devil.

Growing up, I was not exactly a finicky eater, but there were certain foods I just couldn't stomach, namely cooked cabbage, cauliflour, broccoli, and spinach. My dad had a sort of table rule that we should eat at least a small portion of everything Mom cooked for us. (Easy enough for Dad, he'd eat just about anything that didn't get up off the plate and walk away.) So I always had to take a little of even these hated foods. It was all I could do not to barf when I ate the aforementioned veggies. I'd chew and chew and chew. Then the gag reflex would take over and I'd retch and cover my mouth. I couldn't help it. It was automatic. I'd usually finally manage to get a mouthful or two down – just enough to satisfy Dad – but I never liked it. Nothing against my mom's cooking; it was just a gut reaction, a chemical incompatibility, maybe.

Well, I got served all those "delicacies" at various times in the D Company Mess Hall and I ate them– all of them. I practically licked the plate clean. Was it because they were better prepared? No. It was because I was always so famished after a day of training that I would devour anything that was placed in front of me. Hell, after a long, cold day on the rifle range and a five-mile march back to the company, I would have eaten a plate of boiled horse turds if they warmed me up and filled my stomach.

And there is one particular food that will forever be associated in my mind with those frigid, wet, windy days we spent on the firing range that November. Green pea soup. It was one variety of Campbell's soup that I could never stand in my other, civilian, life. But when the mobile field kitchen showed up at the range and we got in line with our metal mess kit cups with their folding handles, and each of us got a big steaming ladle of green pea soup, I swear nothing had ever tasted so good to me in my life. And I savored every last drop of it. I still like a hot cup of that soup occasionally. I sip it slowly – and remember.

Other than remembering how hungry I always was and how good everything seemed to taste after a full day of training, it's very difficult to remember any particular dish that I favored, except maybe one – SOS. Shit-on-a-Shingle was the affectionate nickname of that mainstay of the military diet then and now. The official menu designation for the dish is creamed chipped beef on toast, but it was usually just cooked hamburger in a white flour sauce served over toast that really *was* often the consistency of a shingle. But the hot white sauce softened the toast, and by golly, I *liked* it. On Sundays, I'd sometimes go back for seconds and thirds when there was enough.

There was a reason that I only got seconds on Sundays. During the training day, weekdays, we were given about five minutes flat to eat a meal, then we had to clear out of the mess hall. A slow eater would never survive basic, so we all learned quickly to gobble and run.

When I was in basic training camp, I never could think of much to write home about, although plenty of things were happening to me. At the time, I just didn't realize how my everyday activity might be of interest to a civilian. It just seemed grueling, intense, and, sometimes, even a bit terrifying, and once I'd survived it, I preferred not to think about it anymore. So, when I wrote home, I'd say, "Nothing much to write about here" or words to that effect, and I'd tell my folks to ask some questions in their return mail so I could answer them and have something to write. My mom always wanted to know what I was eating, whether I was getting enough, and whether it was good. Well, here's your answer Mom, better late than never: I ate *every*thing they dished up. I *never* got enough (except on Sundays). And I didn't *care* whether it was good or not, but I *was* partial to the SOS.

Lemme see: food, clothing, shelter. I guess I've covered the basic needs. Now I need to talk about the training.

There was so much material covered during BCT that I can't possibly remember it all. Especially forty years later. But here goes.

Close order drill, or marching in formation. We began learning to march almost immediately upon our arrival at the FLW reception camp. Its a fairly basic skill, you'd think, right? If you can walk, you should be able to march, right? It's just walking in a large group, right? Well, yeah, sort of, to all of the above. Except as I sit here now trying to remember how all those moves are executed – left face, right face, about face, various column movements – I can't quite remember. So I stand up, here in my study, and try a couple facing movements. Ten-HUT! One. Left FACE! One-two. Right FACE! One-two. Now it's coming back. All these movements and commands, properly executed, are done "by the numbers." Some are simple one-counts: Ten-HUT! Others are two-counts, like facing movements – even the about face command, which always tripped a lot of troops up, because of its backward, pivoting motion. I can't seem to get it right at all now, and I'm not sure if that's because I'm older and my balance isn't so good, or because I'm in bedroom slippers on a carpet. Oh, what the hell! I don't need to do those movements anymore. Hell, I'm happy if I can cleanly execute a smooth bowel movement these days. Suffice it to say that those seemingly simple commands and movements did require a considerable amount of practice and drill. And drill we did, every day, until the movements became automatic and marching in formation became second nature.

Since I was one of the tallest men in our platoon, I was usually at the back of the formation, except when we executed a "to the rear march. " Then I would briefly be at the head of the line, until the same command was executed again. Traditionally, the tall troops were kept at the rear of a formation, since we were usually lined up according to size for most parades or formal marches. There were certain disadvantages to marching at the end of a column of troops. If you were marching on a dirt or gravel trail, you ate everyone else's dust. If it were wet and muddy, you struggled through the already churned up mud trying to keep pace as the mud sucked at your boots. And even under the best dry and temperate conditions, marching on blacktop or pavement, there were certain problems you had to deal with. With ten to fifteen troops marching ahead of you, in the column, one or more of them always managed to fall out of step, causing every recruit behind him to also lose the rhythm. To get back into step with the man ahead of you there was a movement called a "change step" or "chain step" which requires a shortened stutter step or a skip. Probably, "chain step" was the more accurate term, because if someone near the head of the column lost the step, then corrected himself, an observer could watch the chain reaction skip all the way back down the line. So I became something of an expert chain-stepper. Sometimes, when I got bored I'd execute a few chain step skips just for the hell of it. The platoon sergeant or drill instructor seldom looked at the back of the formation anyway.

Marching was tiring and could also be boring, but it could also be kind of fun on a sunny day with the bright colors of fall surrounding you. Especially if we sang as we marched. Yeah, we sang– marching songs. Our songs weren't exactly wholesome alpine "Valderee, Valderai" kinds of tunes (though I often did have "my knapsack on my back"). Army marching songs tended toward the raunchy call and response like this one:

> *I got a girl who lives out west*
> *She's got mountains on her chest*
> *Sound off – one two*
> *Sound off – three four*
> *Break it on down*

One two three four one two
THREE FOUR!
Or....

I got a girl who lives on a hill
She won't do it but her sister will
Sound off...
etcetera, etcetera, etcetera.

There were many other marching cadence-counting songs like these, some *much* raunchier. By today's politically correct standards, I know such ditties are extremely impolitic, but this was an all-male environment. There were very few women around a BCT regiment and also very few females in uniform in 1962.

There were a couple good reasons for marching songs and counting cadence. One was to establish a sense of esprit-de-corps among the men. And these songs and cadences were shouted at the top of one's lungs, so another reason was fitness – it developed stamina and lung power. It worked well on both counts and we usually enjoyed it. By the time we'd half-completed our training, many of the men had composed their own marching songs and the DI's sometimes allowed them to use their compositions and count the cadence.

Close order drill and marching were disciplines we practiced for the entire period of BCT. One other integral and continuous element of our stay in Company D was weapons training, which began when we were issued our rifles just a few days into the training cycle.

The standard infantry weapon during most of WWII was the Garand M-1 Rifle, first developed around 1934. A solid, durable weapon made of wood and steel, the M-1 weighed eight and a half pounds and featured a bolt action that could fire a single round or an 8-round clip. It was a semi-automatic rapid-firing, gas-operated, .30-caliber rifle and was indeed a formidable killing machine in the hands of a trained marksman.

M-1 rifle

27

In the fall of 1962, the M-1 was in its final days as the weapon of choice for the U.S. Infantry. In fact, by the end of that year, I think the M-1 was officially replaced by its successor, the M-14.

But for our company the M-1 was still the weapon and we came to know it intimately over the next eight weeks. The rifles were kept in a locked rack just inside the entrance to our barracks. Only the platoon sergeant or the platoon leader had access to the keys for the padlock that secured the weapons.

Each recruit was issued his own rifle and he was responsible for keeping that particular piece clean and in proper working order for the duration of our basic training cycle. We were issued the rifles the first week of the cycle and didn't officially turn them back over to the battalion armory until the final days of training. Your weapon was your personal responsibility, and a gravely serious one at that.

I had never had much experience with firearms of any kind before this. My dad and my oldest brother did a little deer and rabbit hunting when I was young, but they had pretty much given up hunting themselves by the time I was of an age to hunt. We had a few air rifles, or bb-guns, around the house while I was growing up, but they were just passing novelties for my brothers and me. When they were new, we bought bb's and did some target practice and tin-can shooting out back of the corn crib, but it never became a passion for any of us. Once the original bb's were all gone, we mainly used the empty rifles for playing war or cowboys. They had impressive lever actions and made a satisfying thunking sound even when they were empty.

Now, suddenly, I was personally responsible for the care and maintenance of a very real and potentially deadly weapon. It wasn't an easy pill for me to swallow. It would probably even be accurate to say that I was a little bit frightened by the rifle and the awful responsibility that went with it. But I was stuck with it and we began taking it just about everywhere with us, even well before we learned to shoot it. I think the idea behind this was to get us to feel comfortable carrying a weapon, and also probably to get us used to the added weight. In any case, wherever we went, the M-1s went with us. While we trained at other things, whether inside or outside, we would "stack arms" and leave our rifles in the formation area. Stacking arms meant placing three to several rifles in a tepee-shaped configuration on the ground muzzle up by hooking the sling swivels together. It was a little tricky to do until you learned how to properly stack them, but practice does make perfect.

And we began learning the basic "manual of arms" – commands like, "order arms," "right shoulder (or left shoulder) arms," "port arms," or "present arms." All of these commands represented by-the-numbers three- or four-count movements to get your rifle from the butt-on-the-ground position up onto either shoulder or held diagonally across the body or straight up and down in front of the body, and then back again. It required a considerable amount of drill to achieve group unity in even these simple movements. We didn't even begin to try more complicated things like the Queen Ann Salute that you see professional drill teams doing, which involves twirling and throwing and catching your weapon.

The one basic movement I had the most trouble with in the manual of arms was "inspection arms." The object of this movement is to lock open the chamber of the rifle while in port arms position and then surrender it to the inspecting officer, who might then peer into the chamber or upend the rifle and look up the bore to check for cleanliness. If you muffed the move and failed to properly lock open the chamber, the bolt would spring forward violently and trap your thumb in the chamber, leaving you with a very painful (and colorful) condition known as "M-1 thumb." It happened to me only once. Once was enough, believe me. After that, I practiced inspection arms most diligently to avoid a repeat embarrassment.

In addition to learning the manual of arms in our pre- firing phase with the M-1, we also through frequent practice learned to disassemble, clean, oil and reassemble the weapon.

I made a friend during this training phase. He was in my squad and slept just a couple bunks down from me in the barracks. We shared a table in the training room where we first tore down our weapons into their component parts. My friend's name was Fred Wilkerson. He was a good ol' boy from the hills of Missouri and handled the rifle components with such loving care I could tell he was a hunter and experienced with firearms. He was very impressed with the M-1 and its various parts and named his "Marilyn." Blonde and ruddy-complected, Fred was a hulking, normally rather slow-moving guy. But even the smallest components of the rifle, like the spring or the firing pin, showed an immediate affinity to the caressing touch of his sausage-like fingers. The weapon parts just seemed to leap together in the proper order under his hands. Slow and lumbering at practically everything else he did, Fred was probably one of the fastest in our platoon at breaking down and re-assembling his beloved "Marilyn."

Since I wasn't nearly so adept with my un-named and unloved piece, we formed a kind of unofficial alliance. Fred could never quite get the hang of making up a tight bunk, a skill that came easily to me, since my mom had taught me about hospital corners years before. So I helped Fred with his bunk in the mornings and particularly before barracks inspections, and he helped me out with the care and maintenance of my weapon. The arrangement worked out well for both of us.

In case you haven't noticed, I have refrained completely from ever referring to my M-1 as a "gun." There's a good reason for this, and also a lesson to be learned. I learned that lesson by watching and listening. Calling an M-1 (or and M-14 or M-16) a "gun" in the military is a definite no-no. You may call it by its proper alpha-numeric designator. You may call it a rifle. You may call it a weapon. You may even call it a piece. But you must *never* call it a gun. Gun, to the firearms purist, is a common, vulgar term reserved for other things.

Let me illustrate. Just a day or two after we'd been assigned our weapons, we had just fallen out of the barracks to our regular formation area one morning and formed up into four ranks. Suddenly there was a loud clatter from the rear of the ranks. Sergeant Mac, in his usual unhurried, unflappable manner, peered in the direction of the noise and inquired softly, "What is going on back there?"

The culprit who made the noise – we'll call him Private Jones – replied, "I'm sorry, Sergeant. I dropped my gun."

Sergeant Mac looked at Jones narrowly for a moment in the pre-dawn gloom, then said quietly, "Private Jones, I want you to come up here, front and center, right now."

With a nervous clatter, Private Jones bent and retrieved his weapon and hustled quickly around the formation and stood before

Sergeant McKinnis, who seemed to sadly consider Jones for a long moment, then said, "Stand over here beside me, Private Jones, and face the platoon." Private Jones nervously complied.

"Now, Private Jones, I want you to grasp the front hand guard of your weapon firmly in your right hand and hold your weapon out at arm's length at your side."

Jones did.

"Now, Private Jones, I want you to raise your weapon higher and repeat after me, 'This is my rifle.'"

Jones repeated the phrase.

"Louder, Private Jones. I can't hear you."

Jones shouted, "THIS IS MY RIFLE, SERGEANT!"

"Again, Private Jones."

Jones shouted it again, his skinny arm beginning to visibly tremble under the strain of waving the eight and a half pound rifle.

"Now, Private Jones – No, keep that weapon raised high. Now I want you place your left hand firmly around your privates, Private Jones."

Eyes now nervously darting from side to side, Jones gingerly grasped the crotch of his fatigues.

"*Firmly*, Private Jones."

Jones squeezed.

"Now, Private Jones, I want you to alternately wave your weapon and squeeze your privates and repeat after me:

This is my rifle.

This is my gun.

This is for killing.

This is for fun."

Upon hearing this, the whole platoon erupted in spontaneous, unrestrained laughter, which Sergeant Mac allowed for only a brief moment, then silenced us with a withering look up and down the ranks. "I'm waiting, Private Jones," he said softly.

Waving his weapon and squeezing his "gun," Jones stammered out the rhyme, blushing furiously. Sergeant Mac made him repeat the process several times at the top of his lungs, then finally gave him an order arms command and told him to get back to his squad. Jones did, by this time red-faced and quivering with embarrassment and exhaustion, and the day's training commenced – or rather *continued.* Never again did anyone make the egregious error of calling his weapon a gun. Lesson learned.

Did this incident really happen? Maybe it did, and maybe it didn't, but this "rifle vs. gun" tale is legend in the army, and anyone who has survived BCT has at least heard the story, so I felt it needed to be included here.

Of course, we also learned to shoot our guns – *Oops!* I mean we learned to fire our weapons. In our first live-fire training we learned how to use the front and rear sight mechanisms and "zeroed" our rifles, or calibrated the sights. The range cadre and platoon sergeants helped us do this to insure our weapons would aim and function properly.

My very first experience with firing the M-1 was not a particularly positive one, and it never got a whole lot better. It wasn't just that I was a lousy shot; I just couldn't seem to get the hang of the whole process. Part of the problem was my eyeglasses. I've worn specs since the fourth grade, so I was certainly used to them, but they just didn't mix well with shooting that M-1.

First of all, I had trouble getting that proper sight picture, which involves lining up the front and rear sights on the target while squinting down the barrel. My vision would get dim and fuzzy, and the sights and target seemed to swim in and out of focus.

And there's a special grip you're supposed to use for firing (all explained in the training manual) that brings your trigger hand, cheek and the stock of the weapon all snugly together, so that when you take that breath, let half of it out, then slowly squee-eeze the trigger (never *pull* it), there should be no noticeable recoil. The fact of the matter is, the M-1 has got a kick like a Belgian draught horse if you don't use it correctly. I don't think I ever quite got it right, because, inevitably, every time I *ska-weezed* the trigger, I got kicked by that damn horse. And when I got kicked, my steel pot helmet would jiggle forward just enough to knock my glasses halfway down my nose, and the gas-operated cylinder would squirt out a dollop of oil onto the lenses of my glasses, further obscuring my already fuzzy sight picture of the target. So my firing sequence went something like this: ready, aim, ska-weeze, *FIRE*, kick, jiggle, bump, slide, squirt, blur – *damnshitpisshellfuckingsonofaBITCH!* Then I'd push my helmet back up into place and do it all over again. Needless to say, my firing scores were distinctly unimpressive and often downright abysmal, a fact that did not go unnoticed by Sergeant Mac and the range cadre.

Marksmanship and basic weapons training were, of course, skills that made up the very foundation of BCT, and it was absolutely paramount that every recruit do his best to qualify with the M-1. There were three skill levels recognized in weapons training, all based on accuracy and numerical scores achieved on the range. Badges awarded for weapons qualification were, in descending order: expert, sharpshooter and marksman. A recruit who failed to qualify at all was referred to as a "bolo." I have no idea where this term originated, but it was a term weighted with shame and disgrace in the BCT environment. We had learned the word almost immediately upon being issued our rifles that first week. A bolo was someone who had failed, a person who had let down his comrades, who had shamed himself and his team, his squad, his platoon. Bolo was a tag to be avoided at all cost.

Given my usual marginal and sometimes downright miserable performance on the rifle range, I was scared shitless that I would bolo when it came time to qualify, or fire "for record." I was trying my best. I really was. But that mix of M-1 and me was like oil and water. Several weeks were devoted to practice fire with the M-1, so I had ample time to grow accustomed to my weapon, and I suppose I did. I just never improved much or achieved any great level of proficiency, despite firing probably hundreds of rounds of live ammunition. I simply was not a natural with firearms. They made me just a wee bit nervous – all that deadly potential, I suppose. I have to give Sergeant Mac and all the range personnel credit. They observed me closely, made helpful suggestions and coached me individually.

During practice fire we learned to fire from various positions: prone (lying flat on your stomach), standing, kneeling, sitting, and from a foxhole. I was frankly a pretty poor shot from all these positions, but continued to learn all I could. And I prayed a lot during that last week or two before we marched that one last time to the range for record fire. I felt like I was literally walking "the last mile."

During all the weeks of practice firing our scores were toted up at the end of each day and given to us so we could see how well (or how badly) we had done. On the day we fired for record we were not given our final scores at the end of the day, although many of the men – the natural shooters – kept their own informal running tally in their heads and discussed them enthusiastically with each other afterwards. The guys like me – and there *were* other recruits struggling too – just did the best they could and hoped and prayed for the best. Well, I didn't pray for the *best*, just for the bare minimum score needed to qualify, *Please, Lord.* And I tried mightily not to curse too much when my helmet bumped my glasses down and the hot oil fouled my vision, or the kicking rifle stock bruised my cheek and shoulder, because I was still having many of these same troubles. I just endured it all and kept sighting down the barrel and squeezing the trigger until it was finally over and I could honestly say I had done my best.

In order to qualify for the marksman badge, the lowest of the three medals, your total score had to be between 36 and 49 (out of 112 targets). I honestly didn't know how many targets I'd hit. I hadn't even tried to keep track. I just tried to keep cool. I was too nervous to count anything. The pressure felt overwhelming.

The following afternoon our scores were posted on the company bulletin board. I didn't even bother to look at the expert and sharpshooter lists. I went right to the marksman list, and there – at the very bottom of the list – I found my name, my service number and my rank, PVT E1. My total score was 36, the rock bottom minimum score needed. I had been awarded the "marksman badge w/ rifle bar" for the M-1 rifle. I remember going weak in the knees and my eyes filling with tears. I had not boloed. I had qualified. I was so immensely relieved and grateful that I suddenly felt lighter, and even a bit light-headed. My inner prayer gyroscope was fluttering frantically up and down and side to side with *ThankyouthankyouthankyouLord*s.

The marksman M-1 award.
The actual badge is long lost.

Had I really qualified on my own merit? Was it the power of prayer? Or did the range cadre, who had coached and helped me for weeks and gotten know me some and seen I was doing my best, taken pity on me and tacked an extra target or two onto my final score? I don't know. If they did, then God bless 'em, because I know I was happier than any of the guys who had earned an expert badge. It was a giddy feeling. It was November 13, 1962, and there were only a couple more weeks to go in basic training. I was over the hump. Praise the Lord! Life was good!

I've spent a lot of time talking about rifle training and weapons qualifications because it is probably the single most important part of basic training. But there were so many other skills and lessons crammed into those eight short weeks that I need to try to touch on some of those too.

There was classroom training in subjects like military courtesy (how, when and whom to salute) and the UCMJ, the uniform code of military justice. The latter course taught us about things like courts martial and Article 15's (formal reprimands and disciplinary actions sometimes involving fines and loss of rank that were entered into your permanent record).

There was also a mix of classroom and practical training in map reading and orientation and land navigation. In this phase we studied the Universal Transverse Mercator System (UTMS) and learned how to use a compass, then spent some time wandering around in a pine forest and swamp trying to find our way out. I guess we must have succeeded, but I don't really remember much about that training anymore.

We were introduced to basic radio procedures and played about with hand-held walkie-talkie type radios, as well as larger backpack and vehicle-mounted model transceivers. *Red Dog, this is Gray Wolf. How do you read me? Come in. Over.* Great fun.

We had courses in basic first-aid and learned about tourniquets, applying pressure bandages, treatment for sucking chest wounds, and how to inject atropine and administer morphine. We became familiar with all the contents of the first-aid kits we wore on our web belts when dressed in full field gear. The day we had classroom instruction on first-aid was an unseasonably hot one. As we sat sweltering in semi-darkness watching slides and films on how to treat for shock and apply field dressings, I remember a disgruntled and disembodied voice muttering from the back of the room, "I come here to learn how to kill, not to be no Florence fuckin' Nightingale." An astute commentary on the dichotomy of our roles as soldiers, to be sure. (The backwoods malcontent who made this comment was tagged with the unfortunate nickname of Florence for the rest of the cycle.)

PT, or physical training, was a recurrent theme throughout BCT from start to finish, beginning with an edict in the reception camp that anytime we were on our own in the unit area we were to RUN, not walk. Some of the official PT I could do, but some of it was extremely difficult for me. At that time there were several separate elements to the PT regimen and we were tested on all of them. There were sit-ups, push-ups, pull-ups, the crab crawl, the run-dodge-and-jump, the horizontal ladder, or "the bars," and the two-mile run.

Most of these fitness-building exercises are self- explanatory, except for perhaps the crab crawl. For this event you were required to scrabble on all fours, belly up, up and down a sand-bed course as fast as you could go. (Hell, you did *all* these damned things as fast as you could.) To me it seemed the most ridiculous of all the events of the PT test, but I somehow managed to survive its unnatural contortions.

I probably would have done best at the two-mile run, since I ran cross-country in high school, but that event was usually saved for the last, after everything else had pretty much winded and drained you, and you weren't allowed very much recovery time between events either. As it was, I always did pretty well on the run, but knew I could have done better had I been fresh and rested. The fortunes of war, I guess.

I also did well enough in the run-dodge-and-jump, which consisted of a timed run in which you zig-zagged around obstacles and leapt across a trench. I felt particularly sorry for one very short recruit whom everyone called Shorty (naturally), who couldn't quite make the jump and often fell into the trench, then had to scramble back out again. This really hurt his time in the event and also affected his overall PT score.

Shorty was a hell of an athlete otherwise, highly competitive, and really excelled at the bars. He hurtled up and down those rungs like a monkey on speed, racking up additional points to compensate for his difficulty with the RD&J.

The bars were probably the hardest event for me, because my upper body strength was never that great to begin with, but also because I was too tall. When you swing from one rung to the next, dangling from the ladder, you can't help developing a slight pendulum motion from side to side. The taller, or "longer" you are, the more pronounced this side-to-side motion becomes, until it eventually just tears your hands loose from the rungs. We practiced these events at various PT fields scattered over the regimental training area and there were a few of these ladders that were built too low for someone as tall as me. By this I mean I could actually hold onto the rungs and walk along the ground underneath them. Of course, this wasn't allowed, so the drill instructor just told me to bend my knees to hold my feet up off the ground. Yeah, sure. No chance. I was just fucked. I was lucky to make it even halfway down the ladder on those days, while guys like Shorty would fly up and down the length of it three or four times in the alotted time.

Sit-ups I had no trouble with, and could often achieve a maximum score on that event. Pull-ups (chinning yourself on a bar) were the pits for me – again my height and poor upper body strength were working against me, but I worked my way up to doing at least the minimum eventually.

Push-ups didn't come easily for me either. They usually don't for tall people. Our backs are too long. I did the best I could though, and experimented with ways to try to shorten my length by bringing my feet up closer to my hands in the down position, but then ended up with my butt sticking up in the air. The DI always noticed this and would soon wander over and place a heavy boot on my upraised ass, collapsing me face-first into the dirt and gravel. Somehow I finally managed a satisfactory number, but I still hate push-ups.

One common disadvantage we were all faced with back in 1962 was that we wore our combat boots for all these activities. The boots were standard footgear for all training. Today recruits are issued athletic shoes for PT, a practice that I think began not too long after my BCT days. Leather GI boots are stiff, rigid and unforgiving when the wearer engages in strenuous athletic events, and there were several combat boot casualties in our company who suffered various degrees of achilles tendon injuries, some of them serious enough to require hospitalization and/or crutches.

Another training phase covered CBR warfare – that's chemical, biological and radiological. Nowadays I think it's called NBC – nuclear, biological and chemical. Whatever you call it, it's training in how to properly use a gas mask. Today's troops receive training with a full protective body suit, MOP gear, but we just had the gas mask, which we wore in its own case strapped across our bodies. The training wasn't emphasized then the way I'm sure it is now, but was quite thorough nevertheless. After several practice sessions in the correct method for uncasing, donning, clearing and sealing the mask, we all got our turns in the "gas chamber," a sealed room where a canister of tear gas would be thrown down and activated, at which time we put our training into practice. There were a few guys in the company who didn't get their masks properly sealed or cleared, who ended up throwing up in their masks. Upon hearing the warning, *GAS!* our first action was supposed to be to stop breathing, but the natural impulse when you know you have to hold your breath is to take one final gulp of air. A lot of us did just that in the excitement of the moment and in spite of our training, so even the guys who successfully donned and cleared their masks still came out of the chamber afterward with eyes and noses streaming. For some odd unexplained reason, I was not affected at all, even though I got a good lungful of the stuff. Just serendipity good luck, I guess. Nevertheless, another training phase successfully completed.

Another memorable training phase bore the innocuous-sounding name of the "confidence course." Hey, that didn't sound too bad, at least on paper when we saw it posted on our training schedule. The reality of the confidence course was a rude awakening to the possibilities of what actual combat and being under enemy fire might be like.

Picture an area roughly a hundred yards wide by fifty yards long. Most of this area is pock-marked with what look like small hummocks of dirt and gravel alternating with craters and shell holes, some filled with stagnant standing water if there's been rain recently. There is a sprinkling of scrub growth – small stunted trees and shrubs, none more than a few feet high. At irregular intervals throughout the area there are lengthy obstacles of rolled and barbed concertina wire. Along one end of the course runs a long wide trench about five or six feet deep. This is where the massed recruits are brought in and spread along the length of the trench to await the command to go "over the top," much like the doughboys did in the trench warfare of WWI. We'd been given some general instructions and some inklings about what to expect, but the only specific and ironclad orders were to stay low and crawl – *DO NOT STAND UP* – as we negotiate our way as quickly as possible the fifty yards to the opposite end of the course. At the opposite end of the course are three or four platforms holding swivel-mounted belt-fed .50-caliber heavy machine guns *which will be firing live ammunition* while we attempt to cross the no-man's land of the confidence course.

The object of this exercise is to get from the jumping-off point at the trench to the finish line at the course's opposite end as quickly as possible. We will go in waves, and each wave will be given a starting time and a course cadre member will record the finish time of each individual recruit in the wave.

We had had a couple days of training previously on how to negotiate coiled barbed wire obstacles, but even when you do it right, it's a tricky and always uncomfortable maneuver. It's accomplished by lying on your back and using your rifle barrel to lift up the outside strand of the concertina wire, then continuing to use your entire rifle to hold the wire up over you as you wriggle through underneath, still on your back, until you've cleared the wire completely. Even in practice I had managed to acquire several jagged tears in my fatigues and numerous scratches on my wrists and hands. And these had just been short flat crawls through sand. I was really dreading low-crawling this obstacle-covered uneven overgrown terrain for fifty yards.

But I *did* it! I crawled through the craters and over the rises and wriggled under the wire. I even overcame the sudden shock of a mock land-mine explosion, simulated by a small remotely-operated explosive charge, which showered me with dirt and small pebbles. There were several of these that went off close by as I made my way down the course, low-crawling precisely as prescribed, but only the first one really spooked me when it went off just a couple feet from my right ear, leaving me partially deaf for the remainder of my crawl, and layering the whole experience with a kind of surreal underwater feeling, with bullets whizzing soundlessly overhead. As I crossed the finish line one of the course cadre clapped me on the back, peered at the nametag over my jacket pocket and recorded my time on a clipboard, then said something I couldn't hear at all. I could see his lips moving, then he grinned, so I grinned stupidly back at him.

I had to admit my confidence really *was* bolstered after I completed the course successfully. We had to do it all over again after dark, with illuminated tracer rounds screaming overhead (my hearing was back by then), but I wasn't so worried this time. I had confidence that I could do it again. I remember that I even went a little slower this time on purpose, and, for a few moments, after wriggling under still another roll of concertina wire, I just lay there on my back looking dreamily up at the stars and also at the deadly beauty of the light patterns created by the tracers as they streamed by a scant few feet overhead. It was a kind of epiphany, a stolen moment of absolute peace in the most unlikely place. I knew at that moment that I could survive this madness called BCT which had so terrorized me for weeks now. Confidence course *indeed*.

Maybe I should add here (though I hate to break the spell of my epiphany) that there was another more practical reason I slowed down on my second low-crawl through this artificial no-man's land. I had a painful rash around my crotch and up the crack of my ass from all the sand and grit and burrs I'd picked up the first time through the course. All that low-crawling on both back and belly tended to tug your trousers down and grind all manner of uncomfortable debris into any exposed flesh. Then when you would pause to pull your pants back up, all that stuff would end up down your pants and up your back and in your shorts. If I'd been wearing jockey briefs my rash might have been even worse, but those GI boxers let at least some of that Missouri sand and and other stuff go right on down my legs (and into the tops of my socks).

Bayonet training was actually kind of fun. I know this might sound rather callow and insensitive when you consider the actual purpose of a bayonet. It is, after all, a long sharp knife affixed to the end of a rifle barrel, and it is used to cruelly skewer and and disembowel an enemy soldier. But *BOY* – and I have to say it again – was bayonet training ever *fun*!

It was just a one-day training session, but we finally got to unsheathe that wicked-looking blade from its metal scabbard and lock it onto our M-1 muzzle. (I keep wanting to say, *It was WAY cool!* but that would be so impolitic, I suppose.) There was just something about bayonet training that brought out the kid in you. After all, most of us weren't all that far removed from the days we used to lead imaginary charges over the top from our home-dug trenches and foxholes, brandishing our toy rifles and rubber bayonets and vanquishing make-believe enemies as we played "army."

So when we were suddenly furnished with real rifles with bayonets fixed, then lined up in front of a row of hanging sandbags representing enemy soldiers and told to have at 'em, it was like a kid's fantasy come to life. And were instructed – nay, *ordered* – to scream at the top of our lungs in blood-curdling fashion as we lunged and thrusted at our cowardly burlap-and-sand foes. And we did. We shrieked and screamed and even occasionally threw in a somehow more literate-sounding, *DIE, you commie bastard, DIE!* (This was the Cold War. All Communists were our enemies.) We did our level best to skew and twist the blade as we extracted it, so as to do maximum harm and leave a gaping and mortal wound. Hey, I know this sounds awful, but it really was such *fun*!

The DI's egged us on in our bloodlust, shouting, "What's the cry of the bayonet fighter?" We responded as we'd been taught, "Kill or *be* killed!"

"I can't *hear* you!"

"KILL OR BE KILLED!"

Bayonet training. *Way* cool.

Bivouac. Not a word you hear much anymore. I don't even know if the army uses the term anymore, but they probably do. It is, after all, a military term. "A temporary encampment of soldiers in the open with or without shelter; hence, figuratively, a position or situation demanding extreme watchfulness." Thank you, Mr. Webster. I needed some help.

It rained most of the week our company bivouacked out in the dark piney woods of Fort Leonard Wood. So I always associate bivouacking, or camping out, with rain, cold, discomfort – misery. Remember that playful nickname for FLW, Missouri? Fort "Lost-in-the-Woods, Misery." It captured perfectly the essence of our bivouac. It wasn't really even a whole week. We marched into the wilderness on a Monday and were supposed to come back on Friday. Luckily for me, I was scheduled to pull KP on Friday, so they came and got me in a truck on Thursday afternoon and I got to sleep in my own sweet bunk that night in a largely empty barracks. Even if I did have to get up at 3:30 am on Friday and work until after 7pm, it was a great trade-off, I thought. I'd had enough of bivouac.

For we were indeed a "temporary encampment." As for having shelter, that was itself debatable. Part of our full field pack when we were toting all our gear was a canvas shelter half, with a half complement of poles, stakes and ropes for erecting that "shelter." Another soldier had the other half of your tent. These shelters were basically two-man pup tents. And they were *extremely* basic. My problem with them was they weren't long enough. If I tried to stretch out, either my head or my feet (or portions of both) stuck out the ends of the tent. Same problem with my sleeping bag. IT only came to the top of my chest, so in order to get warm I had to bend my legs enough to get the upper portion of my body down into the bag, no easy feat since it was a very narrow bag. So I slept in my field jacket with the liner buttoned into it. Our tent leaked. Our rubberized ground sheet had holes in it. My tent-mate snored through all the discomfort, oblivious.

And on top of all this, you had to sleep with your weapon – *inside* the sleeping bag with you. If you didn't do this, you might wake up and find it missing – a serious breach for a soldier, losing his weapon. The first morning after making camp several men awoke to find their M-1's missing. Cadre members had been sneaking about after dark and confiscating any untended weapons. Those without weapons the next morning were assigned extra duty filling old slit trenches and digging new ones for our field latrine, an odious detail.

I also remember one unlucky troop being singled out by the DI one morning for having failed to shave. Shaving was not an easily-accomplished task under these primitive field conditions. You had to take your steel pot helmet over to the mobile kitchen and draw a small portion of hot water, then take it back to your tent and shave with a safety razor. It just didn't seem worth all the trouble. Luckily, my own adolescent beard in those days was mostly peach fuzz, nearly invisible, and I could often go two or three days without shaving and no one noticed. (In any case, I used an electric shaver.) I don't think I shaved at all while on bivouac.

At any rate, this unfortunate soul was called up in front of the morning formation and made an example. The DI produced a safety razor then and there and and forced the man to shave right on the spot while we all watched. That was the day I learned the term "dry shave." The poor guy was not allowed any soap or even any water – just the razor. But he had no choice, so he shaved. By the time he finished, his face was an angry red, and covered with cuts, scratches and welts. Talk about razor burn.

As I said earlier, *luckily*, I was slated to pull KP (kitchen police) on Friday. At no other point in our training cycle would KP have been considered a "lucky break," but after those three and a half days of sleeping out in the cold and damp, it did indeed feel like a gift. I was one happy camper when I climbed into the back of that deuce and a half to be trucked back to the company area and the luxurious comforts of our warm dry barracks.

I should probably say a few words about KP. Generally everybody dreaded it, hated it, tried to avoid it. But, as is the case with any army duty, there were good jobs and bad jobs under the heading of "kitchen police." You just had to learn which was which and then try to finagle one of the good ones.

I pulled KP at least twice during basic training, and possibly three times (one of the disadvantages of having a last name starting with B in an alphabetical roster system). The first time was only a week or two into the training cycle. KP's reported to the mess hall by 3:30am, at which time jobs for the rest of the day were assigned. I was too timid to volunteer for any particular job, so I got what was left over. That first time my job was pots and pans. I found out afterwards that this is, of course, one of the least desirable jobs in the kitchen. It meant I was up to my elbows in scalding soapy grease-filmed water for much of the next sixteen hours or so, trying to scrub the crusty grease and residue off some truly enormous pots and pans, some of them perhaps better described as cauldrons – "bubble, bubble, toil and trouble" indeed. When you're cooking – boiling, frying, broiling, baking – for large numbers of people, you use very large containers. So I scrubbed and scrubbed, using soap, cleanser, brushes, chore boys, scouring pads – whatever it took.

Then I rinsed and dried these miniature vats and hung them back up, usually just in time for them to be put back in use again. I probably lost a few pounds that day, immersed in clouds of billowing steam and sweating buckets. Fortunately, I was provided with a pair of rubber gloves, or my hands would have been a real mess. They ended up looking pretty par-boiled and red and puckered anyway. Somehow I managed to keep up pretty well and didn't get yelled at too much. I should probably thank my mom for that.

I grew up on a small family farm (my grandfather's really), but I always hated working out in the garden or the fields – *hated* picking pickles or hoeing corn. So I often finagled a way to work inside the house helping my mom – washing dishes or cleaning the bathroom – and let my brothers do the field work. I learned early how to wash a dish or pots and pans, and to do it right. This skill served me well on KP that first time.

There was one other KP job that was even more onerous than pots and pans – the grease pit. The poor slob who drew this duty was *really* a filthy smelly mess by day's end. His job was to empty the garbage cans and then scrub and rinse them out over the grease pit. But that was the *good* part of the job. The bad part was cleaning out the aptly-named grease pit, or trap. This was the drain out behind the mess hall where all the dirt, food scraps, and, yes, grease and sludge collected over the course of the day. The only way to do the job was to get down into the pit and clean all that shit out of the trap by hand. Yes indeedy – a nasty *nasty* job.

When I got caught up on my pots and pans between meals, I got to take a break – peeling potatoes. There were usually three or four of us doing this. We didn't actually peel the whole potato. We just dug out the indentations and the eyes. Then we dumped the prepped potatoes into a machine that finished peeling them and washed them. I know peeling potatoes doesn't sound like much of a "break," but it felt like one at the time. At least I wasn't enveloped in a cloud of steam, and I actually got to sit down for a little while.

The "good" job on KP was DRO, dining room orderly. I think the mess sergeant remembered me and the good job I had done on pots and pans, because my second time around he pointed right at me and said, "*You!* – Tall and Skinny – you're DRO today." Of course, this pissed off a few other guys who had wanted this cushy job, but I didn't care. I was grateful, and decided I'd be the best damn DRO that mess hall ever saw – and I think I *was* too. The DRO's job was to wipe down the tables and chairs after the meal was over, then stack the chairs on the tables and sweep and damp mop the floors. I'd had plenty of experience cleaning and mopping. I'd spent part of one summer when I was thirteen helping our school janitor at St. Philip's scrub, strip and wax floors. During that time Fred Morris taught me how to use an electric floor scrubber-buffer. So when I had gotten the mess hall floor swept and mopped, before I put the chairs back down I went and got a buffer from the orderly room closet and quickly buffed and polished the whole dining area floor. Let me tell you, Cookie was impressed. He didn't even put me on the spud-peeling gang. He told me to get a Coke and take a break – a *real* break, relaxing at a table with a cold drink in front of me. After pots and pans, DRO was a walk in the park. Maybe I had found a way to beat the system: bust your ass and impress the bastards.

One of the first lessons I learned in basic training was *never volunteer.* One morning the first week of basic our drill instructor said the company needed a few good drivers. Did anyone have experience and a clean driving record? Several guys immediately and enthusiastically waved their hands in the air. The DI picked three of them and sent them to the orderly room. Later that afternoon when we marched back into the company after an

General Orders Card.
"To walk my post in a military manner ..."

45

afternoon of classroom instruction on the UCMJ, we passed the three chosen "drivers" pushing wheelbarrows filled with topsoil in an area where the commander wanted a patch of lawn planted. The only vehicles in evidence were those wheelbarrows.

It was only a few days later that a request was put out by the orderly room for personnel who had experience as firemen, or who would like to train as firemen. There were two recruits in the company who had apparently served as volunteer firemen in their hometowns, so they reported to the First Sergeant to volunteer. Two other men went along and expressed interest in training for the job. These four volunteers and several others who "were volunteered" were subsequently put on a rotating roster to stoke the coal furnaces of the company barracks – at *night.* Yeah, they were firemen all right.

I didn't get roped into these details, but it wasn't because I was wise to such come-ons. I was just too timid to speak up. Not necessarily a bad trait, I found out. I watched and I listened. And I learned – *never volunteer.*

In addition to KP, there were a few other regularly scheduled roster details that were posted on the company bulletin board, ones which we all took our turns filling. One was guard duty, which was more of an adjunct training than it was an actual job that needed to be done. It was an extension of learning our General Orders and putting into practice principles like "I will walk my post in a military manner" and all that went with them. I think I only pulled guard duty once, one night between nine and midnight. I drew my rifle from the weapons rack and was issued a full clip of ammunition from the armory. We were to keep the ammo clip snapped into our field jacket pocket – *not* locked and loaded. I felt faintly like Barney Fife, with his one bullet buttoned safely in his uniform shirt pocket.

I was dropped off at a lonely stretch of the post perimeter fence, a six-foot high chain link barrier topped with three horizontal strands of barbed wire. The post I had to walk was about a hundred yards long, following a hard-beaten path along this fence. Sometimes when I reached the end of my fence section I would meet up with another nervous recruit coming to the end of his section, looming suddenly out of the darkness. The first time this happened we both simultaneously issued a shaky *Who goes there?* our voices shrill and breaking. Hey, being out in the dark piney woods of the Missouri wilderness can be a bit nervous-making. But we both managed to remember the password we'd been given and exchanged them. The important thing was that we didn't shoot each other. Probably it was a good thing the ammo was in our pockets and not in our weapons.

After that initial exchange my guard duty experience petered out into an exercise in staving off boredom and fatigue. I meandered up and down the fenceline humming snatches of church hymns and top forty tunes to myself, sometimes kicking rocks along in front of me like I used to do walking home from school, but this time with an M-1 slung over my shoulder. Even though I was carrying a real rifle and a clip of live ammo, it was somehow not quite as exciting as it had been playing army with my friends and brothers in the big sandpit near our house in Holdenville when I was eight or nine and armed only with a wooden Tommy gun my brother Rich had fashioned on his jigsaw. Was I walking my post in a military manner? I suppose so, but somehow the reality of army life just didn't measure up to the fantasy I used to conjure up after watching Audie Murphy in *To Hell and Back,* or John Wayne in *Back to Bataan* or *Sands of Iwo Jima.*

Perhaps I could have taken my stint on guard duty a bit more seriously that night if I had known about the tense showdown that was taking place in the Atlantic about that time between U.S. and Soviet battleships. It was October 1962, and the Cuban missile crisis was nearing a flashpoint. Then Nikita Khrushchev finally blinked, and the Soviet warships turned back. I was blessedly ignorant of all this as I trudged up and down that fence in the forest, humming to myself and kicking stones. Current newspapers and radios were not a normal part of the BCT environment, and that was probably just as well. If I had had to worry about the possibility of going to war on top of passing the PT test and qualifying with my rifle, I probably would have suffered a nervous and emotional meltdown.

Another roster detail we all pulled a few times was fireguard. This was a safety measure more than anything else, and probably a pretty good idea. Those old wooden barracks with their coal-fed furnaces were undoubtedly real firetraps. The fireguard's job was just to stay awake and walk around in the squad bays, quietly, while everyone else was sleeping. He was to keep his eyes open for any danger or possibility of a fire starting. When you stopped to think that just about everyone smoked, trainees and cadre alike, and smoking was allowed inside and outside both, it was a pure wonder that there *weren't* any barracks fires. A full bucket of water was always kept just inside the latrine entry to be used to douse any small fires that might ignite. And there were also the partially water-filled butt cans placed throughout the sleeping areas. You pulled fireguard for a two- or three-hour shift and tried to walk through two or three times an hour, keeping your eyes open and your sniffer primed for any suspicious smells. (Of course with all those sleeping men there were *plenty* of smells, but smells you were *used* to.) In between walks up and down the aisles you could sit in the latrine and read or write letters or shine your boots and brass. And there was usually someone else up doing those same things in the latrine, which remained brightly lit all night.

And while I'm thinking of it, the late-night latrine was a blessed sanctuary of sorts. It was only there, after lights out in the bays, that you could finally feel safe enough to sit down and have a really complete and satisfying crap – something you'd had to hold all day, because there was always a whistle blowing or a DI or platoon sergeant yelling at you to fall out or fall in, and it was an awful thing to get caught in mid-movement and have to try to break it off and wipe it out and go running out and pulling up your pants all at the same time. There was simply never enough time to shit in the morning (unless you got up a half hour early), and never enough time during the training day either. So probably ninety percent of the platoon became regular late-night shitters. Some nights the whole row of commodes would be taken by exhausted men, pants in a crumpled heap around their ankles, the air thick with cigarette smoke and the putrid stench of too-long backed-up bowels. There would be a mixed chorus of farting, some of it muted and vowel-less, some explosive as rifle reports. After several weeks of communal togetherness, the inhibitions had disappeared entirely. None of us cared what we looked like, sounded like or smelled like. We just wanted relief. We came to laughingly call those late-night fart and shit fests "the pause that refreshes."

The latrine was the scene of one of a few memorable moments that I can still see clearly in my mind. It was early on a Sunday morning, around 5:00, and probably at least a few weeks into our training cycle, because there was nothing at all scheduled for that day – a welcome respite from our usual crammed schedule. Sundays were by this time reserved for church services and leisure activities (read: naps and going to the movies). My internal clock had awakened me anyway just before five, so I decided to go get in a peaceful Sunday morning dump. The only other person in the latrine was our platoon sergeant, who was lathering up to shave at one of the wash basins, already half dressed in tee-shirt, fatigue trousers and boots. He nodded at me as I came down the two steps into the room and went and sat down on the end crapper in the corner. A few minutes later another early riser – I'll call him Smith – came in. We could hear him coming before he entered the latrine. He was coughing – a harsh hacking that sounded so painful it almost hurt just to hear it. Smitty was a soft-looking, slightly overweight kid with thick-lensed glasses and a pimple-peppered face who had been struggling to keep up ever since training began. Like many other recruits, he had also been plagued recently by a persistent cough and other cold symptoms, and it was all obviously beginning to get the best of him. That morning he came dragging over to the middle commode in the row, even in his adversity remembering to observe that unspoken bathroom etiquette that demands you leave a vacant stool or urinal between you and the other guy. For a moment he stood swaying and coughing over the toilet, hawked mightily and tried to spit into it, but nothing much came out, so he turned himself around, dropped his wrinkled boxers and sat down, sighing heavily, then coughed again. He had brought along a pack of Camels and his Zippo. Still coughing, he extracted a cigarette from the pack, put it between his lips and lit up. He managed to stop coughing long enough to inhale deeply, creating a sudden quiet in the room, except for the scrape of Sergeant Mac's razor up the curve of his jaw. At that moment, his lungs filled with smoke, Smitty seemed to slowly deflate, first going limp, his lighted cigarette falling to the floor. Then he jackknifed slowly forward, his butt-cheeks sucking softly away from the toilet seat, followed immediately by the ripe watermelon-sounding thunk of his head as it hit the gray enamel-painted concrete floor, one temple of his smashed glasses jutting out at a crazy angle. He had fainted dead away.

I remember it as if it had taken place in slow motion, but it actually happened so quickly that all I could do was stare open-mouthed as his folded over body then slowly slid sideways from the front edge of toilet and came to rest in a semi-fetal position, facing towards me. Smitty's blue-veined eyelids fluttered. His ragged breath came shallowly. I gaped.

Sergeant Mac, his face still half-covered in shaving cream, turned halfway around at the sink, his razor still poised in one hand. He looked carefully at Smitty's crumpled body and said, in his usual calm unflappable manner, "Private Bazzett, you had better go to the orderly room and tell them to call an ambulance." Doing the world's fastest wipeout, I yanked up my shorts, leapt up the two steps of the latrine, and was jerking open the barracks door when Sergeant Mac called my name again, "Private Bazzett."

"Yes, Sergeant?"

"Put your pants on. It's cold out there."

Why do I remember this small incident so vividly? Maybe it's because it was the first time I had ever seen anyone faint. Or maybe it was the way Smitty went so quickly from being awake, suffering yet sentient, to complete unconsciousness, suddenly no more than a barely breathing slab of human flesh, slipping precariously towards that state we sometimes so cavalierly call "dead meat." Whatever the reason for my remembering, it was an extremely unsettling experience for this Reed City boy, and that slow motion sequence of poor Smitty's collapse was forever burned into my memory cells.

Smith never rejoined our platoon. He was hospitalized, a victim of something called "walking pneumonia," a malady that was, disturbingly, fairly common among basic training troops. You might ask, Why on earth would anyone allow himself to become ill to the point of collapse? Why didn't he report to sick call and get some help? The answer to that question is that such troops were afraid. They weren't afraid of the treatment. And they weren't afraid of being mocked or ragged by their fellow trainees, although there was always that too – the comments and advice of the self-styled he-men and barracks medics: *Don't be a pussy!* or *Suck it up and be a man!* No. They were afraid of being left behind – of being "re-cycled."

Re-cycled was undoubtedly the most feared word in the lexicon of BCT. To be re-cycled meant to start all over again, from week one. No one wanted to do that, not even the jocks and the hunters and sportsmen who seemed to sail so effortlessly through every phase of the training cycle. It was simply too demeaning to have to endure it all again. You were too much under someone else's thumb practically every waking minute. Rarely could you ever relax, really and fully. And you were virtually cut off from the outside world during basic training. – no papers, no radio, no TV. You weren't even allowed any phone calls, except in cases of dire family emergency. Even common criminals were allowed their one phone call. Nope, not us. We were completely at the mercy of the DI's, instructors, sergeants, corporals, or any of the unit permanent party during the time we spent in basic. Even if you were in top-notch physical shape and did well in everything they threw at you, it still sucked. And if you were struggling or out of shape – or both – it *really* sucked. So no one, absolutely *no one,* wanted to be re-cycled. Hence the ordinariness of such cases of chronic bronchitis or walking pneumonia.

Remember that this was in 1962, but I don't think things have changed all that much in the interim. In 1988 my son Jeff went through BCT at Fort McClellan. A few weeks into the training cycle he re-injured an ankle that had been twice broken during his junior high and high school years. Falling victim to the dread fear of re-cycling, he managed to hide his injury and soldiered on for another week, despite sometimes excruciating pain. His BCT was then mercifully interrupted by the Christmas holiday break and he flew home for a two-week leave. His mother and I were shocked by the gaunt shaved-head spectre he presented as he hobbled down the ramp from the airplane, his ankle grossly swollen. It took most of his two-week furlough to semi-rehabilitate his ankle, alternating heat and cold-pack treatments and making frequent use of pain pills. But he managed to successfully complete his basic upon his return to McClellan. He escaped being re-cycled.

And so did I. I kept my head down and persevered. I endured. Mostly I did my best to be as inconspicuous as possible.

It didn't hurt that our "platoon guide" was Dick Kuhn, one of the Gross Isle boys I'd first met in Detroit. The platoon guide, who wore temporary corporal stripes, was a recruit just like everyone else, but usually had some measure of prior military knowledge or experience. Dick's ROTC training had gotten him the job. He already knew the basics of close order drill, marching and the manual of arms, and was a natural for a position of responsibility. He took time to work one-on-one with men in his platoon who were having a hard time catching on to these things. I think he knew about my own fears and insecurities, because he looked out for me and even anticipated some of my difficulties. Of course he couldn't make me a better marksman, but he never stopped offering me encouragement, and I was grateful for that.

Dick was also very effective in maintaining order and discipline in the barracks once the regular training day was over. He was fair and equitable in picking men for work or cleaning details and made sure everyone did his share. The men appreciated this and respected him for it.

You might think that with forty-some men of varying backgrounds and education all crammed together into a relatively small living space with little or no privacy (and the same number upstairs) that there would be temper flareups and fights. But I can recall only one such occasion, and I don't even know what started it. There was just this sudden explosion of a flurry of punches thrown, then a couple bunks and footlockers got knocked askew and the two combatants were down on the floor wrestling for dominance. It was my rifle-cleaning buddy, the big lumbering Fred Wilkerson, who had been suddenly attacked by a guy I didn't know very well. I think his name was Larsen; he was one of those super-charged gung-ho types that generally did everything right and excelled at every phase of training. There must have been some angry words exchanged first, or perhaps some smoldering resentment had suddenly flared. I don't really know, but these two guys were complete opposites in temperament, that's for sure. It happened so quickly that by the time I joined the ring of spectators, looking over the other men's heads, Fred had Larsen down on the floor, a meaty arm locked around his neck. Larsen was flailing and kicking and shouting strangled obscenities. Fred's nose was bloodied and a bruise was already forming under one eye, so I suspect Larsen had thrown most of the punches. Fred was more the backwoods "wrassler" type of fighter, and had finally asserted himself in that manner. He wasn't saying anything, he just stolidly held Larsen down until Dick Kuhn and a couple other guys waded in and separated them, then removed them to opposite ends of the squad bay. Dick then spent several minutes with each man, talking quietly.

As fights go, it didn't amount to much. I only mention it to illustrate how remarkable it was that strict order was usually maintained in the platoon under the combined auspices of Sergeant Mac and Platoon Guide Kuhn. In this case, Sergeant Mac never even came out of his room. Dick settled it and calmed everyone down by himself.

One day towards the end of the training cycle my name was called out at a morning formation, along with several others, including my induction mates from Detroit, and we were ordered to report to the orderly room. There we were put aboard a small bus and transported to the ASA Processing and Placement Detachment . There we spent most of the day filling out paperwork and taking various aptitude tests. The day was unique for a number of reasons.

From my own point of view, I was very relieved to be missing the regular training scheduled for the company that day, which was to be hand-to-hand combat and pugil stick training. Both of these activities could be quite brutal and sometimes caused painful injuries, in spite of safety equipment and precautions. Some guys enjoy this kind of controlled scuffling, but I'm not one of them. I've never been much of a fighter. My temperament wasn't, and isn't, a naturally aggressive one. Pugil sticks could best be described as giant Q-tips, except the ends were definitely *not* soft or fluffy cotton balls. They were more like hard-centered boxing gloves. Picture Robin Hood and Friar Tuck's tussle with staves on that log bridge over the stream, and you'll get a general idea of pugil stick fighting. The combatants were furnished with protective leather headgear much like old-time football helmets. Nonetheless, it could still be a bruising experience, and I wanted no part of it. There were no makeup sessions offered, so we sissy ASA boys escaped the smacking and scuffling in the pit altogether.

Another reason our day away at the ASA Det was significant was the subtle shift in the attitudes of our cadre that we noticed when we returned to the company. We were suddenly being treated with a kind of deference that hadn't been there before. The kid gloves were on, so to speak. We soon realized that to ordinary ground-pounder army types, like the infantry or artillery and armor soldiers who were in charge of conducting our BCT, the Army Security Agency was a kind of mysterious unknown quantity. We were looked upon as future cloak-and-dagger types, who could, conceivably, come back to bite 'em in the ass later on, if they were too hard on us now. We were "spooks," or spies. The BCT cadre had only a very vague idea of what exactly the ASA did. Some of them were obviously concerned that we might be there to spy on *them* and report on their conduct and effectiveness as trainers. Of course this was absurd, but once we realized why we were getting better, slightly preferential treatment, we certainly weren't about to disabuse them of their misconceptions. It was wonderful to be treated somewhat humanely once again, after weeks of the normal abuse that is a normal part of BCT. Too bad it didn't happen earlier.

In any case, during the final few weeks of basic, I was finally able to relax a little. Or at least I didn't live in constant fear of screwing up or being re-cycled. Maybe just the fact that I'd managed to survive to that point gave me additional confidence.

At least on Sundays I had a day to enjoy myself. And, being a good Catholic boy, I never missed a Sunday Mass. Church services were held in a nearby theater. I would usually hike over to attend the earliest Mass, at 8am. The theater was almost always packed for this service, filled with other recruits like me. Then, if I wasn't assigned to any Sunday detail, I could go from Mass to the service club or the PX to hang out or browse the merchandise until the Sunday movie matinees began at noon. Sometimes I would go see an afternoon film in the same theater where I'd attended Mass and received communion just a few hours earlier.

Just to briefly explain a few terms. A service club was a separate building maintained as a place where soldiers could go to get away from their units to rest and recreate. These clubs were staffed by either military or civilian personnel. There were usually pool tables or ping-pong tables to use, and it was always easy to find someone willing to play. There was a service desk where you could check out a deck of cards, checkers, chess sets and other games. Stationery and other writing materials were made available if you wanted to write a letter. There was a TV room, or you could check out a phonograph and records. A coffee urn was usually percolating, filled with complimentary java. Or you could just kick back with a cigarette and a bottle of pop, read a book, or peruse recent periodicals. In short, it was a welcoming refuge for otherwise miserable recruits like me who were waiting for this hell called basic training to be over.

The Post Exchange, or PX, was and still is the military equivalent of a department store, with all or most of its goods discounted and tax free. I mostly just *looked* at the merchandise when I ventured into the PX proper. (There was usually one large main PX and several smaller branch PX's scattered about on a military base.) The PX usually had a snack bar with a grill and pizza and beer and other normal GI treats available. There was often a photo booth where you could have a few grainy pictures made for a dollar. I made use of this service and sent home a couple blurry prints of myself to show my folks I was still alive. I think my biggest enjoyment in going to the PX though was in getting some hot popcorn, or maybe a chocolate shake or malt, small creature comforts that tasted faintly of home.

I had very little money during basic training. The starting pay for a Private E-1 in the fall of 1962 was $78 a month. That sounds pretty paltry, I know, but you have to consider that all our basic needs were already provided for – food, clothing and shelter. All we really needed to buy were basic toiletries. We also had to pay a post tailor out of our first paycheck to sew name tags onto our uniforms and into our hats and boots, and we also had to pay to have our laundry done, since our training schedule didn't allow us time to do it ourselves. (And there weren't any washers or dryers in the barracks anyway.)

We had received a "flying ten" initial pay during our time in the reception camp. That ten dollars was to use for buying soap, razor and blades, toothpaste and whatever else we might need. One thing we didn't really need during BCT was shampoo. Our hair was kept cut so short we just soaped on up over the tops of our heads and rinsed it all on down. The only acceptable hair style during this time was a barely discernible stubble. I wrote home after receiving that ten bucks that I'd bought everything I needed and was down to about three dollars, but I'd probably splurged on a bag of popcorn and an ice-cream bar or some other non-essential extravagance. Every week or two Mom and Dad would put a dollar or two into their letter, and I would be so happy to have that extra buck.

Admission to the movies on post was just a quarter, so a dollar would afford me a whole Sunday of entertainment and enjoyment. (Thanks, Mom. I don't know if I ever told you and Dad how much that dollar or two meant to me then. It was like a lifeline.)

One other place to spend a dime or two a couple times a week was at the "roach coach," which was a snack truck kind of like a Good Humor wagon that came trundling through the company area almost every night when training was over. You may remember that I said earlier that I was always hungry in basic. Well I was, but I couldn't always afford that dime or two you needed when the roach coach came beeping into the yard. But sometimes one of the other guys would treat me to a fudge bar or dixie cup sundae when I was broke, and I would return the favor when I could. It wasn't just me, after all. *Everybody* was always hungry. It may not have been an actual physical hunger. Perhaps it was more of an emotional hunger. Having an after-hours treat was a way of loving yourself just a little, and it made you feel better, even if only briefly.

I spent only one holiday at Fort Leonard Wood. Thanksgiving came the week before we graduated. We had the day off and the cooks in the mess hall prepared a really sumptuous feast of turkey and all the requisite trimmings. We were allowed to take our time eating for once, and could even have seconds or thirds if we wanted to. But it was a sad day for me. It gave me enough time to reflect on Thanksgivings past and I felt quite homesick, enough so that it spoiled my appetite. I was almost relieved to resume training on Friday. And a few days later BCT was finally over.

My graduation from BCT pre-dated the Reverend Martin Luther King, Jr.'s famous "free at last" speech, but even so, if anyone ever understood that phrase and what it meant, it was I after completing BCT. Finally I could breathe more easily. The constricting, often paralyzing fear I had felt more or less constantly for the past two months finally lifted.

I don't remember much about the graduation ceremony itself. We got all duded up in our dress green Class A uniforms, with shoes and brass shined and gleaming, and marched in a final parade before a reviewing stand filled with anonymous officers. We formed up in ruler-straight ranks. We ten-*hut*ted. We raht-*faced.* We forward *harch*ed, and we column-lefted and -righted. We eyes-righted. And we executed militarily correct pree-cizhun marching

*Tim in class A greens,
at BCT graduation.
November, 1962*

maneuvers for the entertainment and edification of our commanders, visiting families and honored guests, and then – Hallelujah, Great God Almighty! – it was *over.*

BCT was over, that is. There was so much more yet to come. But two of the most miserable and harrowing months of my young life were finally behind me. And I suddenly felt quite proud of myself. I had thrown live grenades. I had fired (once) a .50-caliber machine gun. I had found my way out of a dark forest with a compass. I had hiked hundreds of miles. I had qualified as Marksman with an M-1 rifle, the standard weapon of the footsoldier in WWII and Korea. I had pulled KP. I had stood sentry and walked my post in a military manner. I had low-crawled under barbed wire while live-fire tracer rounds whined overhead and (simulated) land mines exploded all around me. I did all these things and more, and I never once pissed or shit my pants or cried. I had endured. I had persevered. *Hell,* yes, I was proud. I was a *soldier*!

AIT: FORT DEVENS, MA

I was crying in the chapel. Unlike the song, however, no one saw me. I was all alone and I was missing my home and my family back in Reed City terribly. It was December 10, 1962, and I hadn't been home since September. Two difficult grueling months of basic training had not made me cry, although I'd certainly wanted to more than a few times, most memorably my first night at the reception camp at Fort Leonard Wood, lying in my bunk listening to the muffled sobbing of some other miserable recruit, and wondering, *What have I done? What have I gone and gotten myself into now? Help me, Jesus, to get through this.*

Post HQ Annex and Training Center at Ft. Devens, 1963.

Well, Jesus hadn't failed me. With what I'm sure was a large helping of His intercession I had survived BCT. The worst was, presumably, over. Nevertheless, with Christmas only a couple weeks away, the terrible homesickness had finally broken me. It was a Monday night. I had called home and talked with my mom and dad only an hour or two earlier and tried to hold myself together and present a brave and manly front, but I think they probably guessed how miserable I was feeling. The sound of their voices coming over the wires nearly unmanned me. It was the sound of home. Upon hanging up the phone, I grabbed my field jacket and cap from my locker and quickly headed out the barracks door of Charley Company to wander the darkened streets of Fort Devens. A few blocks down the hill I found a chapel. There were no lights on, but the door was unlocked, so I let myself in and sat down in a back pew near the door and began to cry. The chapel was deserted, but I tried to be quiet anyway. After all, I was eighteen years old and a soldier in the U.S. Army. Soldiers aren't supposed to cry. Nevertheless, I was wracked with wrenching, shuddering sobs as the tears finally let loose and snot trickled from my nose. It had been a long hard two and a half months since I left my comfortable civilian small town life in Michigan. I had a right to cry. In another ten days I would be headed home on a two-week furlough, but right then, at that moment, those ten days seemed like a lifetime.

Like all military chapels, this one was non- denominational, since it was used by all faiths, but God was unmistakably there, and I took solace in His loving embrace until my tears were finally spent. I had wept myself dry. I heaved a few long sighs, wiped my eyes and nose on my sleeve, and realized that I felt better. There's nothing like a good hard cry to clean you out and give you a sense of, *Okay, then. Let's start over again.* Women are lucky in this respect. They can have a good cry and no one will think any less of them. Men are supposed to hold it all in, bite the bullet, keep a stiff upper lip, and all that crap. Or they can go hide somewhere and let the tears rip, like I did. And a church or chapel is a damn good place to do it. It had worked for me when I was fourteen and a homesick boarding student at St. Joe's Seminary in Grand Rapids, and it worked for me again in this nameless military chapel in Massachusetts a thousand miles from home.

I had arrived at Fort Devens on the first of December. It had been my first time ever on an airplane. The aircraft that brought me was a military two-engine prop job that flew from Fort Leonard Wood to Worcester (which I learned was pronounced *Wus-tah*), with a twenty-minute stopover in Philadelphia to re-fuel. It was a relatively short bus ride from Worcester to Fort Devens, where I was assigned to a transient barracks in C Company – C for casual.

In military parlance, casual means unassigned, or between assignments. Casual duty means shit details, generally, especially if you're from the lower ranks, which I certainly was. When you're on casual status you report to a given mustering point every morning, usually the unit supply room, because that's where all the tools are kept, like wheelbarrows, shovels, picks, rakes, cleaning supplies, or paint and brushes. Whenever anyone in the company or its parent battalion or regiment needs some bodies to perform some manual labor, a call is made to the supply room. The supply sergeant will then say, "I need four volunteers to go wax the floor in the Headquarters Company dayroom." Then he points, "You, you, you and you." And four hapless souls, "volunteers," are carted off to do a day's work.

Actually it might only be a few hours of work, but if you do the job quickly and efficiently and then report back to supply, you'll probably get assigned to another equally unsatisfying crappy detail. So you learn, collectively, to take whatever job you're given and stretch it out over the entire course of the work day. A four-man detail will, for example, learn quickly to work as a cohesive gold-bricking team, constantly cautioning and reminding each other to *Slow down. Take your time. It's a long time yet 'til five o'clock.* We also learned to stretch out our smoke breaks and lunch hour. After all, one detail per day was more than enough for anyone. More on casual duty and Charley Company later.

What was I doing at Fort Devens in the first place? I was there for my AIT (advanced individual training), to learn Morse code, among other things. Devens was at that time the HQ of the Army Security Agency Training Center. When I had enlisted in the Army, I had been guaranteed a slot in the ASA, nothing more. I had hoped to be sent to California to learn a foreign language at the Defense Language Institute in Monterey. It had sounded perfect. I'd had two years of Latin in high school and liked it. I would be learning another language and I'd be in sunny California, land of beaches, surfers and movie stars. How could I go wrong? Well, the first place I went wrong was not getting any of this in writing when I signed my name to enlist. I got ASA, period. That was all. So my actual job or MOS (military occupational specialty) within the ASA remained unspecified. I was up for grabs once I completed BCT. During basic I had spent a whole day at the ASA Detachment taking various aptitude tests, including an artificial language test. I learned later that I scored very high on the language test, but did equally well on the code aptitude test. Apparently the Agency needed a lot more Morse intercept operators at that time than they did linguists. So I was picked to train as a "ditty bopper," MOS 058. In retrospect, I had gotten lucky. There were probably only half a dozen or so men from my BCT company who were picked for language school. They all headed off to Monterey to study Vietnamese. One of them was Dick Kuhn.

In the waning months of 1962, Viet Nam was barely worth a mention on the international pages of U.S. newspapers. I probably couldn't have found it on a world map or globe, and I wasn't alone in my ignorance. It would be another year or two at least before Viet Nam became a regular feature on the evening news. I was blissfully ignorant of my own good fortune, just as I had been when Russian warships had come about and headed back home after the Cuban missile crisis was narrowly averted.

In any case, I landed in casual Charley Company at Fort Devens in early December of 1962, glad beyond words to have basic training behind me, a little apprehensive about what came next, and suddenly homesick as hell with the Christmas season bearing down on us all.

Fortunately I made some friends fairly quickly. One of the best things about being in the military and feeling miserable is that you have plenty of company. Misery really *does* love company, and, before you know it, a commonly-shared misery can develop into a lasting friendship. I have one life-long friend to prove it.

Joe Capozzi was from Yonkers, New York. He was Italian-American, with a headful of thick black hair and a big white toothy smile that made you immediately think of Bucky Beaver, from the Ipana toothpaste commercials shown on TV in the late fifties and early sixties. (You know, the *Brusha, brusha, brusha* one.) He was an only child of doting parents and a big city boy, from NYC.

I, on the other hand, was small town, a Reed City boy. I was of mostly Irish-American stock, blonde and blue-eyed. I was one of six kids, but my parents were also pretty doting, I think.

So what did two guys like that have in common that could result in a life-long friendship? Search me, but it worked. We *were* both raised Catholic. That was something, I suppose. But Joe was kind of short and stocky, while I was tall and skinny. Maybe we complemented each other in physique.

We did have music in common. I was an avid fan of pop music. Joe was too, but he was also a self-taught musician. He played the guitar. He had a rudimentary knowledge of reading music, but mostly he played by ear, and his musical ear was unerring and excellent. He could sit down with his guitar on his knee and listen through a record three or four times, frowning slightly in concentration as the fingers of his left hand moved meditatively up and down the frets of the guitar neck. By the time he had heard the song a few times, he could usually strum along, moving smoothly through each chord change. And after another listen or two, he could usually play the solo of the instrumental break too. I was always just a little in awe of Joe's musical talent.

But it wasn't just the music. Joe had a friendly puppy air and a genuineness about him that was impossible to resist. You just had to like the guy. His good nature went with that Bucky Beaver smile, which, incidentally, saddled him forever with the nickname of "Buck" (later modified to "Buckaroo," or the "Ol' Buckaroo"). My own nickname, acquired about the same time, wasn't quite so warm and fuzzy. I became "Spider," or "Spidey," and not because I reminded anyone of the comic superhero Spiderman. No, it was because my gangly appearance brought to mind a daddy long-legs spider. But I was okay with this. There are a lot worse nicknames than Spider.

Whatever the reasons or the chemistry, Joe and I became friends almost as soon as we met, when we were both doing time at Charley Company. As it turned out, we only stayed on casual status for about a week and then moved to B Company, where Joe and I became "cube-mates."

B Company brick barracks, 1963

What's a cube? A cubicle was a living space in an open bay barracks. B Company, like its adjacent A and C Companies, was one of the new cement block barracks that made up the 1st Battalion of the ASA Training Regiment on the west end of Fort Devens. Those three barrack buildings were so new and shiny that it was almost impossible to ever relax and feel at home in them. The floors were all sheathed in a light colored rubberized tile that showed every scuff mark from the heels of our combat boots. We learned to tip-toe around on these floors, because there was an inspection practically every week and the floors had to be kept absolutely spotless and gleaming at all times in anticipation of these sometimes unannounced walk-throughs.

There were smaller, semi-private rooms in these new barracks too. These rooms housed two to four men, depending on their rank or status. But the non-ranking students like Joe and me were housed in large open squad bays similar to the ones we lived in during basic training. These areas were broken up into "cubes" by grouping wall lockers and double-tiered bunks into smaller living spaces of four men each. The men in each cube were responsible for keeping their own living space and the adjacent aisle space spic and span and shining at all times. So it was indeed hard to relax under these exacting conditions.

I can't remember the names of our other two cube-mates in B Company, but I do remember that one of them was Polish and came from Chicago. I'll call him Kowalski, or Ski for short. Kowalski was short and stocky with blonde wavy hair and an impish grin. He was a rabid fan of rhythm and blues music. His musical hero was

Jimmy Reed. I'd never heard of Reed, which Ski couldn't believe. "Geez, Bazzett," he exclaimed. "You're from *Reed* City and you ain't never heard of Jimmy Reed?" He quickly set about remedying this unforgivable gap in my education. He had a small portable record player and a cache of 45rpm R&B records. I quickly learned to enjoy Jimmy Reed's bluesy sound, particularly his hit, "Baby What You Want Me to Do," which Ski was always singing or humming or slippin' and slidin' to as he putzed around the cube area "getting his shit together," as he liked to say.

Ski also had an irrepressibly filthy mouth on him. If a word was more than two syllables long, Ski would habitually insert a "fucking" between the syllables.

For example, if he found something hard to believe or disagreed with something, he would invariably respond with an "un-fucking-be-*liev*-able," or "im-fucking-*possible!*" But his absolute favorite phrase, his mantra practically, was "Well, fuck me," an affable, friendly uniquely Kowalski variation on the usually more hostile "fuck *you*" that everyone else habitually used. Ski had an infinite number of uses for this comfortable homey little phrase, but it was most often employed to indicate wonder, puzzlement, or admiration. There was a quality of harmlessness, of comradeship, in Ski's use of profanity that made it impossible to take offense. His inflection was all. In fact, it may even have made him a bit more likable. If I had tried to explain this to him, he probably would have been pleased and would have undoubtedly responded, "Well, fuck me!"

So my education continued during my sojourn in B Company, both in the Chicago blues scene and in the myriad intricacies of the mother tongue.

We didn't start our actual classroom training for almost a month. This was due mostly to the timing of our arrival at Devens in early December, but I think it was more due to the army's tendency to always factor in three or four days, or weeks, of slack time at the beginning and the end of scheduled training periods or duty assignments. It happened every time I moved from one place to another.

While we waited for our actual 058 class to begin, we were kept busy with other things. We had a two- or three-day class on the M-1 carbine, for example. We learned to break it down, clean it and reassemble it, just like we did with the rifle in BCT. The M-1 carbine was only about half the size of its rifle counterpart. An officer's weapon, it was famous for its lack of accuracy and general uselessness in a combat situation. But it was rather cute, in a Mattel sort of way, and learning all about the carbine was something to do while we waited to start our real school, which wouldn't be until after the holidays. Our instructor was a middle-aged fatherly sort of fellow, Sergeant First Class (SFC) Squires, who would later also be one of our primary teachers in Morse code school. He was a kindly, already graying, easy-going native of Maine, and his regional accent took a little getting used to. As he named and described the various parts of the carbine, it took most of us a while to figure out that "awl," "awler," and "awlin'" were actually references to "oil" and "oiling" the weapon. SFC Squires was very patient and unfailingly pleasant in everything he did with us. After all the yelling and screaming and obscenities we had become accustomed to from the BCT DI's, his laid-back manner was a truly pleasant change, and we all grew to like and admire him immensely. Never one to criticize much, SFC Squires' most common and perhaps his highest form of praise was, "You done good," a phrase we all quickly incorporated into our own fast-growing military lexicons.

Since we were basically marking time until our class start date in January, and since our Christmas leaves didn't begin until December 20, we also had to pull more casual duty in the meantime, which included KP, shoveling snow, spreading sand and salt on the walks around the barracks, and whatever other unskilled manual jobs that needed doing. There was a period of several days when we reported every morning to the C Company supply room once again. After a few days of this we settled into a routine and became more comfortable (or perhaps a better word would be devious) in these surroundings. Joe and I discovered three rows of boxes, contents unknown, lining the back wall of the supply room that were stacked four to five feet high. I discovered that these boxes were not very heavy, and, with a minimum amount of effort, we managed to slide the first two rows forward a few feet, leaving a gap large enough to conceal ourselves in. We re-arranged some boxes from the back row, stacking some on top of the front row to maximize our cover, and arranging a few more to form a shelf we could stretch out on. Hell, if you're going to hide out to duck details, you might as well be comfortable. No point in lying on a cold floor. There was a high window in the back wall, letting in enough light to read by. It would have been too risky to actually snooze, but we did successfully employ this hideout for a couple of days, popping out to make token appearances occasionally. All those years of reading Beetle Bailey in the Sunday funnies was finally paying off.

But it wasn't all just details and gold-bricking those first few weeks at Devens. After all the restrictions and confinement imposed on us during BCT, it seemed a great luxury to be able to put on a civilian shirt and trousers again and wander freely about the post and surrounding area on evenings and weekends. One of the first things I did my first weekend at Fort Devens was to visit the main PX and buy a pair of pants, a shirt and a package of jockey briefs. No more GI boxer shorts. My boys were gonna be snug and safe from now on. I was still stuck with a GI haircut (although not so extreme as the BCT version), but I was back in civvies again and that felt good.

We went to the movies a lot in our free time. Remember that the price of admission at post theaters was only a quarter, so that much we could afford. We also often pooled our meager funds to purchase a pizza and a pitcher (or two) of 3.2 beer at the nearest snack bar, and fed our odd nickels and dimes into the juke box and munched and guzzled to the strains of the Beach Boys' "Little Deuce Coupe" or "Be True to Your School," or the latest offerings from Elvis, Ricky or the Four Seasons. Nights we tuned in WBZ out of Boston for the latest top forty songs, falling asleep to the idyllic simplistic strains of "Hey Paula," or the mysterious haunting lyrics of Kyu Sakamoto's "Sukiyaki." Things like junk food, movies, music and normal clothing had become untold luxuries following our common two months-plus ordeal of BCT.

We swapped stories about what we'd endured under unnamed monster DI's, whether at Leonard Wood, Fort Dix, or Fort Ord. There was a sameness and commonality to our experiences that helped us to bond. None of my new friends cared that I was a lousy shot and had just barely managed to make Marksman, even though many of them had fired expert. It was all bullshit, we agreed. We were ASA and would probably never carry weapons again. We were the cream. We weren't ground-pounders or grunts. We were *military intelligence*, the original and probably most genuine oxymoron ever coined – something else we all laughingly agreed on. For even at this still-early stage of our enlistments we were beginning to develop an attitude. The rules, regulations and restrictions imposed by the army were beginning to chafe. We hadn't yet reached the full-blown FTA (*fuck the army*) stage of disillusionment, but the seeds were being sown during this, our first chance at feeling like individuals again.

Yes, we were certainly full of ourselves. We were survivors of BCT and many of us were on our own and away from home for the first time in our young lives, and were eager to spread our wings and fly – to grow up. Unfortunately, we weren't quite sure just how to go about being adults. Drinking seemed like a good way to start though, so we went at our beer binges with a vengeance. Since we were all pretty new to it, it didn't take much beer for us to start acting silly – a good thing, since we didn't have much money.

It was about this time I had my first martini. I wasn't even sure what exactly a martini was, only that it came in a long-stemmed glass, usually with an olive. And I kind of liked olives. Mom put olives in her homemade lasagna sometimes, and olive loaf luncheon meat was almost as good as pickle loaf. At any rate, one Saturday evening, feeling eminently grown-up, I took the shuttle bus into Ayer, and after wandering around the small downtown area for a while, I went into a rather fancy-looking (to me) saloon. Well, it was probably actually more of a cocktail lounge than just a bar. It was dimly lighted and quite tastefully appointed. (I realize this *now*; I didn't then.) It was the first time I'd ever been inside a place like that. In Reed City there were only a couple bars, Henry's and the U&I, and of course I'd never been in either one of them. And I was still only eighteen.

I slid into a red leather-upholstered booth near the bar, and a waiter in a white shirt with a black bow-tie brought me a menu and asked if I'd like a drink. I was immediately flattered and somewhat emboldened by the fact that he didn't ask to see any proof-of-age identification. I don't know to this day if that was an oversight or if eighteen was the legal drinking age in Massachusetts. Or maybe it was just that if you were a soldier, which I so obviously was, then the Ayer imbibing establishments made allowances for you. In any case, unprepared as I was for his query, I said the first thing that popped into my head. "Yes. I'll have a martini, please." And just moments later, there it was, placed discretely on a cocktail napkin near my elbow. Yup, yup. In a long-stemmed glass, just like in the movies. And there was that olive too, impaled on a toothpick leaning against the rim of the glass. Immensely pleased with myself and with the relative ease of the whole situation, I savored the moment as I drew my pack of Newports and a matchbook from my shirt pocket. Tapping the filter end of a cigarette briskly and knowledgeably on the side of the pack (as I'd seen the more experienced of my smoker friends do), I then placed it between my lips, lit up, inhaled (only slightly), and blew a thin stream of the menthol-flavored smoke out both nostrils as I looked appraisingly around the nearly empty lounge. Carefully laying my cigarette into the groove of a heavy glass ashtray, I took the olive on its toothpick from the glass and laid it on the corner of the napkin. I'd save that for after the drink. Raising the glass to my lips, I took a long sip.

BLECCHH! My *GAWD*! It tasted like *bug spray!* Like *insecticide!* With perhaps a pinch of 10-W-30 *motor* oil! Christ all-fucking-*mighty,* it was nasty! Was *this* what a dry martini really tasted like, or was the bartender playing some kind of a horrendous joke on me? I wanted to go wash my tongue. Eating soap at that moment just might have been a pleasure. Judas-fucking-*PRIEST!* How could this *be*? I mean, *come-ON!* I'd seen countless cool people like Cary Grant and Ingrid Bergman and Charles Boyer and Rock and Doris sip these things and seem to really *enjoy* them! *YUCK!*

Of course, you've got to understand that this somewhat unpleasant reaction was entirely internalized. On the surface I remained completely cool, suave and cosmopolitanly debonair. I was *Bond, James Bond,* and if I'd just made a really awful face, then it must have been a sneer of displeasure at the obviously inferior quality of this martini.

I managed a couple more tiny sips of the oily-tasting shit, then carefully spilled as much of it as I could onto the napkin. Then I ordered a beer to go with my burger and fries and managed to wash away most of the disgusting residue. My first – and last – martini. True story. Well, of *course* it's a true story. *All* of this stuff is, more or less. It's a *memoir*, remember?

Martinis and beer aside, probably my favorite drink then (and now) was a nice thick chocolate malt. One of the things I'd missed the most since I'd joined the army was the kind of malt I used to enjoy regularly at Reed City soda fountains. The best place to get one was at the Bonsall's Drugs fountain, where they mixed it up from real ice cream, milk, chocolate syrup and malt powder in that tall silver mixing cup. Then they poured half of it into a tall soda glass and set the glass *and* that still frosted and chilled aluminum mixing cup down in front of you. It was *soooo good!* And the second best thing about a soda fountain malt like that was knowing that once you'd drained that glass you had enough left in the cup to fill it up again! It was like getting two malts for the price of one. Of course, Jay Williams also whipped up a fine malt at the Dairy Queen down on South Chestnut, but once you'd sucked that tall paper cup dry, it was over.

The first time I ate at a burger joint in Ayer, I was a little upset that there were no malts listed on the menu, so I asked the waitress about this discrepancy, and after some initial confusion, I learned that in Massachusetts a malt is called a frappe – same ingredients, just a different name. What a relief! I wouldn't have to go without my manly malt beverage after all.

I did get back to Reed City twice while I was stationed at Fort Devens. The first time was a two-week Christmas leave, my first furlough since I'd joined the army in September. I remember vividly the homesickness and the anticipation leading up to that long-awaited return to the homeplace. Strangely enough, however, I remember almost nothing of the time I spent at home that holiday season. It was pretty much an all-day bus ride from Ayer, Massachusetts, to Grand Rapids, where I think my brother Bill picked me up to bring me the last seventy miles home. That two-week period is pretty much a blank in my memory. I suspect it was plagued by the ticking clock syndrome that most military furloughs fall victim to. Every day you wake up thinking, *I've only got nine days left* – or six or three days. You get the picture. It can almost ruin a vacation.

I must have enjoyed myself some though, because in February I made the trip home again over a long Washington's Birthday holiday weekend, braving snow and ice storms. That time I traveled in a car with Lynn Pontz and Rick Smeltzer (from Beulah,

At home in Reed City, Christmas, 1962.

Michigan). I think we came across Canada and through the Upper Peninsula on the way home, and then went back via Toledo and the Ohio and Pennsylvania Turnpikes. We were only home for a scant two days (out of our four-day weekend) and spent two days driving. Again, I have no memory of what I did while I was home. It must have seemed important and worth while at the time though.

Finally, in January 1963 I began my official training as an 058, which was the MOS number for a manual Morse intercept operator. The class lasted nearly six months. When we began our training in January, I think we numbered nearly fifty men, but by the time the class graduated in late June, there were less than thirty of us. The men who didn't finish 058 training were usually funneled into other jobs or training schools. Some washed out due to a lack of aptitude, or a lack of interest and consequent bad attitude. Some were earmarked for similar jobs, like teletype operators or intelligence traffic analysts. Some of them I never knew where they went; they just disappeared into other army slots. One of my early friends at Devens, Joe Bohn, was transferred to Fort Gordon, Georgia, but I can't remember if he went to signal school or became an MP (military policeman), and I lost touch with him soon after he left.

Our initial training as 058's included a beginning typing class. It was actually a bit more than a standard typing class, because we were using a military-style typewriter called a "mill." There were no lower-case letters on the mill, only capitals, or "caps." There may have been some other special keys or idiosyncrasies of the mill, but I can't remember any of that. What I do remember is that you had to strike those keys *hard*, and our instructors emphasized this, telling us if we wanted to make a distinct impression when it came time to type on five-ply or six-ply paper with carbons, then we had to *BANG* those keys! So I learned to raise my hands high, wrists stiffened, and really bash at the keys, a habit I had to un-learn years later, first for using an electric typewriter, and, much later, to use a computer keyboard. But at that moment in time we all learned to type Liberace-style.

I probably had a certain edge over some of the guys, since I had taken a term of personal typing in high school, so was already somewhat familiar with the keyboard layout at least. But I kind of enjoyed the class. Sometimes the NCO instructors would bring in some martial music, like John Philip Sousa, and we would type along in time with "Stars and Stripes Forever," or something similar.

We started learning code at the same time. We'd have typing class in the morning and code practice in the afternoon. Morse code is fairly easy to learn. It just involves memorizing combinations of sounds representing the letters of the alphabet, numbers, and punctuation marks. Then you practice, practice, practice. The letter *A* is represented by *dit-dah. B* is *dah-dit-dit-dit. C* is *dah-dit-dah-dit*, and so on. (If you want to learn it all, consult a Boy Scout handbook.) We were given a group of letters or numbers to study and learn each day until we had committed the alphabet, numbers and various other symbols to memory. Then we would practice, first with an instructor just reading the sounds, then later by listening to recordings of actual Morse code transmitted by a key.

While we were still learning to type, we would practice taking down groups of letters or numbers by hand, using a pencil. Once we'd completed our typing class, or tested out of it, we began to take down code groups on the mill. After that it was just continuous practicing, with the speed of the code transmissions gradually increased. We started out at about five words per minute (wpm), and gradually increased the speed throughout the course. I think I was up to twenty or twenty-five wpm by graduation time.

This may sound a bit difficult, but once you've learned the code and the mechanics of the mill, it becomes basically a

Pavlovian stimulus-response kind of activity – hear this sound, hit this key, BANG! It becomes a kind of automatic monkey-work job. A really seasoned operator could carry on a conversation and take down code at 25wpm or more all at the same time.

The good thing about this kind of training course was that once you'd committed the code to memory, which only took a few weeks at the most, the rest was just practice and increasing your speed. So – no homework! Yay! There were, of course, a few guys who just couldn't seem to learn the code, or couldn't handle the mill (or maybe they didn't *want* to). These guys, for whatever reason, dropped out and disappeared along the way. In government-ese, they "attrited." In other words, normal attrition was factored into the training equation.

There was a rumor while we were in code school that a small portion of these "attriter critters" were channeled into another ASA MOS that provided communications security (comsec) for our own forces. In other words, they listened in on various U.S. military communications, and if our operators committed any comms security breaches, they would report it to headquarters, and the guilty operator would be disciplined or relieved of his duties. The failed 058's who performed this service were most commonly known as "buddy fuckers." I suppose it was a necessary job, but not one I would have wanted. It takes a certain kind of weasel mentality to inform on your own people.

The no-homework aspect of 058 school was a truly wonderful thing. As long as you were progressing at a normal rate, school was pretty much a nine-to-five affair like any job. Of course, the army liked to emphasize you were a soldier twenty-four hours a day, and always subject to "other duties."

Those duties were the usual things – KP, CQ (Charge of Quarters, or unit "go-fer"), and guard duty. I'm not sure why guard duty was necessary in the middle of Massachusetts in the year 1963, but there it was. I know I pulled it several times during my tour at Fort Devens. As I remember it, we weren't issued any weapons or ammo for walking guard. Maybe we got a whistle on a cord to wear around our necks.

We were usually tasked with making a walking circuit around and in between the barracks block where we lived. I remember spending a couple cold hours one Saturday night pacing around flailing my arms trying to keep warm and softly singing, "Another Saturday Night (and I Ain't Got Nobody)" a la Sam Cooke, and feeling thoroughly stupid and generally miserable and disgusted.

KP wasn't nearly the ordeal it had been in basic. Although it still was a very long day, the mess sergeants and cooks tried to treat you like a fellow human being instead of a maggot. Nevertheless, no one particularly liked KP, so there was a healthy trade in that particular detail. The mess hall cadre didn't care who reported for duty, as along as they had the required number of bodies. So if you drew KP and didn't want to do the the duty, you could pay someone else to do it for you – if you had the money. And there was a small core of willing mercenaries around who would pull your KP for you, for the right price. I think the going rate was five or six dollars, but it could go as high as ten. When you consider that most of us only made eighty to ninety dollars a month, five or six bucks was a chunk of change back then. The guys willing to pay usually got extra money from home or had a separate source of income. I never paid anyone to do KP for me. I couldn't afford to. But then I never took money to do anyone else's KP either. You had to have *some* standards, after all.

Those first winter months of our training we lived in B company, which was part of a new barracks complex situated on a hill. Every morning we marched to class at the main training center, which was probably a little less than a mile from our barracks. Once the streets and sidewalks became snow- and ice-covered, the marching could get a bit dicey. Try keeping in step with forty-some other guys who are themselves slipping and sliding around and you'll get the picture. If one guy lost his footing on the slope and went down, there was often a chain reaction as the men immediately following tripped over him, or tried to avoid him, and ended up on the ground too. It wasn't unusual for a whole column to go suddenly from vertical to horizontal, cursing and hollering at each other, but then finally laughing at the ludicrousness of trying to march under those icy conditions. Usually a command to "route step" would follow such a falling-down clusterfuck, once we'd all gotten back on our feet, sometimes laughing and chucking snowballs at each other. Route step just means stay upright and keep moving, and forget keeping in step.

By early March, winter was showing no signs of retreating. In a letter home about that time, I noted that it was snowing and there was still nearly three feet of snow on the ground. That long harsh winter might have gotten me down except for one thing. I found a kind of home away from home nearby with some old friends of my Grandma and Grandpa Bazzett.

While I was home on leave in February, Grandma told me about Art and Leone Smith, who lived in Harvard, a tiny village just a few miles from Fort Devens. Leone had been a Steeby from Wayland, Michigan. My grandparents had been tenants on the Steeby farm outside Wayland, but the Steeby and Bazzett families were also close friends. One of my dad's best pals in high school had been a Steeby, one of Leone's nephews. My grandma and Leone had been best friends for many years by the time Leone and Art Smith "adopted" me, an orphan of circumstance a thousand miles from home.

Art and Leone had lived many years in New York City, where Art had been an executive with DuPont. By the time I met the Smiths, they had retired to a comfortable cottage on the banks of Bear Pond, a small lake outside Harvard. Their daughter Arly lived with her husband Chan and four little girls in South Acton, only about ten miles from Harvard.

I had been rather reluctant to contact the Smiths, even though Grandma had assured me I'd be welcome at their place, as she'd written Leone about my posting to Devens. I'm sure she'd given glowing recommendations for her little "Timmy Jim," but I was like any teenager, reluctant to seek out the company of anyone over thirty. But finally one lonely March Saturday, with the hard Massachusetts winter winding slowly down, I made the phone call and explained who I was. Leone seemed genuinely pleased that I had called, and she immediately dispatched Art over to Ayer to pick me up at the USO Club, which was where I'd placed the call from. She had a hot lunch waiting for all of us when Art brought me into their warm cheery house, and it seemed so much like coming into my Grandma's kitchen that I nearly cried. We visited over lunch and Leone told stories about her long friendship with Grandma, and pumped me for information about Grandma and Grandpa's health and how things were going for them on their farm in Reed City. Art talked about how glad he was to be retired and told me a little

On Art and Leone Smith's patio at Bear Pond in Harvard. June, 1963.
Left to right: Leone, Arly and her four daughters, Art and Tim.

something about his life too. When they found out I had a weekend pass, Leone insisted that I spend the night, and even provided me with a new toothbrush and a spare pair of Art's pajamas. I was shown into a guest room that became "Tim's room" for the rest of my time at Fort Devens.

The next morning they took me to church with them. I can't remember now if they were Catholic, but I was so pleased to have been accepted into their home that I would have gladly attended any Protestant church, synagogue or mosque with them. Church services were followed by an enormous and scrumptious brunch that Leone "just threw together." I even lingered over coffee with them afterwards, and I didn't even *like* coffee, but at the Smiths' table it tasted good, like everything else. At Leone's suggestion, I just kept adding more sugar and cream until it did taste good to me. (I still like a little coffee with my cream and sugar.) Then we perused the different sections of the Sunday papers from both Boston and New York. Later I went outside and shoveled a little of the new snow off the paths and driveway for Art, although he told me not to bother. I was just so *grateful* to these wonderful people for making me feel so at home. Still later that afternoon Leone fixed a home-style roast beef dinner, then Art drove me back to post, filled with good home-cooked food and a wonderful sense of well-being.

This was the first of several visits I made to the Smiths' home over the next four months. They issued me a standing invitation to come and make myself at home anytime I could get away from base, but they didn't pressure me. I think that's why I came to visit as many times as I did. That, and the fact that my cube-mate Joe Capozzi often went home to Yonkers for the weekend.

On one weekend that spring we went and spent a day at Chan and Arly's place in South Acton – an estate of sorts, actually. Chan had nearly forty acres of land and had even dredged a pond near his house. I'm not sure, but I think Chan may have been a museum curator or something similar in Boston. Whatever he did, he was doing well, obviously. He and Arly and their four girls, aged eleven on down to three, all made me feel welcome. We enjoyed cookouts together, at both places. I tried to do little odd jobs for them whenever I could, even washing dishes after meals. I enjoyed playing with the kids, and watched TV with them. It was about as close as I could have come to being back home again.

When spring finally arrived I spent a couple of visits helping Art with jobs around the the yard. We raked leaves and pruned trees and bushes. We put the dock back into the lake for the summer and carried his aluminum fishing boat down to the water and moored it to the dock. Art worked on tuning up his outboard motor and I picked up trash and brush that had collected in the yard and along the shore during the winter. We made trips to the local dump, Art letting me drive his new Buick, probably easily the nicest car I had ever driven. I was flattered by his trust in my driving skills.

Art and Leone were both serious bridge players, and Friday night was their bridge night, but they never let that preclude my weekend visits. At least three or four times they invited me for the whole weekend. Art would come pick me up at the barracks around 5:30 and bring me home for supper. Then he and Leone would leave for their bridge group around 7:30 and sometimes wouldn't get home until 11 or 12:00, still discussing their game and what they could have played or should have done instead of what they did. I have never learned to play bridge, and was a bit mystified over a card game that could so preoccupy a person, not just while they were playing it, but for hours and sometimes days afterwards, because they would often continue their strategy talks the next morning over breakfast.

What I enjoyed most about those bridge nights though was the luxury of having a whole evening to myself in a comfortable house, free to read or listen to music or watch TV with a big bowl of homemade popcorn, sitting on a couch or in a recliner instead of lying on an army bunk.

Popcorn was a Sunday night family tradition at our house when I was growing up in Reed City. We never had a supper on Sundays. We'd have a big country breakfast after Mass, then Sunday dinner around 3:00, usually something heavy and filling, like roast beef or pork, with potatoes and gravy and a vegetable or two. I mean it was a *big*, lie-around- groaning-afterwards kind of dinner. As a kid, I didn't really appreciate those big Sunday meals. It wasn't because they weren't good. No, I was always afraid if I ate too much I wouldn't be hungry enough to enjoy the popcorn later that night. Of course, I needn't have worried. I *always* enjoyed the popcorn. What I did *not* always enjoy was *The Ed Sullivan Show* (nee *The Toast of the Town*), a Sunday night TV staple in homes all over America in the fifties and sixties. The problem with Ed wasn't just his famously stiff delivery, but that his show started at 8:00. *The Wonderful World of Disney* started at 7:30 and ran until 8:30, so when Dad turned on Ed Sullivan, we would miss the second half of Disney's story about Davy Crockett and Mike Fink, or whatever was on that night. Most kids of the era hated Ed Sullivan anyway, because he was a sure reminder that it was Sunday night and we still hadn't done that homework that was due Monday morning.

But I was talking about popcorn. I had missed it during my first few months in the army, so in January of '63, when I got back to Devens from Christmas leave, I went to a hardware store in Ayer and purchased a small electric-coil corn popper that I could use in the barracks on weekends. At the same store I also bought a large aluminum six-quart pot with a lid. You had to have a metal pot to dump the hot corn into. That popper and pot saw many years of service. They traveled overseas with me and back home again. The popper itself finally burned out and was discarded many years ago. But the aluminum pot, now dented and stained from forty years of hard use and and hot oil, still survives. My children all remember it fondly. Whenever we popped corn, the popper was always emptied into that pot and the kids all filled their smaller bowls from it. When I'd popped the last popper of the night, I would eat my portion from that pot myself. Only rarely were the kids allowed to eat directly from that revered vessel. As they grew older they came to call it the "sacred silver pot." Considering the places that pot has been and its many years of faithful service, it seems a fitting name.

The purchase of that popper and pot made barracks life a bit more bearable. It also made me suddenly a lot more popular, for who can resist the sound and the smell of popping popcorn. I could never make just one popperful. I met a lot of guys by making popcorn in the barracks. Some of them enjoyed it so much they would buy me a whole bag of unpopped corn, just to have a fresh bowl now and then. It was a mutually satisfactory arrangement all around, and we all got a small taste of home in the bargain.

In mid-April my 058 class relocated from Company B across post to Company G in the 2nd Battalion of the Training Regiment. The barracks we moved into was one of the old WWII era wooden buildings, much like the one I'd occupied at Fort Leonard Wood, only it had been re-modeled and improved with insulation and sheetrock and a better heating plant. It was also much lower maintenance, being as old as it was. There was no way to make that old building gleam or shine like the newer barracks did. We were

Tim in his G Company cube

able to relax and feel more comfortable in our "new-old" quarters. And we were closer to our classroom area too. We still marched to class every day, but it was a shorter flatter route.

Marching wasn't such a chore for any of us by this time. It had become second nature for most of us. About the same time we made our move to G Company I remember this guy in our class (I think his name was Roberts) took over the duties of platoon guide and began calling cadence for us in our march to class each day. He was a little older than most of us and had already served a stint in the Marine Corps. I guess his particular "diction" for calling cadence was a result of his training in the Corps. Whatever the origin, we all loved it. It was a loud guttural growl, and sounded something like this:

Buddle-a-LE'L,
(pause) *LE'L,*
(pause) *LE'L,*
REE, LE'L.

I know it looks like nonsense, but it sure was easy and fun to march to. I'm not sure what that initial "Buddle-a" means, but of course the "Le'l" means LEFT, then a beat to put your right foot down, then repeat, followed by a final "Le'l, ree, le'l" (left, right, left). It was so different and so *cool*, and was unique to our marching formation, to our class, and we were strangely pleased with ourselves over this small thing. We all tried to emulate Roberts' cadence delivery, but he was one of a kind. Semper fi, Man.

We had a lot of time on our hands on evenings and weekends, but we never grew bored. When the holidays were over, several guys brought their cars back to Devens with them, so we could usually find wheels when we wanted to go somewhere. I didn't have a car myself but some of my friends did.

One of the coolest cars in our circle, hands down, was a bright red 1955 Thunderbird convertible, with both the self-stowing soft top and a snap-on hardtop. It belonged to Mike Campbell, a fellow Michigander from Battle Creek, the cereal capital of the U.S. Mike was (and still is) an avid car buff, and his red T-bird was already a classic in 1963. Its only shortcoming was it was only a two-seater. Nevertheless, I can remember at least a couple of times that spring and summer when we had four guys jammed into that car, Mike

Bill Couture with Mike Campbell's '55 red T-Bird at Ft. Devens. February, 1963.

behind the wheel, of course, his best friend Bill Couture riding shotgun in the other leather bucket seat, and I and Joe (or someone else) crowded into the tiny space behind the seats. Not very comfortable to be sure, but it was worth the discomfort just to be seen in a car that classy.

Campbell and Couture were a pair. Bill was from the Pontiac area in Michigan. They had both gone through basic at Leonard Wood the same time I did, but were in a different company, so I didn't meet them until we got to Devens. They reminded me very much of the two other Michigan buddies who had been fellow Delta Devils with me, Doug Hura and Dick Kuhn. They were, in many ways, another Laurel and Hardy combination. Mike was slight, blonde and blue-eyed, and tended to be very excitable. And he could quickly ratchet that excitability up to a near hysterical shrillness. He was also a chronic worrier. Bill was the calming influence of the pair. Whenever Mike was somehow provoked into his alarmist screaming mee-mee state, Bill was the one who would gently raise his hands palms out and quietly talk Mike down from his panic, telling him, "It'll be all right, Mike. You'll see. Don't worry." And Mike would gradually calm down under his friend's soothing admonitions. These two guys were tight, and made many day trips to Boston and its various attractions, and also made several long-haul weekend trips home to Michigan in the T-bird during those months of training.

Bill Couture was a really interesting guy. He was very well-read and interested in just about everything, particularly the arts. He had spent a year or so in college before enlisting and was a few years older than most of us. He had a solid well-muscled wrestler's build that was offset by an intelligent, bookish-looking, square-jawed face, tightly- curled dark hair, and a pair of horn-rimmed glasses. He had a wry, quiet sense of humor and was usually slow to anger. But once that slow fuse was ignited, you'd better get the hell out of the way.

I went to a lot of movies at Devens. We all did. But my most memorable movie matinee there was one I attended with Bill one Saturday afternoon. *West Side Story* first came to the screen in 1961, but it was still playing army theaters in the spring of '63. Bill knew the story and the music from its stage version and had already seen the film, but was excited about seeing it again. He talked it up to me enough to convince me to go along. I knew some of the music already from records and radio – beautiful songs like "Tonight" and "Maria," which had already been recorded by numerous artists. Most of our friends passed on this film, because it was a musical, with lots of dance numbers, something "real men" weren't supposed to be interested in.

So it was just Bill and I from our bunch, but the theater was packed with GI's nonetheless. Bill had been right. *West Side Story* was (and is) a beautiful film, visually and musically. I was immediately engaged by the *Romeo and Juliet* theme and the affecting performances of Richard Beymer and George Chakiris from the rival street gangs of New York. The Bernstein-Sondheim score was riveting, and I even liked the dance scenes. But mostly I was entranced by the still-young Natalie Wood as the tragically beautiful heroine, Maria.

Bill, of course, loved every part of the film. But there was a problem. A lot of the GI audience fell into that category of guys who felt dancing was sissy and that singing unnecessarily interrupted the flow of the story. In other words, they didn't understand or appreciate musicals. So every time the story segued into a song or dance number, they began to groan and complain audibly, and even erupted into ridiculing catcalls at the on-screen dancers a couple of times. Bill was appalled and angered by such behavior in the presence of such an obviously superior artistic performance. His fuse had been lit and he was doing a slow burn. He gave the noisy detractors sufficient time to to mend their ways, but instead they got worse. They became bolder, louder and increasingly more obscene in their comments about the "fairy" dancers and "faggot" music.

Finally Bill could bear this boorish behavior no longer. He reached flashpoint. Enough. Now Bill was not ordinarily an adherent of profanity, and was normally a very soft- spoken gentle guy, but he had taken the measure of this audience, so when he finally exploded, he addressed them in their own language. Erupting from his seat in the middle of the theater, he ripped into all those uncultured, ill-mannered buffoons.

"YOU *STOO-PID* MOTHERFUCKERS, SHUT THE FUCK *UP*! WHAT THE FUCK ARE YOU *DOING* HERE IF YOU DON'T LIKE MUSICALS? SHUT THE FUCK UP OR GET THE FUCK *OUT*!"

Then, still trembling with barely contained outrage, he sat back down. And, miraculously, except for the music from the screen, the theater was quiet. And it stayed that way until the film was over. Couture had cowed the uncultured masses. The stupid motherfuckers shut the fuck up. Un-fucking-be*liev*able.

I have viewed *West Side Story* and listened to its music numerous times in the past forty years, and I can never watch this beautiful film or listen to its soundtrack without thinking of Bill Couture and the first time I saw it. And it's not a *bad* memory, Bill. It's a good one. Art triumphant, sort of.

There was another not so good film that I remember *almost* seeing that spring called *The Chapman Report.* I had recently read the book in paperback and had been somewhat engaged and pleasantly tittilated by its salacious, pseudo- scientific research approach to examining the sexual mores and practices of modern-day American women. I guess what I really mean by that is that it was chock-full of juicy sex scenes held together by a rather thin and contrived plot, at least in the book. Hell, the real reason I wanted to see the film was to see Jane Fonda again, whom I'd fallen in love with when I saw her in *Tall Story*, and also in *Period of Adjustment,* which had both been adapted from stage plays and were actually *good* films. *The Chapman Report*, or what I saw of it, was nothing more than a trashy potboiler, but it offered the possibility of seeing Jane with at least some of her clothes off.

But I've gotten a teensy bit ahead of myself. I had taken the bus into Boston on a bright spring day to do some sight-seeing. I went with a casual friend from the barracks, a short slender fellow named Edgars, I think. Or maybe his first name was Edgar, I can't remember. We were doing the tourist thing. We walked all over downtown Boston, following the Freedom Trail and visiting the Paul Revere House, the Old North Church, and other points of historical interest. We stopped for lunch at a delicatessen where I had my first ever hot pastrami sandwich on rye, a new taste treat. There were big bowls of kosher dill pickles on each table to go with your sandwiches, and they were so good that Edgar and I polished off the whole bowl.

Afterwards, feeling full and a bit sluggish, we went in search of a good movie. There were undoubtedly much better films playing in Boston than *The Chapman Report*, but the outside posters of a frustrated and juicy-looking young Jane Fonda sucked us into that particular downtown theater. We sat through the previews of coming attractions and then settled in for the feature, which turned out to be excruciatingly slow and rather boring, as scholarly-looking sex researcher Efrem Zimbalist, Jr. began his painstaking data gathering. Edgar and I were sitting near the middle of a back row in the half-empty theater. Jane Fonda's character had just made her appearance in the film when I noticed a tall man in an overcoat get up from the end of our row on the other side of Edgar and move over to sit down one seat away from him. We both glanced over at him, then turned our attention back to the screen. Several minutes later, the man got up again and this time sat down in the seat right next to Edgar, a flagrant and obvious breach of "guy etiquette."

When two guys go to a movie together, they don't sit in directly adjacent seats if there are enough empty seats in a row. They leave an empty seat between them. There are a couple of reasons for this. One is so you've each got arm-rests on both sides and a little more room in general to spread out – elbow room, or breathing room, if you will. The other reason, and probably the more important one, is kind of related to that bathroom etiquette thing I talked about earlier, where it's considered guy good manners to always leave an empty urinal or toilet stall between users. It's a matter of establishing a personal comfort zone. But let's be honest. There's also an unquestionable if unspoken element of homophobia at work in these "guy etiquette" situations.

In any case, when this shadowy stranger shifted into the seat next to Edgar's, Edgar immediately stiffened. Well, maybe that's a poor choice of words. Let's say he shifted minutely in his own seat, trying to move *away* from this guy without actually changing seats. He also shot me a look of conscious alarm, which I caught, even across the correctly vacant seat separating us. Monitoring the situation out of the corner of my eye, but still trying to get an eyeful of Jane on the screen, I could see the whites of Edgar's eyes as they shifted nervously back and forth from the screen to the stranger to me.

Edgar's alarm escalated quickly when the overcoated creep eased his knee to the left until it made contact with Edgar's knee, which he promptly jerked away as if he'd been burned. Edgar shot me a silent *help-me* look and was still looking at me with both knees pressed tightly together and turned in my direction, when Overcoat reached over and laid a large hairy-knuckled hand on Edgar's thigh. Uttering a high-pitched *"Mother-FUCK!"* of distress, Edgar leapt upright from his seat and scuttled quickly past me and over the laps of an older couple seated at my end of the row and, without breaking stride, headed up the aisle for the exit. I was no more than a step behind him.

Talk about freaked out. We both were, *tot*ally. I don't know about Edgar, but I had never had any kind of homosexual encounter before, and the near-miss feeling of this one quite unnerved me, so I could only imagine how poor Edgar was feeling. We continued our headlong flight through the lobby and out into the afternoon-bright street, never even considering stopping at the box office to lodge a complaint or request a refund. Edgar was visibly shaking and muttering to himself as we walked quickly down Hanover Street away from the theater. "Goddamn motherfucking cocksucking *fag*got!"

And poor Edgar's very bad, horrible, no-good day (to paraphrase the title of Judith Viorst's popular children's book) wasn't over yet. Just as we'd begun to calm down and started walking a little slower, Edgar reached up and felt his crew-cut hair and asked, "Hey, Bazzett, is it raining?" Glancing up at the bright sunny sky, I said, "No." Then I turned to look at Edgar, who was looking at his hand, which was now smeared with the same greyish-white viscous slime that was also running down over his ear and into his shirt collar. Putting his fingers to his nose, Edgar sniffed, grimaced, and let out a pained last-straw cry, "Ee-*YEW! BIRDSHIT!* Goddamn motherfucking cocksucking *PIGEONS*!" (Edgar was a man of few words, and apparently he employed the same ones over and over, whatever the situation.) Sure enough, poor Edgar had been bombed by the birds ubiquitous to downtown Boston. Just like Viorst's hapless hero, Alexander, Edgar was having a truly crappy day.

I *did* feel sorry for Edgar, but at the same time I couldn't stop myself from laughing at him either, as he stood in the street trying to shake the shit off one hand and wiping the shit off his neck and shirt with the other, and passers-by made wide careful detours around us. Finally, giving up on it all, he started laughing too, and we found a drinking fountain where he cleaned himself up as best he could with a dampened handkerchief.

Ironically, although I got into Boston a few other times during my tour at Devens, this is the day I remember most. And, like Bill Couture and his outburst will be forever linked in my memory with *West Side Story,* any mention of Boston will always conjure up that image of poor shit-spattered Edgar and faggot-filled movie theaters. Next I would remember those delicious deli dills and hot pastrami sandwiches. These things quite naturally override other memories of re-tracing the Freedom Trail and the city's other famous historical landmarks. Sorry, Boston Fathers. We make our own memories, and my memories of Boston will always be pastrami, pigeon shit and homos. And I never did see the end of *The Chapman Report* either.

I once visited Nashua, New Hampshire, and therein lies, if not much of a tale, at least a lesson. There was a recurrent rumor circulating in the student units at Devens that there was a girls' academy of some sort in Nashua, and that (of course) the girls there were wild, and just *loved* GI's. It was the kind of rumor we all wanted desperately to believe, since female companionship was an extremely scarce commodity during our training days. Sure there were the occasional organized dances at the USO Club in Ayer, but the local girls that attended them were certainly not "wild," at least in my experience, and often seemed to represent the dregs of femininity. I admit I only attended one USO dance, but that was enough. The girls were outnumbered by the guys by at least four to one. I spent most of the evening munching unhappily on the complimentary cheese and crackers and sipping cokes, as I lurked along the shadowy fringe of the dance floor. I affected a cosmopolitan indifference whenever one of the painfully plain girls looked in my direction, dragging deeply on a butt like (I hoped) Bogey or Gable. I was too shy, and so were the girls. It was a miserable bust.

So one sunny Saturday morning when a couple of my buddies proposed a trip to Nashua to find the fabled girls' school and try to "hook up," as kids today call meeting a member of the opposite sex, I was ready. (To me "hooking up" sounds too much like two dogs who have become stuck together in the mating act and need to be doused with a bucket of cold water. I can't remember what we called it then – probably "meeting girls.") None of us had access to a car that day, so we went to a bike-rental place just off post and each rented a state-of-the-art three-speed bicycle. Today I can't even remember who my co-conspirators were in this ill-fated venture, but we all had high hopes. The sun was shining and off we pedaled, bound for New Hampshire.

I should probably mention here that I had never been an accomplished bicyclist. I knew how to ride one, but barely. I had never even owned a bicycle of my own while growing up. I know this probably sounds almost un-American, but it's the truth. I had learned to ride on friends' bikes though, so I could pedal and steer and generally stay upright. I had very little experience with bikes with shifting mechanisms. My friends' bikes had been mostly the old-fashioned one-speed coaster brake models – Schwinns with fat tires. When I was twelve or thirteen, my brother Rich brought home his bike from Michigan State for the summer. It was an "English racer" with a three-speed transmission, hand brakes and really skinny tires. My brother Bob and I used to ride around on it on the lawn and the turnaround near our garage, and were very impressed with this high-tech machine. One day while Rich was working I decided to ride his bike downtown. Our house on West Church sat on top of a hill and our rutted sand and gravel driveway sloping down to the street was nearly a block long. I quickly picked up speed as I coasted bumpily down the drive. When I reached the bottom of the driveway and tried to turn right onto Church, that ridiculously skinny front tire sank into the deep sand that had washed down the drive and stuck. The bicycle stopped, but I did not. I went airborne over the twisted handlebars and landed abruptly on my face, hands and knees in the graveled roadbed. I lost a surprising amount of skin off my face, hands, arms and even my knees, when my overalls split open at the knees on touchdown. I was picking bits of debris and gravel out from under my scabbed-up skin for weeks afterward, and was never too keen on bike-riding after that either.

So why didn't I remember this misadventure before I plopped down cash to rent that bike in Ayer? I dunno. I probably had visions of clean-limbed, full-breasted, rosy-cheeked private school girls dancing in my head at the time. Or, in the common GI vernacular, I was afflicted with "shitferbrains."

None of us knew for sure where Nashua was, but we got ourselves a roadmap and, full of optimism, headed off on a roughly northeasterly course, bound for glory. Now Nashua is probably at least twenty miles from Ayer, and if you haven't ridden a bike in three or four years, and then abruptly undertake a twenty-mile expedition, you probably really do have shitferbrains. And we soon found out that most of the roads that looked so flat and easy on the map in actuality went up hills and down hills, and up and down ad nauseam. Mostly up, it seemed, so we spent a considerable amount of time walking and pushing our bikes up grades we couldn't pedal up. There was also very little shoulder to the road, and we were often intimidated off the pavement into the ditch or brush by large noisy trucks roaring up behind us. The sun kept shining as it rose higher in the sky and we were all soon sweating profusely. No one had thought to bring along any water, so we made frequent stops at filling stations or anywhere else we could get a drink.

The rental bikes were very similar to Rich's English racer, with ultra-thin tires and also a very narrow saddle. Before setting out, I had adjusted the seat height to accomodate my long legs. Unfortunately, after traveling several miles, the seat had gradually slipped back down and I had no wrench to readjust it, so I was stuck riding it the way it was, and the pedaling got harder and harder as my leg muscles grew tired and cramped. On top of all this, my ass was getting red and raw from that narrow saddle digging into it.

But the implicit promise of possible poontang was a strong incentive, so I kept on. Miraculously, we actually made it to Nashua. Once there, we walked and pedaled aimlessly about town for perhaps an hour or more, but we never did find that school. We even asked a few people we met there about its whereabouts, but since we didn't know its proper name, no one could help us. A few older residents regarded us suspiciously when we asked them bluntly where the "girls' school" was located. Probably they figured these sweaty groaty-looking young punks were up to no good.

Well, shee-*it*! Twenty miles of suffering and no girls in sight. No payoff. What pathetic gullible *dick*-heads we were! We'd been suckered by a military version of an urban legend. We were hot, hungry, dehydrated and *dis-GUS-ted* – and twenty miles from the home and hearth of our barracks and mess hall, which sounded pretty inviting by then.

There's no happy ending or snappy moral to this story. We barely made it back to Devens by dark, sore and weary to our very bones. I had a sunburn, aching muscles and a really painful rash all around my crotch and butt-cheeks from the day-long chafing of that skinny saddle jammed up my equally skinny ass. (Some weeks later Joe Capozzi and I and a couple other guys did attend a dance at a nursing school in Nashua. We went in Joe's car that time. I remember virtually nothing about the dance, so I'm sure none of us "got lucky.")

I guess the only reason I even mention this little bicycle jaunt to New Hampshire, surely a thirty to forty mile round trip over hill and dale, is to illustrate the desperate measures we would take in trying to find a little female companionship. We were robust young males, lonely for the sight, sound and perfumed smell of a girl.

The only women likely to be in uniform in the early sixties were in the administrative and medical fields. Clerks and nurses. And nurses were always officers, making them automatically inaccessible to us enlisted peons. As for female clerical personnel, they were equally rare around Fort Devens. I can't really remember seeing any female military around post in 1963, except on one

Mike Bosse, unknown and Tim in front of Joe Capozzi's Ford convertible.

isolated occasion when a bunch of us went to give blood at the the clinic in order to get a Friday afternoon off. There was a nurse running the blood bank, but she wasn't much to look at.

So what did most of these red-blooded American males do for relief? What was their sexual outlet? Fortunately the latrines in the Devens barracks were more civilized than those in basic training. The toilets were enclosed in stalls, with doors, with latches. Behind those doors you could always find relief – in the welcoming embrace of the infamous but always sympathetic Rosey Palm, who, along with her five daughters, always did a healthy trade wherever there were lonely frustrated men. To paraphrase the Duke, *A man's gotta do what a man's gotta do.* Enough said.

Easter weekend I was fortunate enough to get away from Devens for a welcome breather. My pal Joe Bohn invited me home with him. He lived in Woodbury, New Jersey, which is just across the Delaware River from Philadelphia. Like most weekend getaways in the army, it was marred mostly by the inevitable day-and hour-counting you do from the time you leave post until you start back again. You can't help yourself. You get where you're going on Friday night and immediately start thinking, *Gee, I've just got tonight and tomorrow to hurry up and have some fun. Then Mass Sunday morning and we have to head back.* Bummer.

*Joe Bohn and Tim outside
G-Compnay*

I remember that Joe was kind of smitten by a young girl he knew from high school. I think she was no more than a sophomore, but very cute and sweet. I could understand his tongue-tied enchantment with her, and could also sympathize with his embarrassment at being gone on a fifteen year-old girl. I don't think he even realized how charmed and flattered she was by the attentions of this older "man in uniform," or how much she obviously liked him. She had an equally cute friend who tagged along with us, and managed to render *me* pretty tongue-tied too. I felt like I'd finally gotten a date with Karen Sahlin, a golden nymphette three years younger than me who had haunted my guilty fantasies throughout high school. I can't remember either of those Jersey girls' names now, forty years later, but I'll bet if I could find Joe Bohn again, *he* would sure remember.

What I do remember from that long-ago Easter weekend was eating my first cold-cuts-with-everything hoagie sandwich. I had always been a strictly hamburger-with- mustard or hot dog-with-ketchup kind of guy, and my bland midwestern tastes were changed forever by eating that exotic Philly sandwich concoction. I have since heard a variety of names for these six- or twelve-inch bunned beauties: hoagies, heroes, gyros, grinders, subs, romeos. Whatever they were called, I was hooked for life. Years later Subway sandwich shops were born. I'm a frequent customer there, but for me it all started in Philly and in Woodbury. I remember telling Joe,

"I don't think I'd like all those onions and peppers and tomatoes and olives and lettuce and oil and vinegar and mayo and stuff." He just smiled and said, "*Try* it. It's *good*!" *Man*, was he right! Thanks, Joe. I hope you married that sweet little girl and lived happily ever after.

In early June my folks came to Fort Devens to visit. My sister Mary and brother Chris, who'd just completed their school year at St. Philip's, came too. They were twelve and ten, respectively. It was a kind of vacation for them all, although driving nearly a thousand miles one way probably wasn't much of a picnic for Dad. But Dad did have a brand-new 1963 Pontiac that year, so perhaps the trip was a kind of extended road test too. I was glad to see them all, and appreciated their making the trip. I showed them where I lived and where I ate and went to school. I think Dad wanted to sample the mess hall cuisine, but I wasn't able to arrange that. I remember the mess sergeant staring at me in amazement when I asked about it, and responding, "Why the fuck would anybody wanna eat here if they don't *have* to?" Hmmm ... That didn't exactly speak well for his own self-esteem, did it?

I showed my family around Ayer a bit (not many impressive sights there), then we drove to Gloucester, because Mom had read about its picturesqueness and also its reputation for good seafood. Full of high hopes for a truly memorable New England meal, as we drove into Gloucester we smelled something foul. The closer we got to the waterfront, the worse the smell became. I mean it was *bad*! We soon came to realize that it was Gloucester itself which smelled so putrid. The sea breeze was carrying the distinctive odor of rotting fish guts and other offal from the fishing docks. Deciding we didn't really like seafood all *that* much, we rolled up the car windows and got the hell out of Gloucester. We had dinner instead in Essex, several miles away, where the wind just smelled like the sea. I think I had a burger, but little brother Chris had shrimp, so at least *someone* in the family had some authentic New England seafood.

On Sunday we all went to nearby Crane Beach. Mary and Chris wanted to swim in the ocean, which they'd never seen before. It was June, but the water was bone-chillingly cold and raised goose-bumps on all three of us and cut our swim accordingly short. Even so, the kids were happy they'd done it. Now they could tell

*Chris, Tim and Mary Jane
at Crane Beach.
June, 1963.*

*Tim and mom
outside of
G-Company,
Ft. Devens.
June 1963*

*Dad at Crane Beach.
June, 1963.*

*Dad and Tim outside Catholic Church in Ayer, MA.
June, 1963.*

*Mary, Chris and Dad's '63 Pontiac.
June, 1963.*

their friends back home that they'd swum in the Atlantic Ocean. Not many Reed City kids could make that claim. Chris, even at ten one who noticed the small things, thought it exceedingly odd that he had to take a shower after swimming. He had, after all, grown up spending his summers swimming in Indian Lake, and often didn't take a real tub bath or shower from June until September.

Sunday night my family reluctantly deposited me back at my barracks and departed for home (via Canada), apparently satisfied that I was being adequately fed and looked after by our benevolent Uncle Sam.

Looking back across the years, my time at Fort Devens seems nearly idyllic, and perhaps much of it was. I was nineteen years old and in excellent health. I had made a few close friends and numerous casual pals. We attended classes from nine to five just five days a week, listening to the dits and dahs on our headsets and pounding away on our mills. The rest of our time was largely free, aside from an occasional GI party and barracks inspection. Life was good. We bonded in the barracks, doing guy stuff. We played a little touch football out in the yard on warm days. Sometimes in the evenings my buddy Joe Capozzi would break out his electric Fender and amp and practice a few chords or strum some tunes. A couple other guys in nearby barracks also had guitars, and they would often come by and then the three would trade licks and jam a little. They usually drew an appreciative audience, who would make requests and we'd have impromptu singalongs, butchering recent pop tunes like Tommy Roe's "Sheila," Sonny James' "Young Love," or some Buddy Holly or Ricky Nelson songs. These sessions often went late, and only broke up reluctantly. We were living, indeed we were in the very *midst* of "the good ol' days," but I doubt that many of us realized it at the time. *Now* we know it though.

Because of the way we were billeted, many close friendships sprang up in our class that year. Many of the alliances may have been due to simple alphabetical groupings. There were cubemates Bazzett and Capozzi, best friends. Campbell and Couture, ditto. There were Joe Bohn and Mike Bosse, and also Abner and Baker.

Chuck Baker was an army brat. He had grown up near Fort Bragg, North Carolina, his dad a career man. Dark haired and good-looking, he was athletic and very disciplined and organized – what we called "strak," a military slang term for someone who *always* kept all his ducks in a row and his shit together. You would never see Baker with dirty brass or scuffed shoes when he was in uniform, and he was equally careful about his appearance when in civvies, with shoes shined, clothes pressed and his gig line straight.

I should digress briefly here. A "gig line" is the straight line formed down the front of your uniform by the buttoned edge of your shirt, the edge of your belt buckle and the edge of the fly on your trousers. Most guys who ever did a hitch in the military continue to check and adjust their gig line whenever they get dressed up for the rest of their natural lives. It's one of those minute parts of the training that just seems to stay with you.

At any rate, we often teased Baker (who tended to take himself too seriously) about being "lifer" material, which he endured good-naturedly. I would not be surprised to learn that he put in his twenty-plus years in the army.

His buddy and cubemate was Abner, *Beverly* Abner. Initially Abner took a lot of shit about that first name (and it really *was* Beverly), which he took in stride, usually responding with a cheerful "Fuck you and the horse you rode in on." So we all liked him and we called him Ab. Abner, who hailed from Germantown, Ohio, was probably one of the hairiest human beings I had ever met. He was one of those guys who had to shave the whole front of his throat, all the way down to his tee-shirt neckline. Even then the dark coarse hair often curled up out of his shirt, and even *through* his undershirt. His arms and legs were covered with dense dark fur, and so was his *back*. I remember how he used to holler in pain when he'd peel off his tee-shirt after getting all sweated up playing ball or wrestling with Baker. All those hairs would catch in the weave of his shirt and some would inevitably pull out as he pulled the shirt over his head. "OWW-OWW-OWW, *OUCH*!" Abner the yowling Yeti. Where are you now, Ab?

I hope at least some of these friendships have endured. Mine and Joe's has. Well, perhaps I should clarify that. We haven't actually *seen* each other in over thirty-five years, but we stay in touch. I've made a lot of friends in the intervening years, but the truth is there is no friend quite as enduring as the proverbial "old army buddy." It's often a much maligned phrase, but it is also often the very best way to describe a very best friend.

Left to right:
Campbell, Couture,
Baker, unknown,
Bazzett, Abner.
May, 1963.

Mike Bosse,
Joe Capozzi
and Tim
Bazzett.
May, 1963

Mike Bosse and
Joe Capozzi with
Joe's '58 Ford
Convertible and
Mike Campbell's
'55 T-Bird.
January, 1963

Campbell, Abner and Couture. June, 1963.

G-Company, Barracks group shot Top row, left to right: Jim Farra, Bev Abner, Chuck Baker, Bill Couture, Tim Bazzett, Mike Campbell, Dick Gatlin, unknown, Mike Fitzgerald Bottom row, left to right: Charley Little, Shep Evans, unknown

Baker, Capozzi and Abner on the firescape on the back of our barracks.

G-Company, Fort Devens 1963

I was still an avid reader in the midst of all this training and other pursuits. I won't say I was too discriminating a reader, but there were so many authors I hadn't discovered yet. After seeing the film version of *To Kill a Mockingbird,* with Gregory Peck's riveting portrayal of Atticus Finch, I searched out Harper Lee's book at the post library and literally devoured it. Books are always so much better than their movie adaptations. (Except for John Grisham's work. I can't abide his books, but love the films they become.) I also discovered Harold Robbins, reading first his then-bestseller, *The Carpetbaggers*, then backtracking to read several of his earlier lesser known novels. My favorite of those was *A Stone for Danny Fisher*, which had been loosely (*very* loosely) adapted to the screen as *King Creole*, an early Elvis vehicle. It was probably one of Presley's better films, but certainly didn't reflect the fine Robbins story at all. (My *favorite* Elvis films were the ones he didn't sing in, and did some of his best acting: *Wild in the Country* and *Flaming Star*.) Robbins is probably not a great writer, but he did spin a great yarn, one you could lose yourself in for hours at a time, and that's not a bad thing when a reader has time on his hands and wants to be entertained. In any case, my life of the mind was still intact, and I got to know the Devens library pretty well.

I hadn't entirely abandoned my spiritual life either. How could I? I had spent nine years in Catholic school and had been thoroughly infused with a major dose of good old- fashioned Catholic guilt. So I did my best to get to Mass every Sunday. I went to communion whenever I could. I even snuck off to confession when I felt I needed to. And, always, I prayed. I didn't do much conventional praying anymore, but when I had a quiet moment now and then, I'd talk with God, or al least talk *to* Him. Sometimes you're just not sure if He's listening, you know? But then something might happen, maybe even months later, and you know He's getting back to you.

I had plenty to pray about my last several weeks at Devens. In late May I got my orders, that is I received my duty station assignment. I would be going to Asmara for an eighteen-month tour. *Asmara?* What the hell, or rather *where* the hell, was *Asmara?* Well, it's in Africa, I soon learned. In Ethiopia, to be exact. Reading up on it a bit in the post library (where else?), I also learned a little something about Haile Selassie, Ethiopia's emperor, the "Lion of

God," who had been in power since the thirties, and was looked upon by his subjects as a kind of half-god. Hmmm ... I wasn't at all sure if this sounded very promising as a place to spend the next year and a half of my life. But what was even worse, from my perspective, was the fact that I was the only one in my class to get orders to Asmara. I would be going to darkest Africa alone. Most of the class got orders for northern Japan, considered to be a plum assignment. How in the heck had I drawn *Africa*, for cripes sake? What had *I* done wrong? Why *meeee?*

So *hell* yes, I prayed! I prayed that I would be able to handle this unexpected turn of events. I prayed that I could make some new friends when I got there. I prayed for strength and for courage. And I'll admit the mere prospect of *Africa* itself was more than a little intimidating to my nineteen year-old self. It was, after all, called the "dark" continent. I mean, I didn't exactly think I'd end up in one of those big black pots over a fire surrounded by hungry cannibals, but I was more than a little uneasy. So I prayed.

In the meantime, I was shuttled here and there around post and even into Boston where I applied for a passport and a visa. I got more booster shots for things like yellow fever, cholera and malaria. I worried. I mourned the imminent separation from Joe and all my other friends. I felt sorry for myself. I fretted. When I would hear the other guys talking about all the stuff they would do in Japan – *together* – my spirits would sink and I would feel so alone and abandoned.

A few weeks later, around the middle of June, my prayers were answered with an unexpected turn of events which was to affect more than just me. I received a new set of orders which rescinded my posting to Asmara. And I wasn't the only one in the class whose plans were abruptly changed. Ten of us were called into a departmental office at the school and summarily informed that we had been specially selected for additional code training and that all previous orders were canceled. We would be going to Fort George G. Meade (FGGM) in Maryland for this special training. After that half of us would be posted to Shemya and half to Sinop.

HUH? Mouths dropped open all over the office. Most of the other guys had been looking at an extended cushy tour in Japan. Saki and geisha girls. Houseboys to clean their rooms and shine their shoes. What the hell was this sudden shit about *Shemya* and *Sinop*? And where the hell *were* these places anyway?

The department head, a busy no-nonsense Master Sergeant, didn't allow any time for carping or questions. He told us new orders would be cut for all of us, TDY (temporary duty) orders to Fort Meade. While we were in training there someone would sort out which of us would go to which permanent duty station. He told us Shemya was in Alaska and Sinop was in Turkey. That was all. We were dismissed and sent back to class muttering and confused.

The ten of us were stunned by this sudden turn of events. I was probably the only one who was actually kind of happy about it. After all, I had been looking at an eighteen-month tour in a remote place I knew virtually nothing about, and I would have gone there by myself. Now I would be accompanied by at least four of my buddies to a *different* remote place I knew virtually nothing about. Things were definitely looking up for me.

Although the department head had said we had been "specially selected," we soon figured out that the military powers that be had picked the ten of us quite arbitrarily, perhaps even alphabetically, from the top of our class roster. The group included Joe Capozzi, my best pal, so we stood a fifty-fifty chance of staying together, whichever place we went. Also in the group were the two other Michigan men, Mike Campbell and Bill Couture. Chuck Baker, the always-strak army brat from Bragg, was in the group, as was Jim Farra, an easy-going Kentuckian, and Dan Dillon, a married fellow from Massachusetts, whom I knew only slightly, since he didn't live in the barracks with us.

I felt as though a great weight had been lifted from my shoulders. I would be staying among my friends after all. God had come through for me again. The power of prayer. It was even more powerful than the U.S. Army.

As it turned out, Shemya was just *barely* in Alaska, and ditto for Sinop and Turkey. We found some maps at the library to learn more about our eventual fates, and learned that Shemya was a tiny speck of an island at the western end of the Aleutian chain, which extended out into the Bering Strait almost all the way across to the northern land mass of the Soviet Union. It was a tiny frigid atoll which sounded most unpromising as a place to have fun. We found Sinop at the northernmost tip of the map of Turkey, on a point jutting out into the Black Sea. Since none of us knew much about Turkey, the most we could hope for was that at least it couldn't be as cold there as it must be in Shemya.

When you're only nineteen or twenty years old, you bounce back quickly from disappointments or abrupt changes in plans. So instead of moping about their lost tours in Japan, most of the guys started planning exploratory trips from Fort Meade into Washington, D.C., where the legal drinking age was eighteen. Not that we'd experienced any difficulties getting served in Massachusetts, but I can't remember if that was actually *legal* imbibing.

On June 26, 1963, our class graduated. We had successfully completed our course in manual Morse intercept. True to its usual fashion, the army factored in casual time for some of us. Our little group of ten had to move from our comfy "home" in good old G Company back across post to Charley Company, where we languished until after the July 4th holiday, pulling KP, cleanup details and guard duty. But by that time we were all seasoned veterans and goldbrickers, and managed to duck more details than we pulled. We were also all newly-promoted Privates First Class (PFC), or E-3's, so we outranked most of the recruits just arriving at C Company from their basic training units. It was our first taste of enjoying the RHIP part of military life – "rank has its privileges."

I spent a couple of those casual company days at the dental clinic, getting cavities filled. During those visits I made a wonderful discovery – virtually painless dentistry. I discovered novocaine. When I was growing up I'd had plenty of teeth drilled and filled, but my dentist in Reed City, Dr. Brown, either hated kids, or thought novocaine was wasted on them, or both. So, naturally, I grew up terrified of the dentist. I'd had countless cavities filled without any anesthetic or pain-killer administered. Dr. Brown would just say, "Oh, quit crying. Don't be such a baby." The heartless bastard. Of course I cried. It *hurt!* The military dentist at Devens was astounded when I told him I'd never heard of novocaine. He asked me, "How'd you get all those fillings then, if you've never had a shot of novocaine?" I told him I'd cried a lot. He just shook his head in wonder that that kind of barbaric dentistry was still being practiced in the hinterlands of America. I was more than a little pissed myself when I thought of all that pain and all those needless tears. But then I thought what the heck. Life keeps getting better.

ASA Certificate from Fort Devens

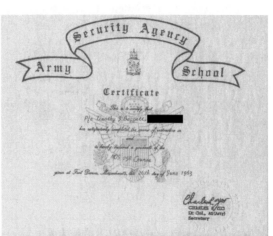

Graduation Day at Devens, June 1963, Class 27-058
Top row; Left to Right:
Dick Gatlin, Phil Martin, Stu Clark, William Johnson, Wayne Roberts, Dwain Jones, Tim Bazzett, Gene Maloney, Bob Roark, Fred Schaming, Tom MacWilliams, John Wolden, Ron Greathouse, Chuck Baker, Bill Bennett, Gerry Levinsky, Mike Fitzgerald, Bub Kennedy,Shep Evans
Bottom row; Left to Right:
Charley Little, Ray Geis, Bob Heikkila, Mike Campbell, Bill Couture, Bev Abner, Jim Farra

TDY: FORT GEORGE G. MEADE, MD

We finally got our TDY orders for Meade, and on the fifth of July we boarded a bus for Maryland. We traveled down the eastern seaboard, passing through New York City and Philadelphia, and finally arrived in Baltimore around 2:00 in the morning. Our group leader – it may have been Bill Couture – telephoned Fort Meade from the bus terminal to see about getting us transport to the post. He was told we'd have to wait there until 6 or 7am, when a military bus would come get us.

The Baltimore bus station was downtown, right near the then-famous "strip." This was an area two or three blocks long of bars, honky-tonks, and clip and strip joints. There were probably a dozen or more burlesque clubs on the strip, featuring a bevy of beautiful "exotic dancers." As a matter of historical fact, one of the clubs was home turf for Blaze Starr, probably the most famous stripper in the country, who had gained notoriety in the fifties for her affair with Louisiana governor, Earl Long.

Cut loose by the army for a while, our little group of ten trickled out of the terminal and meandered on down the strip in our summer khaki uniforms, much wrinkled from the day-long bus trip, our mouths gaping at the lurid posters pasted outside the doors of the strip clubs, all of which were still doing a booming business despite the wee hours of the morning. There were still a surprising number of people out and about on the strip, and there were fast-talking barkers of sorts working the crowd in front of each strip joint, grabbing passersby by the elbows and spouting their rapid-fire spiels about the feminine charms and pulchritude that awaited them just inside the doors of their establishments. A few of our group succumbed to these come-ons. I don't know if they were the bolder or stupider ones. I still had too much of the small-town pessimist and the good Catholic boy in me to to go inside and sample the shows – but I *wanted* to. I was just a bit too timid to do it. I had been to that burlesque show at a county fair with my brother and a friend when I was just sixteen, so I had some idea of what was in store. At that particular show I had seen my first nearly-naked woman, and it had certainly seemed worth while at the time. So, yes, I was definitely tempted, but the loud, flashy, big-city aura of the strip intimidated me more than a little. I was practically hanging onto my wallet with both hands.

In any case, after "window shopping" up and down the bright neon-lit strip a time or two, most of us retreated back to the bus station to wait for our morning ride to Fort Meade. And, interestingly, we never did venture back into Baltimore during our short stay in Maryland. D.C. always seemed more inviting, and perhaps just a teensy bit safer and more wholesome. There was something seamy and dangerous-feeling about Baltimore and its strip that kept us away.

We were billeted at the ASA Student Company on Fort Meade, and it was a liberating experience from the very start. All ten of us were newly-minted PFC's and hadn't had much experience with real freedom during our ten months or so in the army. BCT, of course, had been extremely regimented, with no leave or even a weekend pass. Fort Devens had been much better, but we had still had weekly inspections and morning formations and marched to class every day.

Upon our arrival at the student company we reported to the orderly room where a duty NCO took copies of our orders, then sent us to a small supply building next door where we were issued linens, blankets and pillows. Then a corporal led us across the company yard, pointing out the mess hall and a nearby chapel. Then he showed us into an empty two-story wooden barracks, one pretty much identical to the G Company barracks we had lived in on Devens. Yes, that's right. It was *empty*, as in completely *unoccupied.* It was a standard, open-bay type of arrangement, furnished with rows of steel bunks and lockers. The corporal told us to pick out some bunks and make ourselves at home. He told us the shuttle bus to NSA (the National Security Agency, where our classes would be held) would be at the orderly room at 8:00 Monday morning to pick us up. Then he left.

For a few minutes we all just stood there looking at each other, still holding our bedding, our duffel bags at our feet. It slowly dawned on us that we were on our own here. Nothing had been said about platoon sergeants, or GI parties or inspections or morning formations – *nothing*! And they were sending a *bus* to take us to class each day. Un-fucking-be*liev*able!

Not quite believing we were all alone, we walked down the length of the empty squad bay. We looked behind a row of empty wall lockers and peered into the empty latrine. We went up the stairs, almost tip-toeing, still not quite ready to believe that we were the only ones here. Upstairs it was the same – empty bunks with rolled mattresses and dusty lockers with doors hanging open. We really *were* the sole occupants of this whole barracks. Ten guys in a building that would normally house eighty or more men.

One of the group, I think it was probably Mike Campbell, suddenly let out a spontaneous whoop of pure joy and leaped onto Couture's back, and they rolled scuffling on the floor, Bill blustering and half-laughing, "Goddamn it, Mike, get the fuck off me!" It must have been contagious though, because all at once we were all whooping, jigging impromptu dances, and filling the empty squad bay with echoing shouts of "Fuck *ME*!" and "This is *GREAT*!" We felt like slaves who had just gotten word of the emancipation proclamation. Remember Balki and his cousin Larry on that TV sitcom, *Perfect Strangers*, and how whenever something wonderful or unexpectedly great happened Balki insisted on doing the "dance of joy"? Well, our joy pre-dated that show by twenty years or more, but that Saturday morning, in that empty old echoing barracks, we did the dance of joy. We were home, and we were free at last, great God Al*mighty*, free at last!

And that first impression of virtually total autonomy during our stay at Meade proved to be an accurate one. As long as we got to class from 9 to 5 Monday through Friday, all the rest of the time was our own to do as we pleased. Again for good measure – un-fucking be-*LIEV*-able!

The training itself, which ran from July 8th through August 2nd, or about three and a half weeks, was not anything very difficult, a bit of fine tuning of the code skills we had already learned during our several months at Devens. More monkey work, with perhaps just a bit of puzzled head-scratching thrown in here and there, but we all eventually figured it out satisfactorily.

The near tropical temperatures and humidity we experienced that summer were brand new to many of us. Throughout July and August temperatures regularly rose into the nineties, and even topped a hundred degrees a few times. And the humidity made it almost difficult to breathe at times. You felt like you were walking underwater as you trudged across the vast tarmac parking lots that surrounded the NSA complex. Nights weren't much better when the temps barely dipped down into the seventies. Because of this stifling heat, we all tried to find and seek relief in any air-conditioned refuge available. Our old barracks was *not* air conditioned. Thankfully, NSA was thoroughly cooled, but as soon as we emerged from class in the afternoon, that horrific heat would hit us like a brick wall.

We quickly discovered an air-conditioned bowling alley only a half-block from our barracks and spent many hours there just to escape the enervating heat of the Maryland summer. Bowling was cheap at post alleys, only a quarter a game, and there was no rental fee for the shoes. Some afternoons we bowled game after game, until our thumbs and fingers were blistered and raw, egging each other on with, "Come on, just one more game, then we'll go." The fellows that ran the desk got to know us pretty well, and if the alleys were mostly empty and we ran out of money, sometimes they'd even let us bowl a free game or two, rather than send us back out into that awful heat. I had just taught myself to bowl, after a fashion, when I was at Fort Devens, and my game improved steadily with all the practice we got that steamy summer.

There was also a roomful of pinball machines there which some of the guys challenged regularly, pounding on them and cursing when the tilt sign would flash, but usually steadily running up their scores. They would pool their nickels and dimes for "just one more game," just like the rest of us were doing over on the lanes.

In this fashion we would beat the heat in the late afternoons or during the day on weekends. But the real charm of our Fort Meade summer was the Washington night life. There was always something going on in downtown D.C.

We attended a couple of free concerts that summer. One was the Marine Corps Band performing on the steps of the Capitol building. All you had to bring was a lawn chair or a blanket and make yourself comfortable on the lawn. The music began around 8:00 and would continue past dark. I can still remember lying on my back on that lush green lawn and looking up at the stars as the artillery pieces bashed and boomed at the conclusion of the "1812 Overture."

It was, of course, a simpler more innocent time in our nation's capital, a time before all the concrete barriers and complex security measures had been put into place. We were free to wander practically anywhere in D.C., including up and down Pennsylvania Avenue and the broad park-like mall between the Lincoln Memorial and the Washington Monument, and along the edges of the reflecting pool. We sampled the sights and explored the natural and man-made treasures and inventions in the buildings of the Smithsonian. We attended another free concert on the banks of the Potomac, just outside the Watergate complex, the same Watergate that would figure so prominently in our country's political history and the downfall of a president some years later.

I figured I ought to at least mention these wholesome touristy kind of leisure activities we engaged in first, but they aren't really the things we all remember the most fondly. No, when those of us that have kept in touch over the years do get together on the phone we talk about other, baser things. We remember fondly the boozing and the wild carousing. We talk, invariably, about the Speakeasy.

The Speakeasy was a really unique club we discovered on one of our first jaunts into downtown D.C. It was a beer joint primarily. They probably served the harder stuff too, but we were a part of the pitchers-of-beer crowd. And we did put away many, many (or "minny, minny" as George Gobel used to say) pitchers – I mean a *lot* of beer. What made the Speakeasy special was its ambience, although in retrospect ambience may be too classy a word to describe what we loved about the place. The floor was strewn with sawdust and littered with peanut shucks which came from the mammoth bowls of salted peanuts in the shell placed on every table. These bowls were replenished regularly, or as quickly as the patrons devoured their contents. Hey, the proprietors here were no fools. Salty peanuts make you thirsty! *Another pitcher of brew over here, Sweetheart!*

Sawdust on the floor. Free peanuts on the tables. And that was just a small part of the Speakeasy's appeal. The waitresses were pretty and friendly and kept the beer coming. They dressed in Swiss milkmaid costumes with full skirts and petticoats and tight bodices that displayed tempting mounds of delicious-looking decolletage. Just the right outfit to please a tableful of horny appreciative GI's. We really couldn't afford to tip, but after several pitchers of beer we didn't remember how poor we were, so those girls made out fine.

And I haven't even mentioned the entertainment yet. Not that bulging bare breast-tops weren't entertaining enough in themselves, but we weren't allowed to touch those. The real entertainment was something of the participatory kind. Along with the beer and peanuts, we also got songbooks and drumsticks. Not turkey or chicken drumsticks, but the kind you drum with. The sticks were to beat time on the table with while you sang along with the house musicians and watched the girl on the swing.

There was this wide red velvet-covered swing suspended from the high ceiling just above the upright piano near the center of the large cavernous room that was the Speakeasy proper. A beautiful girl in a brief low-cut costume with black mesh stockings and heels would ascend a portable staircase up the side of the piano, climb aboard the velvet-seated swing and then swing in a wide lazy arc out over the heads of the patrons, who would follow her progress hungrily with their eyes, heads swiveling slowly back and forth as if they were watching a tennis match. It was great and compelling entertainment as long as you didn't overdo it. I remember watching one poor slob, another GI, who'd probably already overindulged in drink, who sat there and followed the arc of the swing, watching the girl, back and forth, back and forth, until he suddenly projectile-vomited straight across the table onto the shirt of his startled buddy. Actually even *that* was pretty entertaining. *Our* table thought it was hilarious.

There were two musicians. One played the piano, and the other played a banjo. Both men were in costume too – straw boaters, red and white striped shirts with high starched collars. They wore sleeve garters and blue and white pin-striped pants. Quite a colorful (and, probably not incidentally, *patriotic*) ensemble, to say the least.

The music was that great traditional kind of stuff that Mitch Miller and the Gang used to do, tunes like "In the Good Old Summertime," "Let Me Call You Sweetheart," and "Down by the Riverside." And our Lexington lad, Jim Farra, often requested "My Old Kentucky Home," another crowd favorite.

Of course, in addition to the pianist and banjo player, there was also an enthusiastic chorus of amateur drummers and singers, bashing away at the table tops and edges, often until their drumsticks broke or splintered, and singing, or rather bellowing drunkenly, at the tops of their lungs. The morning after a night like this, most of us could only communicate in hoarse whispers, and for some reason we were thirsty all day too.

Our stalwart little group did sample a few other bars and night spots around D.C., but we always seemed to end up at the Speakeasy. We felt welcome there. Country singer Toby Keith has this song, a kind of drunks' anthem he does, called, "I Love This Bar." Although I do like some country music, I'm not crazy about Toby Keith, but I have to say that when it came to the Speakeasy that summer of '63, we *loved* that bar.

Looking back now at that summer, it amazes me how stupid – and how incredibly lucky – we all were. When you're nineteen or twenty years old you feel immortal. All kids that age do, and we were no different. "Designated driver" was not a phrase that you heard much back in 1963. Whoever owned the car drove it, and he didn't sit sipping Cokes or tonic while the rest of us got plastered either. He kept right up with us and had just as much fun as we did. And then he drove us home. Yeah, it really is scary to think about all that now.

We only had a few cars between us at Fort Meade. Mike Campbell had his two-seater T-bird, which wasn't much good for a big group. I don't think Joe Capozzi brought his Ford convertible with him to Meade. He left it at home in Yonkers. The car we probably used the most was Jim Farra's. Well, technically the car belonged to Jim's mother, but she had gone to England for the summer, so Jim got to use her car, with his dad's permission, of course.

Farra's car was perfect for our purposes. It wasn't the kind of car a teenager would normally want, because it was a station wagon, one of those suburban mom-type vehicles. It was perfect because you could haul seven or eight people in it. It was a 1962 Buick wagon and had a third seat that faced the rear. That back seat took a little getting used to, but we quickly adjusted to it. We sometimes wrangled with each other over whose turn it was to ride in the back, but that was only for the trip into Washington. On the way back to post no one cared. When you're stinking drunk or passed out, which seat you're in becomes a rather moot point, although sometimes watching the road rush *away* in front of you when you had a load on could make you feel a bit queasy – or queasi*er*.

I have this one memory. I'd like to call it a vivid one, but I'm pretty sure I was practically blind drunk at the time (as usual), so I'm wondering, is it possible to remember anything "vividly" if you were that thoroughly inebriated? Well, no matter. Anyway, I have this memory, this series of mental snapshots with motion and sound effects. We were headed north on the Baltimore-Washington Parkway on our way back to post after still another successful night of carousing at the Speakeasy. It was Farra's car, so Jim was undoubtedly driving. Joe and I were riding in that rear-facing back seat, Campbell and Couture were in the middle, and I can't remember who was riding shotgun, maybe Baker.

It must have been a Friday or Saturday night, because both northbound lanes of the Parkway were filled with traffic and we were probably doing sixty or more when Campbell suddenly piped up with a plaintive, "I gotta piss!" Farra, probably a little annoyed, asked, "Can't ya wait 'til we get home?"

His voice rising slightly in pitch, Mike shot back, "No! I gotta piss right *now*!"

Shaking his head disgustedly (or maybe just drunkenly), Jim slurred back, "Okay, I'll pull over." And without further ado – as a matter of fact, without even *braking* – Jim *swerved* off the Parkway, bumping abruptly up over the curb, causing the whole vehicle to bounce high into the air and back down again – a *couple* of times, once for each axle. None of us were wearing seatbelts. I'm not even sure if seatbelts were standard yet back then. So we all bashed our heads against the ceiling of the car – a *couple* of times.

Luckily there was a not-too-steep grassy embankment running alongside the expressway which helped to slow down our speeding vehicle as we plowed merrily up the hill. Jim finally remembered to brake and we came to a shuddering halt near the top of the bank, the car leaning precipitously sideways down the hill with headlights beaming up into the dark, star-studded sky. I don't know if Jim turned off the engine then or if it just stalled, but into the sudden stillness Jim asked, "Is anybody hurt?" Fortunately, probably even miraculously, none of us *were* hurt, and for some reason Jim's concerned query struck us all as being incredibly *funny*, and we all started giggling, then began roaring in outright laughter. Probably a nervous reaction to a near-death experience.

Flinging open the doors and popping open the rear hatch, we all fell laughing out of the car onto the grass, groping for our zippers as we rolled and floundered about, finally regaining our feet, dicks in hands, and pissing in all directions, on ourselves and on each other, in full view of the passing traffic on the Parkway. No one took any notice of us – just another carload of drunken GI's. Luckily for us, there were no police cars in the steady stream of vehicles that continued to pass us as we fully relieved ourselves and zipped up, or mostly up, and piled back into the wagon, slamming doors and hatch. With our fearless driver Farra back behind the wheel, we eased down the embankment and bumped back over the curb and then he floored it, merging smoothly into the flow, leaving behind only the ugly furrows of tire marks up the manicured shoulder and probably a gallon of recycled Speakeasy beer sparkling in the starlight as it soaked slowly into the grass.

One more mental snapshot of our misspent Maryland summer. My best friend Joe Capozzi kneeling at a toilet in the barracks latrine, wretching convulsively and puking his guts out as he clutches the raised black enamel seat with both hands, wrenching and twisting it with each new wave of alcohol-induced nausea until finally it snaps off in his hands with a loud crunching crack. His gut finally empty, Joe sinks gasping and flubbering back onto his heels, draws the broken toilet seat to his breast and crosses his arms over it, embracing it like a long-lost friend. After a long pause, he gets to his feet, still clasping the black shitter lid to his puke-stained white shirt. He climbs the two steps up out of the latrine with his eyes barely open to pained slits. He wobbles unsteadily down the aisle of our mostly empty squad bay, somehow manages to locate his bunk and collapses onto it, dead to the world. Joe was never really much of a drinker, and seldom got so stinking drunk, which is probably why I remember this particular episode so well. Good show, Joe.

Not that I was such a paragon of virtue myself. The only reason I don't have any stories of my *own* drunken escapades is, of course, because I can't remember them. Someone else will have to recall my nasty behavior that summer. I sure can't.

I feel like I should slip in some kind of disclaimer somewhere here, something like, "This kind of behavior is reprehensible and and just plain *BAD*!" But I won't. It was *our* summer and *our* time, and it was the first taste of such freedom in our young lives, and by God we had ourselves a *TIME*, getting soused and sowing our wild oats.

Well, truth be told, most of those oats went down the toilet, with one notable and memorable exception. Jimmy Farra, our Kentucky boy, actually "got lucky" once that summer, and therein lies a tale – of a first "piece of tail," as we might have crudely put it.

Like most young men that age, we spent a lot of time talking about sex, discussing the merits of various women both real and imagined, and swapping outrageous lies about our own sexual escapades and experiences. I strongly suspect that most of us were virgins. I sure was. Lots of dreaming, lots of fantasies – no action. My cherry was intact. It wasn't something I'd have owned up to at the time. None of us would have willingly admitted to such a grievous deficiency in our experience. So we blustered and swore and lied a lot when we discussed sex and did our best to gross each other out with the depth and breadth of our so-called sexual expertise.

There was a bar right off post, along "the strip" in Odenton, that we often repaired to for a cold one when the NSA shuttle bus would drop us off after a hard day of deciphering dits and dahs. I can't remember the name of the place, if it even had one. It was just one of those long cave-like dimly-lit dives that you can find anywhere along the strip of any army town in America, with a few booths and tables and a bar. The particular attraction at this bar was a very cute and very friendly bartender (bartender-ess?). I can no longer remember her name, but she was really sweet-looking, so I'll call her Candy. After we'd only been there a few times, she actually remembered us, and would greet us each by name when we'd take our stools at the bar. A little thing like that can mean a lot to a lonely GI in a strange town, so, of course, we were all a little in love with Candy.

But the real reason we liked this bar was the entertainment. A *dive* with entertainment? you ask. Well, yeah. See, Candy *was* the entertainment. Besides tending bar, she also danced – up on top of the bar, right above and in front of our hungry appreciative eyes. She didn't do this *all* the time. I think she just did it if she was bored, or if she felt like it. We liked to think she only did it when *we* were there, but that was probably wishful thinking. But how we did *love* it when she would dance for us. It was like a private floor show she was putting on just for our edification. Because it was usually just our small group of five or six guys sitting at the bar when she performed. The rest of the place would be empty. We would feed quarters into the jukebox when we came in, and, after she drew our beers, if the music moved her, she would step up onto the bar and begin to groove. Usually dressed in just a tight tee-shirt and shorts, the nearness and the *heat* of her was mesmerizing. I wish I could remember what songs would set her off. Some of the hits that summer were Little Stevie Wonder's "Fingertips" and Little Peggy March's "I Will Follow Him" and the Angels' "My Boyfriend's Back," but I can't associate any of those tunes with Candy's sinuous bar-dancing. More than likely she moved to numbers like "Fever" by Peggy Lee, or David Rose's "The Stripper," because when Candy danced she was *hot*."

Like I said, we *all* fell a little in love with Candy, but after several visits it became fairly obvious to almost all of us that she was zeroing in on just *one* of us, and paying special attention to that one guy, Jim Farra. Whenever she put a little extra *oomph* into a bump or a grind in her bar-dance, it was usually right over the wide brow and upturned blue eyes of Farra, who would turn pink and embarrassedly avert his gaze.

Jim was one of those fair-haired wide-eyed innocent-looking guys that "bad girls" just naturally want to corrupt. He was a solidly built, good-looking guy with one of those full-lipped mouths that girls want to sample first-hand. But he was just a little on the bashful side, and, being fair- complected, blushed easily – one *more* thing in his favor, dammit! This could have been the story of *my* de-flowering, gosh darn it, but Farra was just flat handsomer than me.

Now I'm not saying necessarily that our Candy was a "bad girl," but it was a fact that she was probably a bit older than us and she could have had her pick of any of us, and she knew that, so there was undoubtedly something of the predator in her. At any rate, she picked Jim, who finally realized – with a little encouragement and gentle ragging from the rest of us – that maybe, just maybe, this was his big chance to divest himself of the awful burden of his virginity. So he asked her out, and she accepted.

Luckily, Jim had wheels, his mom's station wagon, remember? I don't remember where they went on their date, or if any of us even knew. Jim primped and prepared himself for this big night, with lots of obscene advice from us, his "experienced" advisors. He wore brand new khaki shorts and a madras plaid sport shirt and looked his shiny virginal best when he departed. It was a Friday or Saturday night, and we all went out for our usual carousing. When we got back to the barracks Jim still hadn't returned, so we waited up for him. It was like he represented our great white hope. *Some*one in our intrepid group just *had* to get laid that summer.

Well, Jim did. But it wasn't pretty. If it had been a normal "boy meets girl, boy gets girl, boy gets his gun off" kind of thing, we all would have long since forgotten it after all these years. But Jim's appearance on his return from that date made a lasting impression on all of us – unfortunately. He wore a worried, somewhat exasperated look on his face and drying brownish-red stains all over the front of his new Bermudas and the front tails of his untucked wrinkled shirt. We all stared. Finally someone, Couture maybe, blurted out, "Geez, Jim, don't tell me she was a *virgin!*"

"Fuck, no," Farra shot back. "She was in her fuckin' *period!*"

"And you fucked her *anyway?"* Couture asked incredulously. "Way to *go*, man!"

"Well, shit, she never told me nothin', and we were already gettin' it on, and I couldn't just *stop*, so we finished up what we started. Man, she was so *hot*, but it sure was *messy!* I don't know, man."

"Whadda ya mean, 'you don't *know*'? You *did* it! You're the *man!*" Couture congratulated him.

"Where'd ya do it, man?" This from Campbell.

"In the back seat of the Buick, and we got this shit all over the seat. My mom's gonna fuckin' *kill* me if I can't get those stains out. I gotta go clean it up right now before they dry!"

So we all trooped after our new hero into the latrine where we helped him fill a bucket and find some scouring powder, a brush and a sponge. Then we went with him out to to the parking lot where a couple of us held flashlights so he could see to scrub the once-scarlet stains of passion from his mother's seat covers – but not before we'd all had a chance to closely examine this irrefutable proof that one of us had finally indeed gotten lucky. Our last great white hope had come through. Bending into the car interior, peering and smelling and murmuring subdued expressions of awe and admiration under the dim domelight of the Buick, we were like lesser dogs of the pack, sniffing up and down the alpha male deferentially immediately after he's covered the female in heat. It may have been messy, but it was also proof positive that there was a stud among us. In some strange vicarious way we had all gotten lucky that night, and Farra didn't just lose his cherry. He became *legend* in our little group.

Just recently, more than forty years after the deed, I talked with Capozzi, Couture, Campbell and Farra on the phone, and, to a man, we all remember that night well. Jim would probably just as soon forget it, but the rest of us won't let him. That night has become a part of our collective memory.

I know that in retrospect it probably sounds rather sordid and seedy, but young men that age really are very similar to a pack of dogs trailing after a bitch in heat, and we were no different. My good Catholic boy upbringing notwithstanding, had I been in Farra's shoes, or shorts, that hot August night, I'm sure I would have behaved no better. I'd have done it too, not just for myself, but for *all* the guys.

Any women reading this might well ask, "What about the girl? What happened to poor Candy?" Hey, I have no idea. We were nearing the end of our TDY at Meade, and I'm not sure if any of us even ever went back to that bar. Maybe Jim did. I don't know. But I do have this theory, developed much later in life, that some women can be just as predatory as men can be. Maybe Candy was one of them. Maybe she got what she wanted too, you know? *Dogs, man. Dogs.*

Our classwork at NSA was finished by early August, but as usual Uncle Sam had factored an extra eight or ten days into our assignment at Meade, so we marked time doing casual duty around the company area for several days. We walked around carrying a rake or a shovel or a paint can and brush, trying our best to look busy. I remember spending at least one of those days with Joe, painting rocks. That sounds funny to a civilian ear, I know, but to most guys who have done time in the army, painting rocks sounds perfectly normal. This particular time the rocks were large mostly flattish ones that bordered a gravel walkway to the company orderly room. I painted every other rock a bright red. Joe painted the other ones white. Honest. And we did a commendable job too. The company commander told us so. By this time we were considered highly trained communications specialists, but we were still painting rocks.

I also spent several somewhat uncomfortable hours in a dentist's chair that last week at Meade. Since there were no dentists in either Shemya or Sinop, we all had to have "class A" teeth before shipping out. I still needed to have several teeth filled. I wasn't nearly so fearful of dentists since I'd discovered novocaine, but it turned out that if you got too many shots of the stuff too close together, like every day for three or four days, it could have an adverse cumulative effect. What happened was the evening of my fourth day of being under the drill, so to speak, I suddenly discovered that I couldn't open my mouth fully. I mean I could open it a little, but not enough to bite into something or to chew. My jaws just refused to cooperate. My dentist, a young captain, had been a bit worried that I was getting too much novocaine in too short a time period, so he had given me his card with a phone number to call in case I should suffer any adverse reactions. Well, the inability to eat, chew, or open my mouth seemed a bit adverse to me, so I called him at home and explained my problem, through nearly clenched teeth. He told me he'd been afraid that might happen, but then he only suggested that I wait until morning to see if the problem fixed itself. I wasn't too happy with that, but as it turned out I *was* fine by the next morning.

In the meantime, Joe and the other guys were teasing me about my sudden close-mouthedness. They decided we'd all go over to the deli on 175, where they made some of the most delicious hoagies in Maryland. I *loved* their Italian-style cold cut sandwiches with all that good stuff on them – just like the ones Joe Bohn had introduced me to in Philly over Easter weekend. But those sandwiches weren't called "grinders" for nothing. You have to be able to open *wide* just to bite into them, and they require plenty of chewing and "grinding." So I was out of luck. I watched Joe and all those other grinning bastards chow down on *my* newfound favorite food while I consoled myself with a chocolate shake.

All good things must end, and so did our idyllic summer sojourn at Fort Meade. On August 12th I set out for Michigan, along with Mike Campbell. He had taken his T-bird home a few weeks earlier and brought back his folks' Dodge sedan for us to drive home in. I don't remember much about that trip. The car had a push-button selector transmission that kind of "clunked" into gear when you pushed DRIVE or REVERSE. It was a trip of several hundred miles through western Maryland, Pennsylvania and Ohio, so we did take turns driving. I had barely driven a car at all in the past year, so I was actually kind of nervous about driving someone else's parents' nearly new car. The first time I took over behind the wheel, somewhere around Youngstown, my right leg was seized with a nervous muscular flutter that made it difficult to keep my foot on the gas pedal. Fortunately, after several minutes I calmed down and the mysterious tremor subsided.

Our trip was without incident, except for some indecision and confusion at a five-road intersection in downtown Toledo where I ended up running a red light because I was so busy reading all the directional signs. It was about two in the morning, so fortunately there was no other traffic. But *un*fortunately there was a Toledo city police cruiser parked nearby. The officer saw me run the red light and swung quickly up behind me with both siren and flasher going. Mike woke up from where he was sleeping in the back seat and we both explained politely to the policeman that we were in the army and were headed home on our last leave before shipping overseas. We showed him our military ID's and leave papers and he was quite sympatico, telling us he'd been in the army himself, then cautioned us to be careful and sent us on our way. No ticket, no warning, just a "good luck." Nice cop.

I spent that day and a night at Mike's place in Battle Creek. I got to meet a girl named Julie, who was a friend of Mike's girlfriend Verna. We had been sort of pen pals since Devens. She was nice enough, but I was pretty wiped out from lack of sleep and probably made a pretty lousy impression. Anyway, I never saw her again. The next morning Mike drove me home to Reed City.

I had two weeks to spend at home. It was my first time back since that long weekend in February. I can't remember much about what I did at home that August. I probably visited and hung out with my high school buddies, Keith and Rex and Art. Keith was working at the Tool and Die, a job he would stick with for over forty years. Rex and Art were students at Ferris, as was my brother Bob. Another brother, Bill, was a student at Michigan Tech. My oldest brother Rich, of course, was also in the ASA, stationed in Germany. It was summertime, so I probably spent some time at our cottage on Indian Lake, swimming and boating with my pal Fred Rohe.

But something had changed since my last visit home, something I couldn't quite seem to put my finger on. Reed City seemed smaller somehow, perhaps because of all those nights spent in downtown D.C. over the past month or so. Chestnut and Upton, the two main streets that made up downtown, had shortened since the last time I walked them. This feeling that things had shrunk bothered me. I made it a point to walk the streets those last days at home and took a close look at all the places that had loomed so large in my eyes as I was growing up. I walked south on Chestnut from the Kent Elevator, where I had worked on and off for Dad since I was twelve years old. I passed Remenap's Hardware, and then the A&P, where I had stocked shelves and bagged groceries during my last year of high school. Turning west on Upton, I peered into Bonsall's Drugs where my brother Bob was working and would later intern during his last year of Pharmacy School. I had sucked up a lot of Cokes and purchased plenty of ten-cent comic books in there, as well as at Dykstra's across the street. I walked on past Kroger's, Gambles, the Ben Franklin, Wing's Jewelers, Starr's Five and Dime, and Doc Halfman's optometry office, where I'd been fitted with eyeglasses of ever-stronger prescriptions for near-sightedness practically every year since I was nine years old. I glanced over at the south side of Upton, at Wright's Bakery, Erler's market and the dry cleaners. Crossing Higbee, I looked up at the windows of the library above the city hall office, then through the window of the Nestle Inn, my favorite place for a hamburger on Saturday or Sunday nights after a movie at the Reed Theater. Maybel Crysler manned her own grill and laid the buns near the sizzling beef patties, giving them a special greasy delicious crispness. No plates necessary. She wrapped each burger in a square of waxed paper that you could lay your burger on between bites, but I rarely laid mine down. I would eat it in several bites, barely chewing, it was that delicious to me. Near Maybel's was DeWitt's, a radio and TV sales and repair business, but more importantly, Reed City's only record store.

I had spent countless happy hours there from the time I was fourteen or so, flipping eagerly through an eclectic collection of the latest albums. In those days records weren't shrink-wrapped and sealed in plastic. You could actually take the record out of its cover and inner sleeve and play it before you bought it. Mrs. DeWitt (Nola) became one of my favorite people of all the downtown merchants. She trusted me to be careful with the records, and allowed me to play anything I wanted on one of the large Zenith hi-fi consoles displayed in the store. I was like a kid in a candy store. I probably spent most of my teenage paychecks at DeWitt's, buying the latest offerings from Ricky Nelson, Marty Robbins, Elvis, Connie Francis and other pop stars and teen idols of the time. Nearing the end of Upton's business district, I shot a quick glance into the dark recesses of Ed's Shoe Repair, a narrow cave where I'd had my shoes re-soled and re-heeled while I waited, breathing in the pleasant smells of leather, polish and glue.

I strolled on up West Upton, past the huge old ornate homes built by the Michigan lumber barons of the past century. I passed the Osceola County courthouse at the corner of Park Street, with its veterans of world wars memorial. I paused in front of the hospital, where my younger brother and sister had been born, and where I'd spent some time as a patient myself at twelve when I tore my leg open in a rather grisly sledding accident. I gazed up across the street at Milligan's place, a house I had wandered yearningly past many times in the seventh and eighth grade when I'd had a terrible crush on Maureen, one of my classmates at St. Philip's School. Now she was a student at Aquinas College and had been dating my brother Bob. My crush was long over. Things change. People change.

That was it. Reed City hadn't changed. I had. I still had all these memories of my childhood there – mostly wonderful, happy memories. But I wasn't sure if it still *felt* like home. I found myself already missing my new friends – Joe, Bill, Mike, Jim – and all those great times we'd had over the past several months at Devens and Meade, in Boston and Washington, I wanted more of that. I was ready to move on. I wanted to see the world.

NSA certificate of training.
August, 1963.

121

PART II

PCS: SINOP, TURKEY
"Yeni" - Welcome to Det 4

"Clean sheets, Ah-bey?" the Turkish houseboy asked, his ghastly, garlic-laden breath sending me recoiling back across my top bunk as I came suddenly awake. My Gawd! What had this guy been eating, anyway? He smelled like my dog's breath after she'd been snacking on cat turds. What an awful way to wake up!

"Uh, no thanks, Ah-bey. My sheets are fine," I mumbled from the far side of my bunk. Ah-bey my ass, I thought. There ain't no way we could be related. I've got four real 'brothers' at home, and the only time they ever smelled that bad was a few hours after we'd had beans for supper, and then the smell wasn't coming out of their mouths.

Main Gate, TUSLOG Det 4

The Turk then made the same offer to my buddy, Joe Capozzi, in the bottom bunk. Joe too jerked abruptly away from the ah-bey's putrid proferral, then turned over and pulled the brown army blanket up over his head, muttering something unintelligible. Sighing, the houseboy padded softly away with his armload of clean linens.

It wasn't even light outside yet. I knew I wouldn't be able to go back to sleep, but settled back anyway into my still-warm sheets, hunkering down under the covers, remembering suddenly that old joke from grade school, the one where a Mexican checks into a cheap fleabag hotel and the desk clerk asks if he wants sheets on his bed, and the Mexican responds with a vicious, "You sheet on my bed, I *keel* you!" Smiling to myself, I wondered if Joe had ever heard that one, but decided against waking him again right then to find out.

Yeah, my sheets were fine. I'd only used them a couple of days. I still couldn't quite believe I was actually in *Turkey*. It was a concept that would take some getting used to. If you've spent most of your life in a tiny town near the middle of the Michigan mitten, you don't really expect to be waking up in Turkey one day. But that was life in the U.S. Army.

TUSLOG Det 4. That was my official mailing address, along with a New York APO number. It stood for Turkish-U.S. Logistics Detachment. Det 4 was located in Sinop, but there were several other TUSLOGs sprinkled here and there throughout Turkey. I think there may have been one at Samsun, which was where we landed en route to Sinop. This was *after* I had flown from New York's Idlewild Airport to Paris. (Yes, that's Paris, *France*, not Paris, Michigan, which is just several miles south of Reed City, and used to have a fish hatchery and park where St. Philip's School had their annual end-of-year picnic. There was also a kind of museum there filled with mounted animals and heads and a diorama of an Indian camp. And way in the back was one of those little machines that you could put a dime in to see some flickering images of scantily-clad women. The seventh- and eighth-grade boys would post a look-out near the entrance to watch out for the Sisters, and take turns peering at the peep show. But back to my overseas journey.) From Paris we had flown to Rome, and then on to Ankara. Since I remember nothing about either Paris or Rome, I guess we

Headquarters, TUSLOG DET4.

just were only there long enough to change planes. In Ankara we boarded a Turkish Airlines flight, which took us to Samsun. From there we traveled the rest of the way to Sinop in the back of an army deuce and a half. That's a two and a half-ton truck, with a canvas canopy arched over the bed with two side benches facing each other. It was pretty full with several of us crammed in there with our duffels and luggage in the middle. Joe Capozzi and Mike Campbell, who had gone through training at Devens and Meade with me, were part of the bunch.

It's an interesting way to travel. You can't really see where you're going, only where you've been, and that through a thick cloud of dust. There weren't many paved or improved roads on the trip north to Sinop. They were mostly gravel or dirt, so the dust constantly billowed into the back of the truck as we roared along the mountain trails, a Turkish driver at the wheel who was either absolutely fearless and confident of his route, or else he was just plain nuts. I'm not sure he knew what the brakes were for, but he sure could use that horn. Every time he approached a curve he would lean steadily on the horn, blaring in warning at any possible oncoming traffic. Luckily, there wasn't much traffic, and the only time I remember him actually braking was when we came around a curve and a cow was standing in the road. This could be more than a bit hair-raising, since there was usually a cliff-face on one side of the road and a sheer drop-off on the other, sometimes of a hundred feet or more.

But one final word about our brief stay in Samsun. There was a small U.S. airbase there in September of 1963. Joe and Mike and I were put to work for part of a day during our stopover. We were handed some tools and told to tighten all the rivets (or nuts and bolts and screws) on the wings, fuselage and engine cowling of a small airplane that was used to ferry the mail and other incidental supplies between Samsun and Sinop, and probably also to Trabzon in the opposite direction, where another U.S. base was located. I remember that all of us on this rivet-tightening detail expressed a unanimous gratitude that we didn't have to *ride* on this plane after we'd been screwing around with it, since we had no idea what we were doing. It seemed to us that this kind of maintenance work should be handled by qualified aircraft mechanics. But that's the Army (or Air Force) – use any free labor that's available, whatever the task. "Good enough for guv'mint work," as we learned to say years later.

Leaving Samsun in our trusty deuce and a half, we dog-legged northwest along the coast toward Sinop. Looking at a map, I see that we probably passed through Bafra on the way. Now I don't remember Bafra the town, but I certainly remember Bafra the *cigarette*. Anyone who has ever traveled to Turkey remembers those foul-smelling smokes. Bafras were probably about the cheapest cigarettes on the market, and they were absolutely everywhere, to the point that the reek of a burning Bafra is one of the main identifying smells you remember when you recall your Turkish tour of duty. All the GI's there used to joke that Bafras weren't really tobacco at all. They were popularly believed to be packed with dried camel dung. Most of us at least *tried* a Bafra, and usually a puff or two was all you wanted. The taste was rank and strong. You almost wanted to go wash your mouth out with soap after a few puffs, and inhaling was not a wise option. Of course maybe that's just my own biased opinion, since I smoked Newports, which was considered kind of a girly, pussy brand by GI standards. I only mention Bafras because they were so ubiquitous to the region – the cultural scent of Sinop.

Since I've already mentioned camel dung, I have to confess that when I learned at Fort Meade that I would be going to Turkey, I had this mental picture of camels and deserts. That's how clueless I was about the culture and the landscape of Turkey. I never saw a camel *or* a desert during my eleven-month tour in Turkey. (Of course I didn't see all that much of the country either.) But I think I had my countries mixed up. In Saudi Arabia or Egypt maybe I would have seen those things, but not in the parts of Turkey I saw.

Sinop. How to describe it or characterize it, or even locate it, geographically speaking? I have always told people that it is situated at the northernmost tip of Turkey, jutting out into the Black Sea. This is almost accurate, but not quite, I see, as I study the map more closely. The village of Sinop is nestled at the narrowest part of the neck of Cape Sinop, and if you stood on a hill at either end of town, north or south, you could see just how narrow the cape was at that point. You could easily see the waters of the harbors that flanked the east and west sides of the town. Only ten or fifteen miles to the west is Cape Ince, which actually extends a bit further north into the sea than Cape Sinop. So okay, I've been *slightly* erroneous in my description all these years. But who would care?

To reach the joint military base at Sinop, TUSLOG Det 4, you had to travel through the center of the village. I don't remember much about my arrival in Sinop, other than a vague image of a crowd of skinny, ragged urchins running along in the dust cloud behind our deuce and a half as we rolled slowly through town. They all had their hands out, reaching up towards us, as we peered curiously out the back of the truck. They were begging, in broken English, for cigarettes, gum or money – whatever we had. It was a new experience for me, seeing children begging. Where I came from, kids were taken care of. They were well-fed and clothed, and even had toys to play with, bicycles to ride and games to play. These kids, it was painfully obvious to see, had almost nothing. They were poor. They were hungry. The word "needy" became real to me in Sinop – not just a word in a book or CARE pamphlet. That day poverty was given a face, and a voice that cried out in shrill reedy tones: "Chic-lets, Ah-bey? Cig-arettes, money?"

A few of the guys had some Turkish coins left over from our short stay in Ankara, where we'd exchanged a few dollars. So they threw these, along with a few sticks of Juicy Fruit and Doublemint, out the back of the moving truck toward the reaching, dirty hands. A brief melee ensued as the children scrambled in the street, competing for these small prizes, then continued to run behind the truck, their entreaties undiminished. For the first of many times I felt vaguely guilty and ashamed, and then quickly angry at being made to feel that way. *Shit, I ain't no fuckin' millionaire my*self! I thought. *Why should I feel guilty, dammit?*

As we emerged from the north end of the village, the truck picked up speed and headed up the steep hill towards the base, and the children quickly fell behind and were soon lost in the dust. But that first impression of Sinop – poverty and beggars – stayed with me, and is still with me all these years later.

Our first "home" upon arriving at Det 4 was the "yeni" barracks, a galvanized steel quonset hut, probably a relic from WWII days, when these steel structures were used for shelter and storage throughout both theaters of the war. Fortunately, it was still early September, so cold wasn't a problem, but I strongly suspected that those huts would be pretty difficult to keep warm in the wintertime. "Yeni" was a word we heard a lot those first weeks. It's the Turkish word for "new," hence as new guys, we were automatically labeled yenis. There is always a pecking order on a military base, and new guys are always at the bottom. Of course there's nothing you can do personally to avoid the onus of the yeni

Al and Tim outside their barracks.

or "newk" label, except grin and bear it until someone comes in *after* you, then *he* becomes the yeni. It's not a particularly complicated or cruel system; it's just a fact of life, and you get used to it.

It's hard to remember much about those early days at Det 4. I'm pretty sure there was the usual "casual" time of three to four weeks while all our paperwork and pay records were being processed at the personnel office and we awaited final security clearances which would grant us access into the inner sanctum of the Operations Center, where all the real work, or the "mission," was accomplished. During those weeks we "got orientated" (as the military was so fond of saying) to our new surroundings.

It wasn't a very big base. There were probably no more than a couple hundred men there, mostly Army, but a small number of Air Force and Navy guys too, who pretty much kept to themselves. Besides the Ops building, which was the heart of the base, there were the usual support facilities. There was a personnel office, a very small health clinic, or dispensary, staffed by an enlisted medical corpsman or two. I don't think there was a doctor there, and certainly no dentist. Any serious medical problems were med-evacked back to Ankara, which had a well-staffed military hospital. There was a non-denominational post chapel, which I think was located right next to the metal yeni barracks. Down the hill a bit was a small movie theater where the film offerings changed nearly every day. The film canisters came in on the mail plane, which landed a few times a week at a small airstrip on the other side of Sinop. There was a new gymnasium with a full-size basketball court and a weight room and storage for other athletic supplies. Built along one side of the gym, almost like an afterthought, was a two-lane bowling alley with automatic pinsetters. Near the center of post was a quadrangle, with three cement block construction two-story barracks, where most of the men lived. On one end of the quad was the mess hall, where everyone took their daily meals. Across a paved road from the barracks quad was another small complex of nearly new buildings which housed the Post Office and mail room, the EM (Enlisted Men) Club, and a recreation center with ping-pong and pool tables. There was a PX where you could buy necessary sundries, a limited selection of clothing and food, magazines, records and other miscellaneous items. The PX also

1	EM Club	13	Ops Center
2	NCO Club	14	Chapel
3	Special Services	15	Dispensary
4	APO	16	Yeni Barracks
5	AFES (PX)	17	Warehouse
6	Orderly Room	18	Theater
7	Unit Supply	19	Gym
8	Washington Hall	20	Water Tower
9	Grant Hall	21	MP
10	Jackson Hall	22	HQ
11	Orderly Room	23	PMO
12	Mess Hall	24	Main Gate

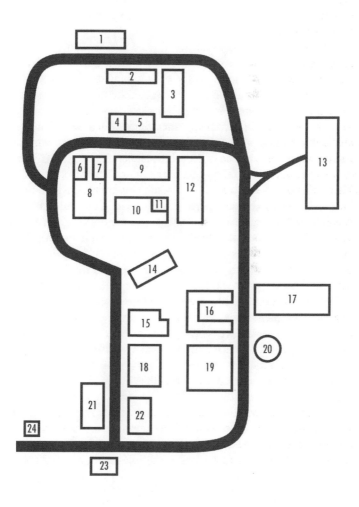

had a small snack bar with a grill. The rec center also boasted a very small library, but everyone was happy when a bookstore opened up in early 1964. Because we were so isolated, books and records were something of a precious commodity (more on that later). There was also a Provost Marshal's Office, staffed by a small contingent of military policemen, who provided physical security to the base. A small cement block BOQ (Bachelor Officer Quarters) was home for the small close-knit group of officers assigned to Det 4. Of course they weren't all bachelors, but Sinop was an "unaccompanied" tour, so any wives or children had to be left behind in the states. Aside from a few other warehouses and storage buildings, that was pretty much it.

This motley collection of U.S.-occupied buildings was completely surrounded by an eight-foot high barbed-wiretopped chain link security fence, which ran all around the perimeter of the base. There was a manned guard shack at the main gate where the road up the hill from town entered the grounds. Along one side of the base outside the perimeter fence there was a small cluster of crude barracks for the Turkish Army troops who were co-garrisoned there with the U.S. troops. Hence the TUSLOG tag.

We had very little contact with these Turkish soldiers. We stayed on our side of the fence – *in*side – and they stayed on theirs – *out*side. Supposedly their presence provided enhanced physical security for the base. Turkish troops kept a continuous guard mount in rotation and walked a regular route around the outside of the perimeter fence. We knew all about this, because we pulled guard duty (a roster detail) periodically on our side, and we would see our Turkish counterparts walking their beat just a few feet away beyond the wire. Sometimes we would try to converse with them, but most of them spoke no English, and we spoke no Turkish beyond a few words. We would exchange cigarettes with them on occasion, but since their brand of choice was usually Bafras, it was more an act of kindness on our part. In any case, officially we were supposed to limit our contact with the Turks and mind our own business, and we usually did.

So that was the physical layout of the base. Exactly how these various buildings and facilities were arranged in relation to each other I can't really remember, all lost in the mists of memory. But it was not a very big place, and spending nearly a year there did eventually give you a real sense of isolation, if not outright claustrophobia.

I never took any leave while I was stationed in Turkey. Part of the reason I didn't was administrative. There was a dire shortage of 058 operators during most of my tour, so the command was reluctant to grant leave, fearing it would negatively impact the mission. But I think the real reason I never took leave was that same sense of isolation. Where would you go? And how would you get there? Remember we came to Sinop in the back of a truck over narrow, primitive mountain roads. It wasn't a trip we were anxious to repeat. I only knew a few guys who did take leave while I was there. They all went to Greece, but I don't remember any details about how they got there. There was a passenger liner, a big white ship, that used to put in at the main pier in Sinop, that traveled up and down the coast. It was called simply the "white boat." Maybe they took that ship to Istanbul and then flew to Athens, I don't know.

We only stayed in the yeni quonset hut for a couple weeks while our paperwork was being processed. Then we were assigned to a "trick," and moved over into the new cement barracks. Trick was a slang term for a work shift. The work we did was a twenty-four hour operation, so there were four tricks. Three of them would be working while the fourth was on break. We usually worked six days (or swings or mids) and then had two or three days off. Sinop station was probably ideally suited for this kind of operation, because it *was* so isolated and remote. You never felt like you might be missing something if you slept all day while working mids. There was literally nothing to miss. Most of us came to feel that the more time we spent sleeping, the quicker our tour there would be over.

I can say very little about the work itself at Det 4. It was all highly classified. All of us who worked inside the operations center had been thoroughly "vetted," that is a painstaking background investigation of our pasts had been carried out. Once we had been processed onto post at Sinop and our security clearances had been forwarded there, we were issued special badges which we had to show to the guards to get inside our workplace in the Ops Center. Although I can't talk about the work itself, I can say that we were all quite proud of what we did and took great pride it doing our jobs

The Operations Center

well. We were Cold War warriors. What we knew stayed with us. There was a standard joke (or I *think* it was a joke) in the Army Security Agency at the time that said that if a site had to be evacuated for an emergency, the ASA personnel went first, *then* the women and children.

The Ops Center itself was surrounded by its own eight-foot security fence topped with barb-wire, a small ultra-secure island within the wire-enclosed post itself. We used to joke among ourselves that our work at Sinop was helping to keep the world "safe from democracy." We were all well aware of how little we actually knew about the larger intelligence picture, but we were nevertheless extremely proud of our small roles in maintaining the balance of power in the Cold War world.

When we first moved from the quonsets to the new barracks, we were housed in a large open room that was designed to be a dayroom, or community room for the barracks. At that particular time the post was apparently overstrength in personnel, so this billeting arrangement was temporary. The fellows I can remember in our new group at this time were Joe Capozzi, Mike Campbell and Fred Beaver. Mike was assigned briefly to another trick, but then, before he even began work, he was re-classified and turned into a mail-room clerk. Apparently they needed someone in the mail room, so there went nearly a year's worth of training down the toilet, so the army could have a body to sort mail. Mike took it well though, and we managed to keep in touch with each other during our tour.

Beaver was a slow-talking, slow to anger red-headed character whom we enjoyed ragging gently. Early on he shared with us that he had a heart murmur and extremely flat feet, but had somehow managed to pass the physical to get into the army. To these defects we used to add in a joking manner that he also suffered from chronic halitosis and congenital B.O. He also took a tremendous amount of crap about his name, Beaver, which was of course also a slang term for the hirsute female pudendum (a term you don't hear much anymore, so perhaps it has fallen out of fashion). All the guys who knew and liked Beaver (and with a great surname like that, hardly anyone ever called him Fred), never tired of loudly announcing him whenever he entered a room – *BEAV-er!* All heads would turn whenever the announcement was shouted out. Even though everyone knew there were no female personnel at Det 4, hope always sprang eternal. Beaver suffered all this ribbing good naturedly, usually responding to his announcers with either an *At ease, men, I'll be in the area all day,* or an equally mellow and affable, *Fuck yeuww.* Most of the men who shared a tour with Fred Beaver will remember him fondly, if only for his furry surname and his good nature.

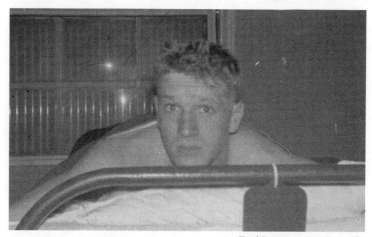

Fred Beaver in Yeni Barracks

* * * * *

I think Joe and I probably spent six or eight weeks in that temporary dayroom setting, crammed in with several other new guys also waiting to be assigned a regular room. In November and December quite a few of the old-timers, or "short-timers," began to rotate out of the base, heading either back to the states or to Europe to finish their terms of enlistment. During those months we became acquainted with the four guys in a room just across the hall, an interesting foursome. Dave Irwin and Chet "Bergie" Bergdale were the two short-timers in the room, both due to leave before the year's end. I'm not sure, but they may have both been from California. In any case, they were close friends, as were the other two guys, Al Trott, from Ohio, and Norm Yurong, from Hawaii. Al and Norm hadn't been there much longer than we had, so they would be looking for new roommates when Bergie and Dave departed. It offered an "in" for Joe and me, an opportunity to get out of the cramped impersonal quarters of the dayroom, so by December we had moved into the room with Norm and Al, and soon found that the four of us were a good fit.

It was important for roommates to get along well in the barracks, because we were, by necessity, living in extremely close quarters. "Asshole to elbow" was, I think, the preferred description. The rooms were originally designed to house just two men each, but the mission and the population at Sinop station had grown much more quickly than anticipated, so what would have been very comfortable two-man rooms had largely become crowded four-man rooms by the time Joe and I arrived. But I can't remember anyone actually ever complaining about this situation. We simply accepted it as inevitable and learned to adapt. The room was not a large one, perhaps twelve by fifteen feet, with a built-in desk and closets and shelves along one whole wall. The rest of the room then had to accommodate two double bunk beds and two additional metal wall and foot lockers, for the two "extra" occupants. So it was a pretty tight fit, but I don't remember ever having any major disagreements or altercations during our residence there together.

It was probably something of a minor miracle that there *weren't* any fights in our room, given the diverse mix of personalities between the four of us. Al and Norm were both real characters, but somehow managed to complement each other. Al

Left to Right: Norm Yurong, Al Trott, Tim and Jim Claunch

was, hmmm ... was what? How to describe Al, probably one of the most colorful personalities I knew at Sinop. He could be a very volatile, explosive sort at times. But at other times he could also be very relaxed and mellow – and *funny.*

One incident that comes to mind was one night when we'd had some kind of cabbage or bean-based dinner entree in the chow hall. Later that evening we were all sitting around in the room together, still in our fatigue work clothes, when I cut a remarkably explosive and putrid fart. This in itself was not unusual, since, like most boys or young men living on their own, farts and other bodily functions are a common source of entertainment and a topic of conversation. Al immediately commented, "Whooa! You shoulda lit that one. You'da been like a human blowtorch." A heated argument ensued about whether or not that old myth about "lighting farts" was just that, a myth. Al asserted vehemently that it was not; that it could be done, and volunteered to prove it then and there, since, as I think he put it, "I feel a real ripper comin' on." With that he grabbed Norm's Zippo off the foot locker and rolled back onto his bunk, feet up in the air. Holding the lighter poised near his bottom, he paused, a look of intense concentration creasing his brow. We waited, bending forward and watching, barely breathing. He flicked the lighter and almost simultaneously blasted what was indeed a "real ripper." Sure enough, a long tongue of blue flame shot away from the seat of his pants. The rest of us *ooooh*-ed, appropriately impressed by this incontestable proof that the lighted fart phenomenon was *not* a myth. Just as our collective *ooooh* died away, we all noticed at once a brighter flame and a puff of smoke coming from the vicinity of Al's still upturned ass. Some loose threads at the seam of his trouser bottom had ignited and were burning! Al must have felt the heat, because he threw the lighter on the floor and started beating at his flaming butt with both hands, hollering, "*Jee-zus Kee-RIST!*" The minute blaze was quickly extinguished by his efforts. Joe, Norm and I were all rolling on the floor laughing by this time. Al quickly regained his cool, stood up, and, brushing off his bottom, said, "See? Just like a blowtorch. Told'ja."

Al blowing sax.

One of the things that caused Al and Joe to connect almost immediately was they were both musicians. Al played the saxophone. He didn't have his own horn with him, but he did have his own mouthpiece, or reed, which he kept in a special little soft cloth pouch. The service club had an assortment of musical instruments that could be checked out for extended periods, so Al kept a sax on hand much of the time, and practiced whenever he could. I think having Joe there, noodling on his guitar, gave him an additional incentive to practice. Of the two, Joe was probably the more natural and talented musician, but Al worked seriously on improving his tone, breathing and technique, and would often blow until he was red in the face from practicing.

But then it didn't take much to get Al red in the face. He was a bit ruddy-complected to begin with, usually had a somewhat impish gleam in his eye, and always ready for some fun. Al wore his hair in a flat top crewcut, with slightly longer hair combed back on the sides, a style commonly called a "Princeton." He was short and stocky, probably about the same height as Joe and Norm, around five foot six or seven.

Al Trott and Norm Yurong in the weight room.

Al and Norm were already seriously into weight training when Joe and I met them. They worked out regularly in the weight room at the gym, spotting each other with the heavier weights on the bench, and competing in a friendly chest-butting kind of fashion over who could bench-press the most. I would say how much they pressed if I could remember, but I can't. I do remember, however, that they both sported some serious muscles, very noticeably in their arms, chests and shoulders, and were working on the other muscle groups too. Soon after we moved into the room they converted Joe to the religion of body-building, so he often went to the weight room with them, although I don't think he ever became quite as serious a disciple as they were.

I didn't get into weights, not with my long skinny string-bean frame. I had done some minor work with weights one year when I played basketball in high school, doing some squats with barbells across my shoulders. This was supposed to build up my legs and help me jump higher. But I ended up straining my back, badly enough to send me to our family physician, Dr. Kilmer, who treated me with heat therapy under a lamp of some kind. So since basketball season at Sinop was already underway, I wasn't very anxious to hurt myself again.

* * * * *

Yes, there was *basketball* in Sinop! There'll be more on my roomies later, but let's talk basketball a bit first. In fact, there was quite a healthy and well-organized intra-mural sports schedule on base. There were softball and touch football leagues in the proper seasons, and there were even a few bowling teams that competed regularly in our two-lane alley. But basketball may well have been the most popular sport at Det 4. I think there were at least five intra-mural teams, which were drawn from the four Operations tricks and Headquarters Company, which provided all the support

Intramural basketball at Synop.

services to the Ops people. Besides these five teams, we also boasted a post team, made up of the best players on station. This team made periodic trips to Ankara, Istanbul and other sites to compete at a Theater level. And a couple of times teams from other stations came to Sinop to play our team too. When this happened it was a really big deal, usually drawing a large crowd, meaning everyone on post who didn't have to work that night. It was during games like this that the base esprit de corps was probably at its zenith.

One of these games – I think it was against a team from Ankara – provided one of the most memorable moments of my tour at Sinop. And I'm sure anyone else who was present at that particular game has never forgotten it either. Our post team was, of course, made up of our absolutely best b-ball players. I think at the time I knew all of them by name, but from this distant vantage point all their names have vanished from my memory. There were two big men on the team. One was a big-boned Nordic type with bright red hair and a flamboyantly long and waxed handlebar moustache. He was probably six foot six or seven and weighed around 250. I think his nickname was Swede. The other big man was black, about the same size as Swede, but a more graceful, natural athlete. I can't remember his name, so I'll call him Sly (short for Sylvester, as in Sly and the Family Stone). Sly and Swede were pretty good friends and were constantly razzing each other and attempting to outdo each other on the court. They could both easily dunk the ball, and neither was above a little showboating, given the opportunity and an appreciative audience. Those conditions were right that night in mid-December when the Ankara team was visiting and all the bleacher seats were filled.

The two teams were still warming up, lined up for layups. Both Swede and Sly had already slam-dunked a couple home coming from the right side of the court, each successive jam followed by ever-more enthusiastic chanting cheers from the crowd of *Sweeed!* or *Slaaah!* The team then switched over to the left side of the court. Swede, in line just before Sly, attempted a vicious left-handed slam-dunk, but misjudged slightly, and the ball caromed high off the back of the rim, actually hitting one of the steel roof beams of the gym. A disappointed mass groan sounded from the seats. Sly's turn. He sprinted forward, taking the pass. Rising gracefully, he turned his body, hang-time personified, and executed a perfect right-handed crossover slam, the ball reaching the floor before Sly's feet did. An appreciative roar leapt from the throats of the crowd, but stopped short when Sly suddenly dropped to his knees upon touching back down, clutching at his right hand with his left. First a trickle, then a stream of bright red blood escaped between the fingers of his left hand. Stunned and confused, Sly took his left hand away, and a small fountain of blood spurted from his right hand. Everyone in the suddenly hushed gym followed his glance up to the basket, and at that moment Sly's pinky, still wearing a heavy gold signet ring which had caught on one of the net hooks, plummeted to the hardwood floor, landing with what seemed an abnormally loud *clunk*. Or *thunk*, or *plunk*. Because how do you correctly describe the sound of a suddenly severed ringed finger when it hits a polished wooden floor falling from a height of precisely ten feet?

After what seemed an eternity of horrified silence (but was probably really only a few seconds), our team manager came running to Sly's side with a clean white towel, which he wrapped carefully around the bleeding hand. Another of our players ran to the bench, scooped a paper cup full of ice from a nearby ice chest and rushed over to where the dark severed finger still lay on the floor under the basket. Hesitating, he reached down, then drew back and looked back at the bench and around the court, apparently hoping for some advice or guidance on how to handle this situation, how to handle his teammate's *finger*, for cripes sake. Finally, after another second or two of looking helplessly about, he plucked the finger from the floor, dropped it ring and all into the cup of ice, and ran to follow Sly, who was by this time surrounded by the coach, manager, other players and a medical corpsman who had come forward from the bleachers, and was being led off the floor towards the locker room.

What I remember most about this grisly incident is the sudden absolute hush, the unnatural *quiet* that filled the gym, a gym packed with normally noisy boisterous spectators, and then the awful physical *finality* of that thud that the severed finger made when it hit the hardwood. And that finality turned out to be very real. Sly was hustled off to the base clinic where his hand and the finger were kept iced until the necessary arrangements had been made to medevac him by air to the Ankara hospital. There a team of surgeons re-attached the finger, but the operation was unsuccessful. The finger was finally amputated several days later.

I have absolutely no memory of the game that followed this awful accident, but I'm quite sure it was played. Only three or four weeks later, Sly came back from the Ankara hospital and was back on the court soon after, shooting around, learning to adapt to his new grip on the ball. You wouldn't think a pinky finger would be too important in shooting a basketball, but it does form a natural part of of the hand's "launching platform," so I'm sure it took some getting used to. I really admired Sly for his immediate return to the court. I hope he adapted and stayed with the game, because he really was a talented player.

I guess I was in the second or third tier of basketball talent at Sinop. I wasn't good enough to make the post team, but I was definitely an asset to my trick team. I probably played better ball that winter than I ever had in high school. I think one of the reasons was that, at nearly twenty, I had finally stopped *grow*ing. I didn't feel so much like I was all knees and elbows anymore, although I *was* still pretty long and skinny-looking. My coordination and reflexes were finally catching up with my size though, and my confidence increased commensurately. The real difference though was that I was playing among friends. I wasn't the Catholic school outsider trying to win acceptance from the tight-knit group of public school kids anymore. We were all just guys in the army a long way from home, doing our jobs and looking for some fun. I was the big man on the team again, but this time I was the "go-to" big man, and I did my absolute best for the guys. Our totals were sometimes almost laughable. Final scores

Second place, basketball gold ribbon

were often only in the forties. But I was usually responsible for half or more of those points, and often pulled down an equal number of rebounds. According to my letters home that winter, I even had a few double-double games in points and boards. All three of my roommates – Al, Joe and Norm – were on our trick team, along with Jim Claunch, who lived just down the hall from us. Jim was probably nearly six feet tall, but my roomies were all only about five and a half feet tall. They were competitive scrappers though, and all those hours spent in the weight room made them formidable competitors when they'd come barreling down the court with the ball, looking for the big man. That was the real difference in my performance. They passed me the ball every time I was open, so of course I scored. Our team was unbeaten for most of the season. We finally lost out in the second round of the playoffs. But I think we were all pretty happy with our season overall. It was a great way to spend some of our free time and build a sense of solidarity.

* * * * *

Basketball was organized recreation, but most of our leisure time was less regulated, our recreation was spontaneous, generated by common interests. When Joe and I were still living in the day room, we met Al because he heard us playing some records one day and came in to listen. Joe had this 45 called "Wild Weekend." It was by one of those obscure one-hit wonder groups, The Rockin' Rebels, and was an instrumental hit with guitars, bass, drums and a really wailing sax solo. Al heard the sax from across the hall and it drew him in like a magnet. He came over to listen and find out who was playing it. It was the beginning of our friendship, and a month or so later, Joe and I moved into the room with Al and Norm.

An unofficial musical collaboration sprang up between Al and Joe. They checked out a saxophone and an electric guitar from the service club and made it a habit to jam a bit and practice together whenever they could. I think "Wild Weekend" may have been one of the first songs they learned to play together. Of course the sounds of "live" music attracted other guys from the barracks, who would drop by and hang around to listen or make requests. Eventually they hooked up with an electric bass player, a drummer, and at least two other guitar players.

One of these guitarists wasn't just another amateur picker. He was a *phenomenal* picker. I don't remember who introduced us to Sergeant Clark. Maybe he just showed up at our door when he heard the music, like the other guys did. At any rate the connection between Joe and him was immediate. They were two musicians who were instantly *sympatico*.

It's embarrassing to just call this guy "Sergeant" Clark, but the truth is I can't remember his first name, and when I asked Joe recently during one of our long-distance "remember when" chats, neither could he. Clark was a staff sergeant (SSG), an E-6, when all the rest of us were only lowly PFC's, so maybe we just always called him "Sarge." If we did, it probably was not just out of deference to his higher rank, but out of respect for this musical talent. Because this guy, who was probably several years older than the rest of us, had talent to spare. I mean he could *pick*! A country boy himself, maybe even from Tennessee, Clark was a huge fan and devotee of Chet Atkins, who was, even in the early sixties, considered one of the premiere pickers in the country. I was familiar with Atkins' music because my brother Bill was a fan and had a few of Chet's early albums. Well, Clark had *all* of Chet's albums, and could pick right along with practically every track on them. Joe didn't know too much about Atkins, and wasn't real crazy about his country sound. He was a disciple of The Ventures, probably the reigning pop instrumental group of the time. And he always kept an ear out for other instrumental hits on the pop scene that he might emulate or put his own spin on – tunes like "Tequila" by the Champs, "Pipeline" by the Chantays, "Let's Go" by the Routers, or (one of *my* favorites) Preston Epps' "Bongo Rock."

At any rate, country met pop when Joe and the Sarge got together, and they began right away to trade licks and teach each other about their respective kinds of music. Clark was also a fan of other traditional country artists and pickers like Merle Travis and Joe Maphis and the Carter Family – folks Joe and I had never heard of, but soon came to respect and appreciate. Clark soon had Joe playing rhythm to tunes like "Wildwood Flower" and "Under the Double Eagle," while Joe introduced him to "Walk Don't Run," "Detour," and, naturally, "Wild Weekend." It was like a musical meeting of the minds between the country mouse and the city mouse.

Sgt. Bud Clark picking on his Fender.

Joe and Al on guitar and sax performing at NCO club. Tim lurking in doorway.

Joe, Al and the Sarge, along with a few other guys who came and went, made a habit of getting together over at the service club that winter to practice certain tunes until they had them down. Eventually, they had put together a pretty respectable repertoire, and by spring they began to perform at the EM/NCO club and were a big success, not only because of their musicianship, but because of their mixed bag of pop and country tunes. They played something for everyone. It was a real treat for everyone to enjoy local talent that could provide live music and even take requests and do justice to them.

Of course I loved hearing the guys play, and even hung around for many of their early practice sessions. There were always a few extra guys hanging around in the doorway and hall whenever they played, swaying or tapping their feet, or even singing along. Once I took a couple of large coffee cans that Mom had packed cookies in, duct-taped them together and turned them into makeshift bongo drums so I could play along too. The guys tolerated my playing well enough, but even I knew it didn't come up to their performance standards, so I only pottered along with them at informal practice sessions, not when they played at the club. They had a real drummer then.

* * * * *

Norm, Al, Joe and Tim outside the gym.

Life seemed pretty good our first few months at Sinop. We were learning our jobs and just beginning to settle into a comfortable routine of work and play. One night in late November we had just finished working a swing shift, grabbed an early breakfast at the chow hall, and went to the midnight movie, a regular attraction to accommodate the shift workers. The feature that night was *Moon Pilot*, a rather silly Walt Disney film with Tom Tryon playing an astronaut. Tryon was a Disney contract actor, who

I remembered from when he starred in a Disney TV series as *Texas John Slaughter.* I had watched the show, about Texas Rangers, as a kid, and still remembered the theme song tag-line: "Texas John Slaughter/ Made 'em do what they oughter/And if they didn't they died." Years later Tryon enjoyed a second career as a novelist. One of his bestsellers, *The Other,* became a box office film success too. But *Moon Pilot*, the film we were watching that night in November of 1963, was a very run-of-the-mill Disney-esque piece of fluff, eminently forgettable.

The reason I still remember it all these years later is that about an hour into the feature the screen went dark, the house lights came up, and the theater manager, an Army NCO, walked out onto the narrow stage in front of the screen and announced rather hesitatingly but perfunctorily that President Kennedy had just been shot while visiting Dallas. He said he didn't have any further information, but had been instructed to make the announcement. He then left the stage, the lights went back down and the movie resumed. We all sat stunned and disbelieving for the next twenty minutes or so. I doubt if anyone who was there remembers much about the ending of that stupid film. When it was over and the lights came on again, the manager again mounted the stage and said everyone was to report back to their barracks and await further instructions from their superiors.

By the time we got back to our room a rumor was already circulating that Kennedy was dead. This was soon confirmed by our platoon leader, SSG Gnong, who gathered us together in the dayroom and told us to get our field gear and put it on. This meant our helmets and steel pots, field packs and web belts with canteens, first aid kits, gas masks and ammo pouches. Then we reported to the small armory across the street from the barracks and were issued our weapons, M-1 carbines, which we had never really used except to fire a few familiarization rounds when we first arrived on base. The reason we only got to fire a couple rounds was that ammunition for the short stubby weapon was in short supply. So even then, gearing up hastily for God knew what, we were only issued the rifles, no ammo. This didn't make us feel any too secure. The carbine wouldn't even make a very threatening club. Cripes, even Barney Fife, with his one bullet buttoned into his shirt pocket, was better armed than we were for any possible enemy attack.

M1 carbine.
No bullets allowed.
Useless even as a club.

Enemy attack? Were we really worried about *that?* You bet your sweet ass we were. When JFK was assassinated, U.S. military forces all over the globe were placed on the highest level of alert status. After all, this was during the height of the Cold War. Paranoia between the superpowers was rampant. The shooting could have been part of a Communist plot, and that was the initial suspicion, even after Oswald was captured, and even after *he* was shot in turn by Jack Ruby. It took a while for things to calm down.

In the meantime, there we sat in full field gear, empty carbines at the ready, wondering what was going to happen next, suddenly painfully and fearfully aware that our deadliest Cold War enemy, the Soviet Union, lay only about 160 miles to the north. Too damn close for comfort. For several days we kept our gear and rifle close by in the barracks, and took them with us back and forth to work at the Ops Center. We continued to receive the latest news by teletype there. It was an extremely uncomfortable and tense time. Everyone who was stationed at Sinop during those days will recall how vulnerable we all felt. We were within range of Soviet missiles and other strike forces. All of us had seen Soviet warships from the Black Sea Fleet lying offshore at various times as they made their patrols. Was I scared? Of course I was, for a while anyway. Everyone was. But after the first few days the actual fear factor lessened somewhat, since nothing had happened yet. Any element of surprise the Soviets might have enjoyed if it *had* been a plot was certainly gone by then. Looking back now, I'm sure that all the U.S. forces throughout Turkey, including fighter jets and bombers, were poised to protect us in our very *un*protected and vulnerable site, on top of a mountain on a point jutting out into the Black Sea. At the time however, I didn't really think about that. I just felt like a sitting duck.

I needed to get this down, finally. Everyone who was around when Kennedy was shot has a story to tell about where they were and what they were doing when they heard the news. Now my kids, and maybe my grandkids too, will know my slant on that historic and tragic time. I was at the movies. But I was also serving my country. I was scared, like we all were, but I was ready to do what I needed to do. As it turned out, I just needed to keep on doing my job. I did, and I'm proud of that.

Eventually the fear and uncertainty passed. More news on the assassination and its aftermath continued to reach us. There were no intelligence indications that the Soviets or the Chinese or any other Communist powers were involved in the shooting. Oswald wasn't talking. He was dead. And so was John Fitzgerald Kennedy, one of the most beloved and charismatic presidents our country had ever known. The Camelot days were done. Lyndon Johnson, a good ol' boy from Texas, was in the White House, was in control. We put away our gas masks and other field gear and turned in our useless carbines. We retrieved our candy bar and Cracker Jack stash from our ammo pouches. (Hey, there was no *ammo*. Might as well have some emergency rations with us, right?) We resumed our basketball practice schedule. We got back to business as usual. But we would always remember this time.

* * * * *

I should be able to remember something significant about Christmas in Sinop, since it was the first time in my young life that that I wasn't at home for that holiday. The truth is, however, I can't really think of anything very significant about that time. I was probably a little homesick, but maybe not. I mean, when you're halfway around the world away from home, you know there's no way you could possibly *get* there, even for Christmas, so I probably just figured, why dwell on it? I know Mom and Dad sent me a box with homemade treats and some presents. We all got one of those and were pretty generous about sharing the booty with each other. But I think for pretty much everyone stuck in Sinop at Christmastime, the overriding sentiment was, let's get it over with and get on with our sentences here. I do remember that I served at midnight Mass on Christmas Eve, and I think I was working days on Christmas day itself, so it felt much like any other day.

A couple weeks before Christmas a rumor started circulating that Bob Hope might be bringing his show to Sinop sometime during the holidays to entertain the troops. Well, I think Hope really did intend to come, but we heard later that he took ill with the flu or something before he could get to us, but he did send a small troupe of entertainers to Sinop, headed up, I believe, by his friend, Jerry Colonna, the bushy-moustachioed comedian. And there was a beauty queen there too. Was it Miss USA? Maybe, I'm not sure. At any rate, a very small bunch of Bob's people did show up just before or after Christmas and put on a show in the gym. There was some singing and dancing and a comedy routine, and the beauty queen signed autographs and posed for photos with some of the guys. Then, and I don't think this was part of the Hope road show, a Turkish belly dancer performed. Well, she wasn't really a belly dancer per se, although she started out with that. She did a kind of dance of the seven veils – i.e. she was a stripper. And, unlike the stripper I had seen at the Ionia Free Fair when I was sixteen, who had only stripped down to a g-string and pasties, this dancer took it *awwwl* off, right down to the skin, much to the delight of the GI audience. Unfortunately, *this* "beauty queen" would not pose for pictures with the guys, although I think a few of the men did snap some photos during her performance. It was fun and tittilating while it lasted, but I think that, ultimately, it just made us all feel a little crappier about being where we were. Not that any of us had beauty queens or strippers waiting at home for us, but it made us feel more acutely the absence of the "real world," or the "land of the big PX and round doorknobs." The stripper being there just kind of rubbed our faces in it. *Merry Christmas, you sorry fuckers. Look at what you're missing.*

As we watched, most of us were probably mentally adding up just how many days we still had left on our tour.

I only spent that one winter in Turkey, but I learned something about the fickleness and sudden changeability of weather that year. In Michigan there's a popular expression: "If you don't like the weather, wait a few minutes. It will change." Well, our winter in Sinop was weird. The sudden changes in temperature were extreme. In December, and even January and February, we had surprisingly mild days when you could go outside in shirtsleeves and be comfortable. It was the kind of pleasant weather that could lull you into thinking, *Wow, I guess this Turkish winter is gonna be semi-tropical.* But then, I think it was late in January, winter suddenly descended with an icy vengeance. Temperatures plummeted from the sixties down into the twenties overnight. The wind began to blow, and down came the snow. It snowed day and night non-stop for two or three days. The accompanying winds were so strong and so swirling and changeable that there was no telling exactly how much snow fell. There were a few areas out in the open where the ground might be nearly bare, and other places, up near buildings, where the drifts were several feet deep. Up against one end of the mess hall the snow drifted into a wave-like formation, with the crest of the wave reaching nearly to the roof. We had to shovel a path through this drift to gain access to the paved path that ran from the housing quad out to the Operations building.

This path ran along the top of a short ridge, where the land fell away into a depression or gully on either side. The high winds that were howling across the base (which was, you have to understand, located on top of a mountain – actually an extinct volcano – on a thin peninsula jutting out into the Black Sea) were so strong that they could easily blow a man right off that path. The snow continued to swirl and blow in blizzard-like conditions, making it almost impossible to see more than a few feet in front of you, even in daylight. Because of these extreme winter storm conditions, the commander had a safety line strung from the corner of the mess hall up the path to the Ops Center gate, something we could hold onto that would guide us that treacherous and icy hundred yards or so and get us safely to work.

Sinop in Winter, 1964

The storm finally blew itself out after a few days. The wind died and the sun came out again. In addition to the deep spectacular drifts scattered here and there around the base, we had probably a foot or more of snow on the ground all around our barracks area – wet, good-packing snow.

Our trick was just starting break, after a set of mids, so we did what kids do under these conditions. We bundled up in our field jackets and scarfs and went out to play in the snow, chucking snowballs at each other, and falling backwards to make snow angels in the clean virgin snow. Soon a couple cases of beer from the EM Club materialized and we all were soon freely imbibing. Someone suggested we build a snowman – a *big* snowman. So we all pitched in and started rolling snowballs of mammoth proportions. A stepladder was brought out to help with the construction, since, after we'd just barely managed to get the second enormous snowball stacked onto the base, we couldn't reach any higher. But we found that even with the ladder we couldn't quite reach up high enough to mount a third huge snowball on top of our creation. And, on top of everything else, we were all getting so drunk by this time that we kept falling off the ladder and staggering around falling into each other and the half-finished sculpture and damaging what we'd already accomplished.

Finally, one of us, probably Al, proposed that we make it a snow-*woman*, a *giant* snow-woman! His suggestion was quickly and enthusiastically endorsed, and everyone immediately started rolling their own smaller snowballs. If we had used them all, our creation would have boasted at least a dozen bulging breasts, but we weren't *that* drunk yet, so we settled on a couple of what we judged to be the best "snow-tits" ever, and mashed them into place, packing more snow around them to hold them in place. Red-faced and panting from the cold and our creative efforts, we all took a break then and stood back to guzzle more beer and consider our creation. It couldn't have looked like much, truth be told, but we were all pretty sozzled by then. It was really nothing more than a couple of giant snowballs several feet high, with a couple more large-ish snowballs plastered onto the front. It didn't even have a *head*, for cripes sake! Of course none of us noticed this obvious deficiency. What we all did notice, practically all at the same time, was that it didn't have a *pussy*! Yeah! Giant snow-woman, giant

Marilyn, the Sinop snow-woman.

tits. Gotta have a giant *pussy*! So we all enthusiastically set to work, excavating a head-size hole in the middle of the base snowball. Finally, judging our creation complete, we all stood back to admire her once again. She *still* had no head, but strangely enough (well, maybe *not* so strange) we never did notice that. She was finished.

So what do a dozen drunken soldiers stationed at a remote post in northern Turkey *do* with a giant snow-woman once they've built her? Why, they *fuck* her, of course! What kind of soldiers – what kind of *men* – would they be if they didn't? So, laughing and hollering and egging each other on, we took turns stretching our wet, snow-covered arms wide, trying to embrace Marilyn's middle (for we *had* to call her Marilyn – those *tits!),* our heads buried and flubbering between those bounteous breasts, our fatigue-clad butts pumping at the gaping hole below, frantically simulating sex.

Al was the only one of us who gave any thought to poor *Marilyn's* pleasure. When it came his turn, he dropped to his knees, spread his arms as far around the base as he could reach and plunged his *head* into the hole, lapping at the packed snow, coming out for air several times and to admonish the rest of us insensitive clods for taking our own thoughtless pleasure without ever once considering poor Marilyn. Well, what he actually *said* was more something like, "Aaaahh, *PUSSSY!* Not only does it *taste* good, but this girl is gonna love me for*EV-ah!*" (Al was always the more sophisticated and experienced among us in regard to matters of love and the opposite sex.) By this time our long mid shift and a full morning of playing and drinking began to take its toll, and we began to straggle back inside the barracks to our bunks.

Marilyn, headless, armless and cruelly mauled and ravished, stood melting in the yard for the next several days, ignored and forgotten. Well, maybe not forgotten. I remember her, and probably most of the other guys do too. For a little while, building her, we were little boys again, playing in the snow together. Then, suddenly we realized we *weren't* little boys, we were *men*, by golly! Then we turned into dogs, mindlessly and unashamedly humping and licking, and, finally, losing interest and wandering away. An interesting progression, no? From snow *angels*, to boys, then men, and finally – *dogs*.

The winter was short but vicious. In addition to the blizzard, there was also a brief period, about a week, of frigid temperatures which caused the watermain from town to base to freeze up, so we had to ration water, which we took from the base water tower. It was a week of few flushes and even fewer showers. It got a little smelly, but we all managed to survive.

The Det 4 water tower

The base water tower deserves a brief mention here. It was much like the ones you see on the outskirts of any small town in America. You've seen them, massive metal tanks made of welded curved plates of steel, mounted on a tall metal framework with a steel ladder that ascends to the top. Usually the name of the town is painted in large letters around the side of the tank. I don't think there was any name or logo painted on the Det 4 water tower, but there was a story, a "legend," that said that sometimes a new guy, a yeni, would arrive at Sinop and become so overwhelmed by loneliness and despair at the bleakness and utter isolation of the base that he would climb to the top of the tower and throw himself off. I doubt that this ever actually happened, but the story circulated and the legend stuck, hence the tower was always called the "Yeni Tower."

* * * * *

It was true that Sinop could be a bleak and desolate place for a young GI thousands of miles from home, particularly in those winter months, so what did we do to fill our leisure time? And there was a considerable amount of time to be filled, for Det 4 was a "working" base. The mission that we carried out on a daily basis within the confines of the Ops Center was the foremost and primary reason for the U.S. military presence in Sinop, and as long as we did our jobs well and efficiently, the leadership, or administration, at the base tried not to bother us much. I do remember, however, one short-lived attempt by a new First Sergeant who arrived about halfway through our tour and decided to whip these "sorry excuses for soldiers" into shape. He instituted a regular PT drill to take place upon the completion of each work shift. I remember vaguely falling out into an open area outside the ops building in the early morning darkness after a mid, with our assistant trick chief trying to cajole us into doing calisthenics, but most of us just lay down on the gravel and half-dozed, until he finally gave up and dismissed us. I think the program only lasted a couple of weeks, and then, after much grumbling by the men, was abandoned. We *liked* being "sorry excuses for soldiers."

So we were left to our own devices to fill the remaining sixteen hours of each work day and the two or three break days that fell between shifts. As I noted earlier, sleeping was very popular, but much of our free time was taken up by enjoying music or movies.

Of course this was long before the advent of CDs, videos or DVDs. Records were the thing. Practically everyone who had any affinity or appreciation for music at all amassed a sizeable personal record collection during his tour at Sinop.

First of all, there were no commercial radio stations to tune in and listen to in our off-duty hours. There was a small self-contained radio station on base that was manned by a few guys from Headquarters Company, who would play records and talk. These "broadcasts" were piped through a PA system into the barracks, clubs and mess hall, but the music played was not really current Top 40 kind of stuff. We were too far off the beaten path to be able to stay current with what was being played back home. The radio station did have a large cumbersome reel-to-reel tape recorder which could play seven- or ten-inch reels of music that guys would occasionally get in the mail from friends or family. My brother Bill sent me a reel of pop music that he taped off the radio in his spare time while he was a student at Michigan Tech that year. I loaned it to the radio station to play, then we played it some more on a machine at work too, when things were slow. There were a few guys in the barracks who owned reel-to-reels too, usually a Pioneer, or heavy German-made machines like a Grundig or an Uher.

Our only commercial window to current pop music was Radio Luxembourg, which we could pick up at night via short-wave radio. We could also tune it in at work, along with a lot of Turkish-language radio. We weren't supposed to listen to commercial radio stations while working, but occasionally we would sneak a short listen when we thought no one was watching. I remember how pleased and amazed I was the first time I tuned it in and heard the British-accented voices commenting on and playing English-language records, mostly Brit artists, but some Americans too. It was on Radio Luxembourg that I first heard the liltingly lovely strains of "Surfer Bird," by The Trashmen. Talk about sudden culture shock.

But mostly our music came from records. The PX manager made, I believe, a valiant effort to keep the shelves stocked with an eclectic mix of music. The trouble was, every time the PX got in a new shipment of vinyl, the word would spread like wildfire, and guys would come running from all over the post, because all the newest and most popular stuff would be sold out in a New York minute. The PX only carried albums, or LPs, no single 45s. So if you wanted to keep up with and own all the latest Top 40 singles, you were out of luck. You could get them (*maybe*) a month or two later, when and if the artist put an album together, by which time the original hit was probably already history.

The standard PX price for an album in the early sixties was $2.35, and sometimes there would be a sale, offering records for as low as $1.65. If this sounds like a real deal, especially compared to today's CD prices, well, it was. Hell, it was a deal even then, when LPs usually sold for four or five dollars a pop in regular stores. I think I went a little crazy buying records that year, not only because of these bargain prices, but also because I found out I could special order records through the PX (from the big Schwann catalogue) at the same low price and with no additional charge for shipping. It was my ambition at the time to own a complete set of Elvis albums. I never did manage to achieve this goal, but I did special order a few of his early movie albums that I'd missed out on before, the soundtracks from *Loving You* and *King Creole*, which were practically played to death by me and my roommates.

The four of us pooled our meager funds early on to purchase a portable stereo for the room. I think it only cost about forty bucks, and it was strictly a phonograph, but it did boast an automatic changer that would hold four or six records at a time, and had two separate speakers. Since we each had our own record collections, the stereo was in nearly constant use whenever we were awake, and usually would lull us to sleep too, with its handy automatic shutoff feature.

I would often spend most of my paycheck on records. Since the PX re-stocked its record inventory at irregular intervals, whenever new stuff *did* come in, you felt like "it's now or never." If you didn't buy something as soon as you saw it, the next day (or even five minutes later) it could be gone, and usually was. On the days when new records were put out on the shelves, it was kind of a free-for-all, with all these guys crowding in and pushing and shoving, reaching under each others' arms and over shoulders to pick a potential prize out of the bin. The tendency was to grab up anything that looked even remotely interesting or promising, and

Music, sodas and popcorn in our room at Grant Hall. L-R:
Unknown, Al Trott, Norm Yurong, Jim Claunch, Tim, Joe Capozzi and Fred Beaver

hold onto it until you had looked over the entire stock of new selections, by which time you could be clutching a dozen or more albums. Then you had to make the hard choices about which ones to put back and which ones to buy. Consequently, if you had grabbed something early on that a few other guys wanted too, then they might be following you around, sometimes unobtrusively, but sometimes in a most obvious manner, depending on how badly they wanted the record. Often a few guys who had gotten there first would stand dickering with each other over trades or two-for-one swaps regarding records they hadn't even purchased yet. If you wanted something badly enough, you learned to be aggressive, kind of like ladies at a bargain basement sale.

As an indirect result of all this fierce competition for the most popular records, my musical tastes gradually began to broaden. Since I had first started buying records, back home at DeWitt's Radio & TV, I had always been a Top 40 kind of buyer. But while I was at Sinop, since the the most popular stuff was always the first to go, I soon found myself looking more closely at and sampling what was left over. And I found things I liked: big band or orchestral arrangements of songs, some of which I recognized and others that I didn't, by people like Les Baxter, Sy Zentner, Gordon Jenkins or Clebanoff. I discovered the sultry and dulcet tones of

Keely Smith, who had just launched her own career, after splitting from Louis Prima. My roommate, Al Trott, picked up a couple early albums by Ann-Margret, whose voice we all liked to fall asleep to. I think at the time we just loved the idea of going to sleep with Ann-Margret in the room, so to speak, but *now* I can also appreciate the small jazz combo arrangements that graced those early recordings by the racy redhead.

Probably a major musical discovery for me that year was the music of Frank Sinatra. Before that time I had always considered Sinatra someone "older people" listened to. He was from our parents' generation, someone the bobby-soxers had swooned over in the forties. But somehow, one record at a time, I became a fan of Ol' Blue Eyes, and have remained one to this day.

Bobby Darin, a budding Sinatra wannabee, also gained my enduring respect that year. I already had known him from his early pop hits like "Splish Splash," "Queen of the Hop," and (my favorite) "Dream Lover." But Darin was experimenting with a little of everything in the early sixties. He had folk albums, country albums, a "'live" album from the Copa, a twist album, and even a tribute to Ray Charles. But what Darin wanted most was the kind of enduring acceptance and respect that Sinatra enjoyed. He finally began to get it with songs like "Mack the Knife" and "Beyond the Sea." His album *That's All*, to my mind, was one of his finest achievements in the Sinatra-mold jazz genre. Sadly, less than ten years later, his career was cut short, when he died following surgery to correct a congenital heart defect.

Al Trott, our sax player, was a kind of pseudo-fan of jazz. He introduced me to artists like Paul Desmond and Johnny Hodges, whom I liked; and Sonny Stitt and Sonny Rollins, whom I did *not* (a bit too squawky and discordant for my taste).

Mac McKenzie was another musician friend of ours who lived down the hall. He introduced me to Miles Davis. Mac was a horn man himself, a very talented one, and Miles was his "main man." He had obviously made a complete and minutely detailed study of Davis's music, for he was able to tootle along with Miles, note for note, in much the same way that Sergeant Clark could pick and strum along with Chet Atkins. What made this even more amazing was the fact that Davis is a primarily improvisational artist. He generally eschewed charts and sheet music and played from "within," so to speak. But Mac had listened to these records so many times and with such painstaking attention that Davis's throwaway notes and casual phrasings became a trumpet duet with Mac. At the time I didn't know about Davis's inclination toward improv. I was just plain astounded at his playing – *and* at Mac's. Mac, a slender guy with dark thinning hair that often hung down over his forehead, and an ever-present five o'clock shadow (he actually *looked* like a jazz musician), had several of Davis's records that he'd brought with him from home, but my two favorites were the now-classic *Kind of Blue* and the scattered effervescent sounds of *Someday My Prince Will Come*. I now own both albums on CD and listen to them often when I want to relax.

It was that winter of '64 that we all first heard of a new English group called The Beatles. We heard *about* them before we actually heard their music. Their trip to New York for their first American tour was headline news, and came rattling across the teletype in the Ops Center: *BEATLES INVADE NEW YORK!* We stood around the machine looking at each other and asking, *What the hell's a Beatle?* Of course, if we'd been stateside we wouldn't have been puzzled, because the Fab Four already had three or four singles on the U.S. charts. Soon after that we began hearing their records on Radio Luxembourg. Then my mom sent me a 45 of "I Wanna Hold Your Hand," which was already, along with "I Saw Her Standing There," a giant two-sided hit back home. My initial reaction to their record was not really favorable. I thought it sounded kind of noisy and amateur-ish. But after a few plays it kind of grew on you. My roommates' reactions were similar. About a month later, the PX got in The Beatles' first two albums, the British Parlophone label versions of *Please Please Me* and *With the Beatles*. I managed to buy both of them, and it didn't take long for the LPs to make fans of all of us. The freshness and energetic enthusiasm of the band was just too infectious to resist. We especially liked their covers of "Twist and Shout" and "Please, Mister Postman," and were also charmed by their rendition of "Til There Was You," the Meredith Wilson love song from *The Music Man*. The Beatles had arrived – even in Sinop, or at least at Det 4 – and I was hooked.

* * * * *

161

The theater in Sinop.

Yes, our lives were filled and made richer by music. And by movies. Ah, yes, the movies. What can I tell you about the movies at Det 4? They were so important to all of us there on the mountain. We called them "flicks," as in "Let's go to the flick," or "What's on at the flicks tonight?" The term was undoubtedly derived from Hollywood's early days, when films were indeed little more than a flickering image across a screen.

I have always been a huge fan of Hollywood and its products. My brothers and I hardly ever missed a Saturday matinee at the Reed Theater when we were growing up in Reed City. For forty or fifty cents we could spend three hours or more on a Saturday afternoon enjoying the adventures of Roy and Trigger or Gene and Champion, and the ridiculous predicaments of the Bowery Boys or the Little Rascals, not to mention all the laughs provided by Bugs and Elmer, Sylvester and Tweety, or Tom and Jerry. By the time I was eleven or twelve, I could go to the movies by myself, and sometimes I would go twice on a weekend. Hollywood spectacles like *The Greatest Show on Earth, Ben Hur, Moby Dick,* and *The Bridge on the River Kwai* were food for my hungry young soul.

Going to the movies at Sinop was different. I'll bet I saw a hundred movies that year, perhaps even more. It was one of the things you did to help pass the time, and to forget, even if for just a little while, where you were.

A new batch of films was delivered to the base every few days. The big metal film canisters would come in on the mail plane or by truck from Samsun. The base theater manager did his best to keep the films coming in on a regular basis so that a new film would show every day. Of course not all the films were actually "new." Many were three or four years old, or even older by the time they began their rotations at military theaters throughout the world. Our theaters were, for the most part, second-run venues for films. Hollywood didn't produce films then in the volume that it does today. And independent films, or "indies," were still pretty much unheard of.

From time to time a film shipment would not arrive on time, or would get lost in the mail. When this happened, the theater manager would dip into his small stash of old stand-by films. This reserve stash consisted of old films from the forties and fifties, including some old Roy Rogers chestnuts. The guys would usually grumble some initially about not having a new film to watch, but then, inevitably, these nights would turn into ones of raucous fun and enjoyment.

First of all, most of the GI's stationed at Sinop had, like me, grown up on a steady diet of Roy Rogers, Gene Autry and other B-western movies. We were grown-up "front-row kids" from the Saturday matinees of the fifties. (Well, maybe not *too* grown-up just yet.) Many of us were too embarrassed to admit that we might still enjoy watching Roy get the best of the bad guys, runaway stagecoaches, or the patently staged barroom fistfights where Roy never even got his pristine good-guy white hat knocked off. But the fact was, we *did* still enjoy all this stuff. You could tell this just by looking around and watching the upturned rapt faces in the reflected glow of the screen, popcorn-crunching jaws working faster as Roy and Trigger narrowed the gap, closing in on the boss bad-guy for that final showdown. We all knew that in just another second or two Roy would launch himself from the saddle like a squinty-eyed li'l human torpedo and blast that black-hatted moustachioed baddie right off his non-descript plain brown horse. Tangled together, they would cannonball down a conveniently located embankment, tumbling round and round all the way to the bottom of the gulch, where, with a few strategically placed punches, Roy would proceed to beat the living snot outa Ol' Moustache. Hell, how could you *not* enjoy stuff like that?

Okay, but remember those later movies Roy did that had *Dale* in them? And those obligatory pseudo-love scenes where there would be a lull in the action, and our stalwart li'l hero in his hand-tooled boots and pin-striped trousers would make goo-goo eyes at Dale and she'd bat her eyelashes back at him? Didn't you just *hate* those scenes? Didn't you wish she'd just shut up and go away, or *some*thing, so we could get on with the chases, fights and shootouts? Well, *I* did. And apparently a lot of other guys felt the same way back then, and I think most of them ended up in Sinop in '64, because whenever one of those "filler" love scenes occurred, the rude comments and catcalls from the crowd would begin.

I remember in particular a film set partially on board a riverboat, a big sternwheeler. I think Roy may have been playing some kind of undercover marshal, or government agent in pursuit of some evil Oil-Can Harry type, as usual. Dale was probably the riverboat captain's daughter, who was also the girl singer with the boat's band. (Oh, all right. I can't remember what the hell the plot was, but who *cares?*) Anyway, there was this tender moment where Roy and Dale were standing at the railing on the upper deck in the moonlight, and she was giving him this raised-eyebrow come-hither sort of look, and Roy was gazing back into her stupid cow eyes, and someone in the theater suddenly yelled out,

"Go for it, Roy! Eat her out!"

Another voice quickly responded, "Yeah! *Trig*ger would!"

Still another voice, "Hell, Ol' Bullet already *did*!"

General merriment and laughter ensued, mixed with more shouted, script-altering suggestions like, "Bend 'er over that rail and put the meat to 'er, Roy!" or "Stick it in 'er *mouth*, Roy! *That* oughta shut 'er up!"

The first time this happened I was *shocked*! You can't talk to Roy Rogers and Dale Evans like *that*! Then someone shouted out, "Do it to 'er doggy-style, Roy! She'll never go back to Bullet!" And I started to laugh. I couldn't help it. This was just too much *fun*. Finally, several years late, all these Saturday matinee front-row kids were taking their revenge on Dale – and all the B-western leading ladies – for slowing down the action and generally ruining so many of their favorite films, and they were having great fun doing it. Sorry, Roy. We all loved you, but the women in your stories were such a pain-in-the-ass. More mayhem and less luu-uv, please.

How odd, that of all the films I watched that year – and there were *scores* of them – that particular night is one of only a few that I remember with any clarity, a memory that still brings a nostalgic smile to my face. (*Not* the image of Roy bending Dale over the riverboat railing, but the memory of all those overgrown *boys* having their naughty fun, finally venting their years-old frustrations.)

Another one I remember seeing is *The Longest Day*, a so-called "blockbuster" movie that claimed to be the definitive film on WWII, and boasted a star-studded international cast. All the guys were really looking forward to it after seeing all the hype in the previews of coming attractions for weeks in advance. Unfortunately, the only reason I remember it is because of the colossal disappointment it was to most of us. Too detailed, too historically factual, too slow-moving, and just plain too *long*. I went to see it at a midnight showing after working a swing, and it may have been we were all just too tired, but I don't think so. *The Longest Day* became the "longest night," and the "biggest yawn." Quite a few guys got up and left halfway through it, and a few others fell asleep and started snoring. I stayed with it and watched it all, mainly because I kept thinking, *It's got to get better,* or *Things will start picking up any minute now.* Nope. It just seemed like the "longest movie" I had ever sat through. It has the Duke in it, along with other great stars like Henry Fonda, Robert Mitchum, Richard Burton and Sean Connery. It *should* have worked, and you'd think a military audience would have eaten it up. The critics liked it, but we didn't.

A movie that *did* strike a familiar chord with the Det 4 audience that year, and would probably have received a unanimous "thumbs up," had Ciskel and Ebert been around back then, was *Soldier in the Rain*, a peacetime army film that we could all relate to much more easily. A spare, no-frills black and white piece, its unlikely co-stars were Jackie Gleason and Steve McQueen. Of course, we'd all grown up watching both of these guys on TV, Gleason as the put-upon and explosive Ralph Kramden of *The*

Honeymooners, and McQueen as a cowboy bounty hunter on *Wanted: Dead or Alive.* McQueen also enjoyed a certain cult notoriety for his starring role in the original 1958 film version of *The Blob.* (And I can't resist including another delicious bit of film/TV trivia here. Did you know that McQueen's teenage girl friend in *The Blob* was played by Aneta Corseaut, who later played Miss Helen Crump, the Mayberry schoolteacher and girlfriend of Sheriff Andy Taylor?)

McQueen and Gleason just clicked marvelously in *Soldier in the Rain,* and the roles they played were of certain army "types" we could easily recognize and at least partially identify with. Gleason masterfully portrayed Master Sergeant Maxwell Slaughter, a "lifer" supply NCO who seemed larger than life, and lived with a flair and panache that the much younger buck sergeant Eustis Clay (McQueen) greatly admired and strove to emulate. The film had a little something for everyone – tragedy, comedy, and everything in between. A young Tony Bill offered some silly comic relief as an aspiring GI marathoner, while a blonde gum-popping teenage Tuesday Weld provided a bit of sexual tittilation. The theater grew noticeably quiet during the scene where Eustis, an orphan, received a letter from his aunt informing him that his beloved Irish Setter had died. To an audience with a median age of twenty or so, that kind of letter would probably be even more upsetting than a Dear John, for, as any boy knows, a dog's love is love in its purest form.

I happened to have a paperback edition of William Goldman's novel, *Soldier in the Rain,* and, after the movie had played at our theater, the book went into heavy circulation and was probably read by about half the post. Yup, I would be willing to bet that *Soldier* was one of the most popular films shown that year.

Running a close second, however, was an Elvis Presley movie. But it wasn't because of Elvis. *Viva Las Vegas* was one of a very few films that was held over and shown a second day, due to popular request. Yes, Elvis was in it, and it pretty much followed the Elvis flick formula, but as far as the guys at Det 4 were concerned, the star attraction was not Presley, but Ann-Margret. Years later you could probably mention *Viva Las Vegas* to any of those guys, and, to a man, they'd say, probably with a fond, faraway look in their eyes, "Oh yeah, that Ann-Margret flick. And maybe they'd even have to stop and think a minute if you reminded them it was an Elvis film. You'd probably get a confused or blank look, and a "Was Elvis in that too?"

This reaction is not really so surprising when you stop and consider that there were no women at Det 4. Zero. Nada. Nichego. It was a completely male environment. There were women serving in the armed forces then, but not at Sinop, which is probably one of the main reasons it was called a "hardship" tour. For a young man at or near his sexual peak to be suddenly plopped down on an isolated mountain top half a world away from home in a place where there were no women was more than a hardship. It was cruel and unusual punishment. It was *unnatural*. And then, suddenly, there was Ann-Margret, larger than life, in Technicolor and Cinemascope, with her mane of flaming red hair, sensual pouty lips and smoldering dark eyes, stuffed or poured into various showgirl outfits with form-fitting bodices that pushed those breasts up and almost (but not *quite*) out the top, and those legs – aaahh, those *legs* (imagine a heavy sigh here) ...

I'm sorry. Where was I? Oh yeah. Those *legs*. Legs that went all the way up to *there*, were wrapped in tights or fishnet stockings, and culminated in wicked-looking stiletto heels that could put a guy's eye out. And I'm confident that there were plenty of guys in that Det 4 audience that would have willingly sacrificed an eye if it would have gotten them that close to the henna-haired goddess.

For those of us who had seen Ann-Margret in her earlier ingenue-type roles in *State Fair* or *Bye-Bye, Birdie*, this smoldering sex-kitten role was something of a departure, but to the deprived men of Det 4, it was nothing less than the perfect role for her. She was sex incarnate. In post-screening discussions over the next few days, I remember hearing guys commenting on and puzzling over the finer points of the film, like the way she filled out her tights.

"So what was with that *bulge* in her crotch, man? It looked like she had a *sock* rolled up in there. Ya think she was on the rag or somethin'? Women ain't supposed to have bulges there, are they?

"*Sure* they do, ya dumb fuck. That was her *mons*, ya know? Her '*mounds* of Venus.' Din't ya see the crease in it? Don't ya know *nuthin'*? Don't ya *read*, man? She was all *woman*, man. I'd like to *bite* that bulge!"

Hmmm ... I couldn't help wondering what kind of literature this guy was reading that made him so knowledgeable about the female form. Was it Henry Miller, or was it something on the back of a candy bar wrapper?

Could Ann-Margret act? I dunno. I don't think anyone cared, or would have even noticed, if she could. In any case, I doubt if the role really required any serious acting chops. She just had to show up. (Several years later she did get a lot of critical attention and rave reviews for her acting ability in a film called *Carnal Knowledge*, a subject that was undoubtedly foremost in the minds of that Det 4 audience, whether they understood the term or not.)

No, *Viva Las Vegas* was not a great film. But it was the perfect vehicle to entertain a bunch of horny, sex-starved GI's stuck in a remote outpost on the Cold War frontier. Was Ann-Margret a sex object? You bet your ass she was, and a damn *good* one too.

Probably one of the reasons I still remember this film over forty years later is something that happened afterwards. I had attended the film at a midnight showing, along with all three of my roommates, Joe, Al and Norm. The theater was absolutely packed, with guys even sitting and standing in the aisles and along the back.

I should probably point out here that there was none of the usual shouting of rude comments during this film. After all, this wasn't any Roy and Dale film. This was *Ann-Margret*. Making light of her beauty and sexuality would have been akin to farting in church. It would have been *blas*phemous. There was a kind of reverence afforded her that Roy and Dale simply didn't rate, and never would.

But getting back to what I started to say, when the film was over and we emerged from the theater, out onto the darkened street, the crowd began to move quickly up the hill toward the barracks. I mean they weren't just moseying or meandering like they usually did, smoking and talking in small groups. No, they were moving out en masse, in what seemed an unusually purposeful manner. We were near the back of the crowd, and suddenly Al started walking faster, almost running. Picking up our pace to keep up, we followed him. Then Al started to run. A little annoyed, I yelled at him, "Hey, Al, what's the big-ass hurry?"

Turning around and back-pedaling quickly, Al blurted out, "Bazzett, you don't under*stand*! This was *Ann-fucking-MARgret*! If we don't hurry, every stall in the latrine will be taken!" And with that, he turned and raced off up the hill into the darkness, bound for glory – along with a lot of other guys who were also running by this time.

Was Ann-Margret a sex object? No question about it, and on that particular night she was *the* sex object.

* * * * *

Once again sex raises its ugly head. Just because there were no women at Det 4 doesn't mean there was no sex. There was no saltpeter in the mashed potatoes, so of course there was sex. Can you say, *solitary sex*? Can you spell *mas-tur-ba-tion*? I think perhaps our common predicament was once best described by Al Trott, our roommate and resident self-proclaimed sex expert. One day, when we were nearing the end of our Sinop tour, we were sitting around at the EM club, drinking, shooting the shit and idly speculating, in a jocular manner, what we might miss about Det 4 and life on the hill. Of course, the acceptable, the correct, the *only* answer to this rhetorical question was *nothing. NO-THING!* There would be absolutely *nothing* to miss about Sinop, if and when we finally managed to escape that "miserable hole." Or at least that was the general consensus. But leave it to ol' Al to seriously consider this question as he pulled thoughtfully on his beer, and to finally come up with a true and honest answer.

"You know what I'll miss, guys?" he said, with a faraway, dreamy look in his eye. "I'll miss that end stall in the latrine. The one where I've beat off so many times that now every time I go in there to take a shit I get a hard-on."

Well stated, Al. We laughed, but it was a knowing, rueful kind of laugh. We all knew *exactly* what you meant. Sex will out, one way or another.

We laughed at other things Al said too, when he tried to put into words the effects of our sexual deprivation, and the serious health risks it entailed. Sentiments like, you *had* to jerk off. Because if you didn't, eventually all that built-up jism would back up into your system until you'd get this big ugly hump on your back, and the skin on the hump would keep stretching tighter and tighter as the hump grew, until finally it would just ex*plode* and blow come all over the walls and ceiling and stuff. And who wants to go around looking like Quasimodo, anyway?

Who indeed? It was no accident then, that the best-selling magazine at the PX was *Playboy*. In fact, the magazine would sell completely out on the first day it was stocked, so quite a few guys had their own subscriptions, just to be sure they didn't miss an issue. At least in a place like Sinop you didn't have to constantly justify your reading *Playboy* with all those lame excuses about the excellent articles and stories, or that important interview with the pope, or Ralph Nader or someone. Nope. In Sinop it was definitely the skin. The centerfolds and pictorials. The exceptional glossy quality of the T&A. It was to look, perchance to dream – of all those air-brushed beauties.

Playboy was in evidence everywhere. The NCO and EM clubs were practically wall-papered with centerfolds and photos from the magazine. And the walls of practically every room in the barracks sported favorite poses, which were changed periodically as new issues arrived. Open up a wall locker or a closet and there would be Miss December or Miss June smiling or licking her lips at you. No wonder that end stall in the latrine was such a popular place.

There were never quite enough issues of *Playboy* to go around, but generally the guys who had copies were pretty generous about letting you borrow them. And you didn't even feel insulted or embarrassed if, when they surrendered the latest issue to you, it was with a comment like, "Don't get anything on it, man. Last month when I loaned it out to some guys, it came back with some of the best pages all stuck together."

Nope. No offense taken. You were just cool (and grateful) about it. "No sweat, man. I'll be careful. Thanks."

So there you have it. Sex in Sinop. We were not eunuchs, after all. We managed. We handled it.

All this is not to say that I had lost my faith, or had rejected my Catholic upbringing and all its teachings. No, I was still plagued periodically by that good old "Catholic guilt." That problematic dichotomy between the ideal of "purity" and fucking reality was still there. I still felt vaguely guilty about my solitary pursuit of sexual relief, but I think by this time I was beginning to rationalize that these sexual urges and "temptations" must be things that God permitted. I mean, if he hadn't allowed them, they wouldn't *be* there, right? And then I would remember about that "free will" thing, and feel bad and confused again. Such was my torn and torturous path of rationalization and guilt. I continued to get to confession regularly, and rotely repeated my "sins of the flesh," so I could receive communion and feel better about myself, at least for a while. Sometimes I almost wished I weren't a Catholic. It seemed like my Protestant friends could be more casual about their carnality, could even joke about it. *And* they didn't have to go to confession. But I continued to profess that not-so-firm "purpose of amendment," and I went to Mass every Sunday, and even assisted as a server at times.

The chapel at Sinop.

The Catholic chaplain at Det 4 (I think he was the *only* chaplain) was a low key, gentle man who was liked and respected by all the men. Father Shadeg was from St. Paul, Minnesota, but he knew where Reed City was when we talked about our home towns. He said that three of his sisters were nuns. Two of them lived in Grand Rapids and the other one in Iron Mountain, so he had passed through Reed City several times while visiting his sisters in Michigan. Just knowing he was a fellow midwesterner made me feel a bit closer to him, and also made me want to try a little harder to be a better person, so I wouldn't have to keep burdening him with all my endless, dirty little sins. I couldn't help thinking that he must get awfully sick of hearing the confessions of all those guys, all the with the same tiresome litany of similar sins. He probably did, but he remained relentlessly cheerful, and was always there, a friendly and sympathetic ear, both in and out of the confessional. Looking back, I'm sure he understood what it was like for us. After all, priests are men too.

* * * * *

Not only did we enjoy our off-duty hours, sometimes we managed to squeeze in some fun while we were working too. On mid shifts particularly, when things were slow, we often amused ourselves with spontaneous, ingeniously devised games. The room in the Ops Center where we worked was arranged in two parallel rows of individual operator positions, or "pos's." There were five or six positions on each side of the center aisle. Each pos had its own radio, a small metal typewriter table holding a mill, and an adjustable chair on casters, all of them an institutional government grey. At the front of the room, the trick chief had his own pos and a separate desk for admin work. As operators, we were each essentially "tethered" to our pos by our headsets (we called them "cans"), which were jacked into the radio. The headset cords were generally no longer than six or eight feet, although some of the guys fashioned longer ones by means of a bit of electronic surgery, splicing on an additional length of cord.

At any rate, on slow nights we would sometimes play improvised games of Ops Center volleyball. We would make a ball out of a large crumpled wad of six-ply wastepaper wrapped with masking tape. Our "net" was a single strip of tape stretched across the center aisle in the middle of the room. The operators in the front would turn and face those in the rear of the room and the competition would commence. The players had to remain tethered to their radio receivers at all times and, ideally, their butts were supposed to stay in contact with the seats of their rolling chairs, these restrictions adding extra elements of difficulty to the game. Of course, these games only took place when the trick chief or supervisor was elsewhere engaged, since they obviously were not officially sanctioned activities. Since the games tended to get a bit noisy, what with the squealing of sticky chair casters, clanging and banging into the metal tables and equipment racks, and the inevitable whooping, shouting and arguments that ensued, they usually didn't last very long. Some passing supervisor or NCO would hear the noise and general hilarity and come bursting into the room and put an end to our fun. Grumbling and muttering, we would take down our net, disassemble and dispose of our ball, and reluctantly return to our assigned duties. But it would be fun while it lasted.

On other nights when things were slow, we often played a tape of pop music that one of the ops had brought in and might engage in a little competitive "chair dancing." Sometimes we even actually untethered ourselves and formed a spontaneous choo-choo train of rolling chairs and would go chugging up and down the center aisle or around behind the racks, grooving and singing along with Little Eva and doing our own improvised version of "The Locomotion." This too was frowned upon and quickly squelched by our bosses. But we all understood implicitly that all work and no play would make us "dull boys," so we persevered in making life difficult for the sticklers for discipline and order.

In addition to our games and stolen musical interludes, we also often played pranks on each other, some of them bordering on dangerous as I look back on them now, but what could you expect? Most of us were little more than kids at the time. A favorite joke was the hotfoot. Some of those swing and mid shifts could seem interminably long and boring, and if you hadn't gotten enough sleep before work it was awfully hard to stay awake. Whenever someone dozed off, he became grist for the pranksters. Fred Beaver was a favorite target. He had a tendency to doze off just about anywhere, even when he wasn't working, so I'm pretty sure he was a hotfoot victim more than once. An Ops Center hotfoot could be a bit hotter than the standard one. Since we all wore combat boots as a part of our normal fatigue uniform, inserting and lighting a single match at that juncture between the rubber sole and the leather upper part of the boot's toe didn't really produce enough heat to cause much, if any, discomfort. Indeed, it could sometimes burn out without even waking the victim, especially with a really serious sleeper like Beaver. Nope. If you really wanted to get a rise out of your victim, you learned to employ a whole book of matches wedged into that boot-toe juncture. When you lighted *that*, it produced quite a blaze, enough to melt the polish right off the boot. This method never failed to awaken the victim, who would invariably blink awake and leap to his feet stomping and swearing, much to the delight and satisfaction of the perpetrators.

One more favorite prank – and this is the dangerous one I mentioned – also involved fire. (Hmmm ... Maybe there were a few actual pyromaniacs in our midst.) Everything we typed on our mills was done on six-ply, which is simply a continuous skein of six layers of paper with carbons in between and perforations between pages, making it easy to tear off. Much of what we typed turned out to be of no particular value, so we often had several pages of scrap paper hanging from the front of our mills down onto the floor. Again, a dozing victim would be identified who had a few pages of scrap dangling from the roll of his mill. One person would set fire to the paper with a match or lighter and someone else would sharply nudge the unsuspecting sleeper, or – even better – pop a blown-up paper bag right behind him, then watch the fun as he jumped up and scrambled around to rip off the blazing paper and stomp it out. Sometimes it would take two or three guys to stomp out and smother the fire and it would leave a tell-tale layer of smoke and a stench that lingered briefly, so everyone had to do a lot of fanning the air. Like I said, a bit too dangerous for *my* taste, and not very smart. I had been taught *not* to play with fire. It's probably a small wonder we didn't burn down the whole damn place.

Still another favorite work-place joke, this one infinitely safer than the pyro pranks, was the wet sponge gag. All you needed was a large very wet sponge, hidden under your rack, but close at hand. Then you would innocently ask the guy sitting at the pos in front of you or across from you to please hand you that patch cord or that box of tissues from the top shelf of their rack. When he stood up to reach for the requested item, you quietly laid the sponge on his chair. There would be an audible "sploosh" when the patsy plopped back down in his chair, usually immediately followed by an even *more* audible, *Mother*-FUCK! *You* BAS*tard!* as he bounced back up off the sponge, plucking the soaked seat of his pants away from his butt. This was probably the most popular prank of all, but it usually only worked once per victim, because once you'd been had, you learned ever after to look at your chair before sitting down. It was a favorite trick to play on our new guys though. It was so comical and so much fun to watch the victim go waddling spraddle-legged out of the room, on his way to the latrine to try to dry himself off.

New guys, or "newks," were of course favorite targets of practical jokes and pranks. They were often given bogus tasks to carry out, the classic one being taking the EMHO count for the morning report. The unsuspecting newk would be handed a pen and a clipboard with a blank form and told to canvas all the ops at the end of a mid shift as whether they had an EMHO to report for that shift. Each of the operators would report, with a perfectly straight face, that yes, he'd had one, or sometimes two EMHO's. The newk would dutifully take down this info from all of the ops, then tally up a total and turn it in to the surprised trick chief or platoon sergeant, who, if he was feeling kind, would gently explain to the poor guy that he'd been had, that EMHO's didn't go into the morning report, that an EMHO is an "early morning hard-on." Amid much snickering and grinning, the red-faced recruit would slink back to his seat. Again, this one only worked once too.

* * * * *

We didn't limit our fun to picking on newks and yenis. We liked to poke fun at each other too, but in a more teasing, gentler fashion. It prevented us from brooding too much over our situation, or from taking ourselves too seriously. You know that old *Reader's Digest* column, "Laughter is the Best Medicine"? Well, it's true. We needed to laugh, and laugh often.

Back in our room, Norm Yurong was often our favorite target, because he tended to sometimes slip into blue moods or go into a dark funk, when he'd just sit and smoke and glower at everything, or at nothing in particular. So Al and Joe and I would try to bring him out of it, usually by means of a little gentle ridicule.

Norm was not a big man, but he could project an illusion of being larger than he was. I always wondered if he was just a little self-conscious about his diminutive stature, because I don't think Norm was more than five foot seven, if he was even that tall. However, because of all the time and effort he had put into body-building and working with weights, he *seemed* bigger (if not taller) than he actually was. Norm had a way of puffing himself up when he wanted to appear menacing or threatening. He would suck in his stomach and somehow inflate his chest and his arms would rise from his sides and his fingers would curl into fists. And if one of us had been poking fun at him, he'd bluster, "Are you makin' fun of me, Joe?" And this display *was* pretty impressive, since Norm's wide, heavily muscled shoulders and chest, which tapered down to a small waist (especially when he was sucking it in), gave him the appearance of a burly inverted triangle. But part of this effect was lessened by his impossibly tiny hands and feet. The arms and shoulders were imposing, but those teeny fists just couldn't manage to look dangerous. In any case, I don't think there was ever any real harm in Norm. We never had any fights in our room, and humor was indisputably key to our getting along in the confined quarters of the barracks.

I can still remember, and probably so can Joe and Al, the first sound I heard every morning was the click and rasp of Norm's Zippo. Before he got out of his bunk, or even opened his eyes, Norm would reach over onto the footlocker next to his bed and fumble a cigarette out of his pack, fire it up, and blow out a cloud of smoke. Then, after a minute or two, he'd swing his feet off his bunk and sit there, eyes barely slitted, enjoying (although there were no actual visible *signs* of enjoyment) his morning nicotine fix. By this time the rest of us would be getting up too, awakened by that Zippo "alarm," and getting together our towels and shaving kits to head down the hall to the latrine. Norm would trail along too, his cigarette half burned down by now, a long ash hanging precipitously off the end, and stop and stand listlessly at a urinal, eyes closed as, like the rest of us, he enjoyed that other early morning perk, that first long bladder-emptying piss of the day.

Norm was the only one in our room who was a confirmed, addicted smoker. I was still smoking some, but was more of a social smoker. One pack would usually last me nearly a week. You wouldn't think that body-building and smoking would go together, but Norm somehow managed to make the combination work for him. Every now and then, Norm's ever-present Zippo would fail to light, and he'd ask Al (I don't know *why*. He *knew* Al didn't smoke), "Hey, Trott, you got a match?"

To which Al would *always* reply, "Yeah. My butt and your *face!*"

Norm would then respond, with no particular venom, "Hey, FOCK you!" and go look elsewhere for a light. This exchange was kind of a ritual between the two of them more than anything else. There was no insult intended or offense taken. I think Norm must have secretly enjoyed that ritual. Sometimes he would try to use that insult himself on me, when I would find myself without matches, but he could never seem to get it right. I would ask Norm if he had a match, and he'd get so excited at this rare opportunity that he would invariably fuck it up and blurt out, "Yeah! My face and your *butt*!" Then, half a beat later, he would say, "No, *wait* ..." But it would be too late. We'd all be laughing our asses off by then.

Norm was Hawaiian, but like many Hawaiians, was also of Japanese extraction. I remember once we asked him if Yurong was a Hawaiian name, and he told us no, it was Japanese. Then he explained further to us that his name resulted from an ancient Japanese custom where a rock was thrown at a bell, and whatever sound the impact made became the thrower's name. Hence, Yu-*RONG*, or, in the case of our platoon sergeant, G-*NONG*. We thought about that for a moment, then Joe asked, "Hey, Norm, if that's true, then how do you explain Yoshimura's name, on Trick Two?"

To which Norm puffed himself up like that fairy-tale frog and retorted, "Hey, FOCK you, Joe! You tryin' to make fun of me?"

Norm, you bullshitter. You know we'd never make fun of you.

Norm and Al were best friends, that much was obvious, regardless of how much they insulted and teased each other. Al was from northern Ohio, near Elyria, I think. He had what seemed like a boundless energy and an irrepressible sense of fun, but he could also get pissed in a hurry. He had an extremely short fuse. His blowups were rare though, and we usually managed to defuse them through humor. Al was about a year older than Joe and me. I'm not sure if he was older than Norm, but he became early on in our "roommate-ship" the senior member of our gang of four. This wasn't because of his age, however. It was more due to what seemed to be his wealth of experience in matters regarding sex. I was still certainly a virgin, and I'm reasonably sure Joe was too. I'm not sure about Norm, but in any case it wouldn't have taken much to make someone in our small group the sex expert, so the honor went to Al. There was a frankness and an openness in the way Al talked about sex. True, there was a bit of braggadocio in his stories, but that was perfectly normal for people our age and particularly in that rarified no-females environment.

Even virgins like Joe and I had a basic grasp, I think, of how sex between a man and a woman worked. Through bull-sessions and reading, we knew about conventional forms and positions of intercourse, and we'd also heard a lot of talk about oral sex, commonly referred to as blow-jobs, hum-jobs (or hummers), cocksucking, and various other crude euphemisms for a female performing oral sex on a male. (I think fellatio may have been too technical a term for us at that time.) The idea of all this was, of course, vaguely tittilating to us – to *any* normal heterosexual young man, if truth be told. Well, Al talked about all these things, but he took it a step further. He educated us, in his homespun manner, about the other side of the sexual coin, the flip-side of fellatio, if you will. I don't remember if the term cunnilingus ever came up, but that's what he was talking about.

I don't think we virgins in the group were quite ready to fully absorb all the implications of this exotic (to us) sexual practice. Like a lot of young guys who were primarily interested in their own sexual gratification (i.e. "getting their rocks off," or "ashes hauled," or "oil changed"), the concept of "going down on" a female seemed vaguely repellent, and perhaps even a bit frightening. I mean, we'd never even gotten up close and personal with whatever it was that a female had "down there," so we just couldn't quite get our minds around the idea of putting our *mouths* on it. (Although, oddly enough, the idea of a girl gumming *our* guns seemed perfectly desirable and okay.) So when Al would wax eloquent about "stickin' your nose right up in there," or "lollopin' your tongue around and lappin' it up," I think we were more put off than stimulated. But still, it was an interesting and novel concept, one that we mentally filed away for future reference. The part of this strange sexual soliloquy that *most* intrigued us, however, was Al's absolute insistence that once you had done this for a girl, she would *never* leave you. She would love you for-*absolutely fucking-EVER*, and do *anything* for you. Hmmm ... Now *that* was something worth thinking about.

I recognize that in retrospect, in the re-telling, this all sounds rather crude, perhaps even disgusting, but you have to consider the context of these conversations. It was an all-male environment. We were stuck away on this mountain-top for a year, in a foreign country where even the native women were all-but invisible. We *desperately* missed having real live women around, even if only just to *look* at. Yeah, we were pretty pathetic. So we talked. We dreamed. We remembered. We hoped – *someday*. I know that the language we employed was extremely crude, and perhaps reprehensible, but then our knowledge of most things sexual in nature was still at a very crude, elementary stage. How else *could* we talk of such things? Intercourse, fellatio, and especially something as mysterious as cunnilingus, were all just vague, wishful, "maybe someday" kinds of pipedreams or abstractions to us. And romantic love was not a concept that "real men" would ever deign to discuss among themselves.

Ironically, years later I would think of Al when I read John Updike's novel, *Couples*, and its infinitely more poetic description of mutual, loving, oral sex. Updike speaks of the mouth "condescending," a marriage of mind and body, and the "sacredness" of the act. At just twenty-one, Al had barely begun to understand this mystery, and only in the crudest, most basic form. Al may have been a little ahead of the curve, but, when it came right down to it, in matters of sex – and love – we were *all* still babes-in-the-wood.

But hey, this is getting a little too heavy, too serious. Let me tell you about another thing Al taught me, something more practical and immediately applicable to our situation. He taught us a quick GI-in-Sinop way to press our pants. Let me explain. At Det 4 you had two options for getting your laundry done. There were washers and dryers in the barracks, so you could do your own. Or you could give your laundry to a Turkish houseboy, one of the ubiquitous ah-beys, who would not only wash your things, but would also starch and press your fatigues, which were the everyday work uniform. This service was dirt cheap, and many of the guys made use of it. I did a few times myself, but I found that the starched and ironed fatigues were too overly stiff and uncomfortable for my taste. When you got them back they were arranged on wire hangers, and both pieces, shirt and trousers, were just as stiff as plywood. The military expression "to *break* starch" was never more appropriate than it was at Sinop. Even stateside military laundries starched your fatigues (or khakis) so stiffly that, in order to put them on, you

179

would literally have to *force* your arms and legs into them, making a tunnel through the heavily starched sleeves and pantlegs. You "*broke* starch." At Det 4 the ah-bey-laundered fatigues were every bit as stiff, but there was an added element that made the experience even more uncomfortable. I don't know what the Turks used for starch, but once you'd gotten the clothes on and worn them for a little while, your skin would begin to crawl, almost like little bugs or mites were crawling on you. I even went so far as to take off the shirt and examine it carefully for fleas or other pests. I never found anything, but the clothes remained distinctly itchy, often unbearably so.

So I quit using the ah-bey laundry service and began washing my own stuff. But then I had to borrow an iron to press my fatigues. (The local GI term for fatigues, by the way, was "gerbs." Don't ask me where it came from, maybe a bastardization of *garb*?) When Al saw me doing this the first time, he stopped me and asked, "Whatcha doin' *that* for?" Then he took my fatigue trousers, pulled the seams of the pantlegs together to align them, then laid them on my bunk and quickly smoothed them out with his hands. Then he told me to lift up the side of my bunk mattress, which I did. He laid my trousers flat out on the springs, pantlegs smooth and aligned, and said, "There. Put it back down. By tomorrow morning they'll be 'pressed'."

And they were, in a manner of speaking. They did sport the tell-tale oblong imprints of the flat steel springs, but that didn't last long once you'd donned the pants and worn them for a while. Neither did the so-called "crease," but by then I'd decided if it worked for Al, it worked for me too. Who wanted to spend time ironing anyway? And who cared, after all, if your uniform was starched and pressed? We were in *Turkey*, for cripes sake. So, one more piece of useful advice from Al. Not only was he a sex expert, but also a garment-care guru. Thank you, Al. I don't press my pants that way anymore, but I do make it a point to always buy wash and wear clothing. I *still* hate ironing – and starch too.

Joe. What about Joe? Joe was just Joe. Never too over the top or outrageous or obnoxious. Joe was the peacemaker in our group. Whenever any tensions surfaced or arguments erupted, he was the voice of reason, the one who calmed the combatants down, smoothed things over. I had never really thought too much about this before now, but I'm fairly certain that it's true. Joe disliked conflict, and I don't think he had a mean bone in his body. And his smile was infectious. You could be in a lousy mood, and Joe would notice it, draw you out a bit, then flash that famous Bucky Beaver grin, and you just couldn't help yourself. You'd start feeling better. Considering Joe was an only child, this seems rather surprising. I would have expected someone raised by himself to be spoiled, self-centered and selfish. Not Joe. His folks did something right, because everyone that ever met Joe liked him and quickly considered him a friend. He was generous to a fault, always ready to spring for an extra round, or treat you to that milkshake he knew you were craving when you were broke near the end of the month.

His musical talent was really quite amazing too, the way he could listen to a record a time or two, then sit and noodle a bit with his guitar, ear cocked to the sounds of the chords, and then quickly be able to reproduce what he had just heard. His ear was simply unerring. We were all quite in awe of his gift, especially Al, who had to work and practice with his sax, but never quite managed that seemingly effortless ease which Joe displayed on his Fender. Yeah, Joe was just Joe, and none of us could have asked for a better roommate or friend.

And what about me? What did I bring to our small band of brothers? What did I add to the mix? I guess I was the "book-ish" one. Ironically, I had fled Reed City and home in order to avoid being pressured into any more official institutional "book-larnin'" – to avoid college. But I couldn't seem to stay away from books. I was always reading something. During my first few months at Det 4, I mined the library's small collection, reading whatever appealed to me, and my mom occasionally sent me paperbacks she thought I'd like to read. Two of her offerings I remember are Kenneth Roberts' *Northwest Passage*, an historical novel which I quite enjoyed and passed along to Al and Norm, who both read it, and *The Cardinal*, a then-bestseller about the church heirarchy during WWII times. Another book she sent me called *Grandmother and the Priests* I don't think I ever did get around to. But two out of three ain't bad, Mom.

In February of '64 the PX opened a small but well-stocked bookstore, a real godsend to me and the other readers on post. It was there I had purchased the one copy of *Soldier in the Rain*, which I then shared with half the readers on post after the aforementioned movie version had played at the theater. I also bought Joseph Heller's *Catch-22*, a book I had tried to read in high school, but just hadn't been able to get into. This time I *got* it. I understood it this time because I was living my own version of the ridiculous surreal world of the military which Heller depicts so vividly in his novel. I could relate to Yossarian's plight, and recognized characters like Lieutenant Scheisskopf (German for "Shithead"). I thought it a marvelous novel and was always bothering my roomies by reading portions of it aloud to them. I don't remember if any of them read it after me, so I'm not sure if they *got* it, but I tried. I have since re-read *Catch-22* a few more times and enjoyed it even more with every additional reading. I even read a few of Ian Fleming's James Bond books that year, primarily because all the guys were reading them, and I guess I wanted to see what all the enthusiasm was about. I didn't *dis*like them, but they didn't really appeal to me all that much either.

That winter I took a class from the University of Maryland Overseas. (I didn't really think of this course as "college." It just seemed a natural extension of my fondness for reading.) I signed up for a freshman English course, which was primarily a composition class, but we were also required to read a novel, Hemingway's *A Farewell to Arms*. I had already read it in high school, but I think I enjoyed it more this time, and also liked hearing what the instructor had to say about the book and about the author too. I even bought a paperback biography of Hemingway written by his brother to learn still more about ol' "Papa."

So I was the bookworm in our room. I'd like to think that I did my small part in promoting literacy and reading, but probably I just bored the shit out of the other guys by always blabbering about whatever I was reading. At any rate, my education continued, whether I realized it at the time or not. I had thought that by joining the army I had escaped education, but it continued to find me, even at a remote outpost like Sinop.

* * * * *

Sinop. I would like to be able to honestly say that I was curious enough about the town, and about Turkish life and culture in general, to get into town and the surrounding countryside at every

Joe, Tim and Al with Sinop and the Black Sea behind them.

opportunity and to learn all I could. But I can't say that. I did go into town occasionally, but always in a group, and, since none of us spoke the language, we never really gained much in-depth knowledge of the area.

Let's see, though. What *can* I remember? Well, just the road down the hill from the post to the town was worth remembering, especially if you ever walked it, which we did at least a couple of times. It was a hard-packed dirt and gravel road, scraped right down to the volcanic rock underneath. Approaching the base, the last half mile or so was quite steep, steep enough that you would find yourself unconsciously leaning forward, just to stay in an upright position as you climbed. And you would usually have to stop a time or two during the climb just to catch your breath. Going down the hill, towards town, was just the opposite. You'd have to lean backward to stay upright. And the road surface was so rock-hard that your descent could be quite jolting. Every step down seemed to rattle your bones and teeth and jar your insides. I think it was Al who made the comment, "Jee-zus, this road just jars the shit outa me. Or it *would*, if I didn't keep my asshole clenched. By the time I *do* shit, it's gonna be all hard-packed into these *tiny* little pellets, one for every step I took down this fucking hill."

The walk into town was probably a bit less than a mile, and wound down the mountainside between cultivated farmland, pastures, and, in the spring and summertime, fields filled with the bright red blooms of poppies, which swayed and undulated gently in the breezes, a scene that could be breathtakingly beautiful. Often there would be men, and sometimes women too, out working in these poppy fields, bent among the blooms, picking flowers, I assumed. I never gave this tableau much thought beyond perhaps wondering idly what they would do with all those flowers. It wasn't until years later that I learned that poppies are harvested to make opium. That kind of knowledge would have put a whole different slant on my walks past all those pretty poppies and all the "flower lovers." But what did I know? Not much. I was barely twenty years old. It was just a pretty scene to me. Too, if I had been aware of what was probably a thriving opium trade in the region, I wouldn't have wondered as much about why so many of the Turks who worked on base were forever nodding off in corners or crouched along a wall outside. They were undoubtedly stoned.

As you came into the northern outskirts of town, off to the right, set back a few hundred yards from the road, at the end of a long tree-lined drive, was a compound with a long two-story building that looked like a dormitory, and probably was one. The prevailing belief among the GI's was that this was a girls' school. I don't know if it really was or not, as I can't remember actually seeing any girls about. It probably was a school of some kind, but a *girls'* school? Remember that perhaps "mythical" girls' school in Nashua, New Hampshire that we never found, on our ill-fated butt-busting bicycle expedition? Maybe wherever sex-starved military morons are stationed, they feel compelled to "manufacture" an unattainable all-girl academy somewhere nearby. At any rate, just in case, we would always peer intently and longingly down that lane at the maybe-school compound, hoping to get a glimpse of a girl. Man, we were pathetic.

Very rarely did you actually see any girls or women around Sinop. Sometimes there would be a few working in the tilled fields, or among the poppies, and occasionally you might glimpse one in town, over the mud walls of a residential compound, or hurrying down a side street. But the women you did see were always dressed in the all-enveloping veils and flowing gowns of *purdah*, which covered just about everything. By the early sixties, purdah was supposed to be a thing of the past, but in remote backwaters like Sinop, it still persisted, unfortunately, at least from *our* point of view. Often the women we saw working in the fields would be wearing a voluminous kind of pantaloon that gathered at the ankles. We used to call these garments "ninety-day shitters." Again, I think it was Al who coined the term, as he speculated that they probably *never* removed those damn pants, not even to crap, but those wide pantlegs were roomy enough to hold about three months worth of shit, and the gathered ankles kept any of the shit from falling out, which also explained the rank smell that sometimes emanated from the wearers. In retrospect, this label, with its accompanying theory, doesn't hold up very well, and sounds pretty dumb, but it amused us at the time, and I still remember it.

One of the dominant features of Sinop was the main pier on the east side of town. It was there that the "white boat," the large passenger ship that plied the northern coastline of Turkey, would put in on a regular basis. Other large vessels used this main pier too. It seems like I remember seeing what appeared to be naval ships tied up there. Were they Turkish or Soviet? Did Turkey *have* a navy? Were Russian or Soviet ships permitted in Turkish waters, or allowed to dock at a Turkish port? I'll be damned if I can remember, or if I even knew at that time. One of the most frustrating things now, about trying to remember this long-ago time, or to get something finally down on paper about it, is coming smack up against my smug, insulated, twenty year-old self, and recognizing my colossal ignorance. But the pier, that long concrete jetty, was certainly real, and was a popular stopping-off place for the American GI's, whenever they ventured into town. It was a good place to take photographs, and was also situated right next to a public park of sorts and a fairly large restaurant, or "chai garden." The park was anchored by an impressive statue or bust of Ataturk, the "saviour," or "father" of modern Turkey. He was kind of the Turkish equivalent of George Washington or Simon Bolivar – a renowned national hero.

Chai means tea in Turkish, and also in Russian and several other languages. Tea was a national drink. Most social gatherings or functions featured tea. Coffee was not nearly so common in Turkey as it was in the U.S. In addition to the large public chai garden near the pier that catered to GI's and to tourists and travelers that disembarked from the boats, there were also numerous other little tea-rooms throughout Sinop's downtown area that seemed to cater mainly to the residents of town. These small, dark "hole-in-the-wall" kinds of tea-houses were frequented solely by men, some of whom wore traditional sandals and long flowing robes like you see in pictures and colored illustrations in the Old Testament. Others wore more modern dress, suits and shoes. There were never any women in evidence at these establishments, only these small groups of stern-looking men, with their "worry-beads," beards and dark sombre-hued clothing.

There was a common custom among these men that, upon first observance, was a bit off-putting, unsettling even, to us homophobic GI's. These Turkish men, obviously friends, and perhaps even relatives, would often walk together down the street holding hands, only not *exactly* holding hands. They would link only their pinky fingers as they walked along side-by-side, conversing quietly. To our western eyes it was an odd sight indeed, but eventually we grew used to seeing it, and even came up with a name for these guys and their custom. We called them "pinky-linkers." It would have been easy to jump to conclusions and just say they were gay. (Except the word "gay" still just meant "happy" back then. We had much uglier words: queers, faggots, homos, etc.) But we didn't think they were homosexual; it was just a custom.

One other point of interest near the park – at least to us westerners – was the public "facility," or restroom. This "convenience" was a *real* culture shock, believe me. You went into this concrete, bunker-like building, which by the way absolutely *reeked* of shit, like a poorly maintained old-fashioned outhouse. Expecting to find urinals and toilets, you found instead a row of several holes in the concrete floor. The holes appeared to be quite deep, and probably emptied into an underground chamber that could be periodically mucked out, but I'm really not sure about that part; the lighting in the facility left a lot to be desired too. Closely flanking each hole were imprints of the soles of shoes (or sandals) , molded into the concrete. No urinals, no toilets, no sinks – no *water* even. Just these holes with the footprints on either side. The idea was you put your feet in the footprints, dropped trou, squatted, and "bombs-away." We called them bomb-sights, and quickly

A Turkish toilet, or "bomb-sight" in downtown Sinop.

learned to use these facilities only to take an emergency piss. Anything more complicated we would hold until we got back to base and a *real* bathroom, with a toilet. I don't think there was any toilet tissue provided in these joints anyway. You would have had to bring your own. (Turkish toilet paper was something else too – so coarse you could almost still feel the bark. The *better* quality was like a fine grade of sandpaper.)

The shops and stores of Sinop were varied and were only alike in their primitiveness. The meat markets, or butcher shops, were the worst. Many were just open-air type shops, but even the ones with plate-glass windows like real stores have were pretty revolting. There didn't appear to be any way to refrigerate the various cuts of meat, mostly goat, mutton or lamb. They were just hung on hooks or laid out for display, some of them already turning a most unhealthy-looking hue, and swarming with flies. It was a most unappetizing array, and we were always glad that the mess hall didn't have to rely on these markets for our meat supply, which was (I believe) shipped in from European commissary centers where it was scrupulously inspected by veterinarians before shipment. Practically all of our food was shipped in this way.

I should note here that the mess hall food at Det 4 was generally quite good, not so very different from mess hall food

The mess hall at Sinop

anywhere, with one exception. There was no fresh milk. Instead we had powdered milk, which was mixed up and set out in individual glasses on the chow line. The glasses were set in a bed of shaved ice to try to keep the milk cold, but it never was quite cold enough to be very good. The only time the mess hall milk was very popular was when there was cake or cookies, or a tasty pudding or dessert to pour the milk over. We drank a lot of tea and coffee. We also ate a lot of canned fruit and vegetables. Fresh produce was a rare treat. There was also ice cream during the hot weather that tasted very much like the homemade ice cream we used to make in a bucket with a hand-turned crank. It was delicious.

Breakfast was probably always the most popular meal, as the grill always offered eggs to order and three or four types of omelets. It was at the Det 4 chow hall that I first discovered and learned to enjoy Spanish omelets, with peppers and onions and stewed tomatoes. Eggs in almost any form have always been one of my favorite foods, and I could always have all I wanted there. Oatmeal, French toast and pancakes were also staple breakfast choices, along with various cereals.

Our food was prepared by a staff of Turks, all garbed in kitchen whites. I think there was a British fellow who was the overall boss of the food services, but the head Turk, or boss ah-bey, was a large rotund man we called "Cisco." I don't know if that was his real name or just a nickname bestowed on him by his GI patrons. In any case, with his dark swarthy complexion and big drooping moustache, he looked more like Pancho than the Cisco Kid. Supposedly the mess hall jobs were much sought after positions among the local residents, and it was rumored that Cisco, with his job of kitchen straw boss, was one of the town's wealthiest men, and also the mayor of Sinop. Like I said, it was a rumor. Looking back, it hardly seems likely, but who knows?

But I was walking you through town when I got side-tracked by that greenish fly-blown meat display in a butcher shop. Remember?

The bakeries weren't a whole lot better. I don't remember any pastries or sweet treats like we normally associate with bakeries, only various shapes and versions of what we came to call "hair-bread." The first hair-bread I saw was in the lunches of the ah-beys who worked around post. Their noon meals seemed to consist largely of chunks of goat cheese, garlic or onion, and a half-loaf of this bread, with usually a bottle of wine to wash it all down. (This lethal lunch combo invariably resulted in the most horrible cases of chronic halitosis you have *ever* smelled.) The threshing or milling processes used to glean or refine the wheat or oats or whatever grain was ground into flour to make these breads was apparently extremely primitive, because long fibrous husks were still visible in the end product. These long hair-like fibers protruded out the sides of the baked loaves, and were even more visible when the loaf was broken open to eat. It really did look like long dirty hairs had been baked into the bread. Most of us squeamish GI's had been raised on soft white breads like Wonderbread or Butternut Bread (the TV sponsor for *The Cisco Kid*, incidentally), so this ever-present display of such crude, high-fiber baked goods seemed particularly repulsive. By today's more scientifically health-conscious standards, however, that high-fiber bread might not rate so badly. I never did taste it, so I have no idea if it was good or not. It was just there – ah-bey bread, or hair-bread.

There were quite a few shops and trades and catered to the tourists and travelers, and also of course to the GI's of Det 4, who were undoubtedly quite important to the local economy. Two items that were extremely popular with the GI consumers were carved meerschaum pipes and puzzle rings.

Meerschaum is a soft material, so it's easy for carvers to work with, and it is also heat-resistant, making it a perfect substance for the bowl of a tobacco pipe. Technically, meerschaum is magnesium silicate, also called *sepiolite*. (O*kay!* I didn't know any of this until I looked it up in the dictionary. *Happy*?) There were a number of shops in Sinop that sold these carved meerschaum pipes. I don't really know if they were produced by local artisans or were shipped in from somewhere else. I *am* pretty sure they weren't "made in China." They were unique Turkish items, and were apparently very popular in pipe and tobacco shops back in the states – *and* very *expensive* there.

There were a few enterprising GI entrepreneurs on base who understood this, and made regular purchases of the pipes downtown, where prices were apparently very reasonable, then shipped them back to trusted "business colleagues" in New York or Chicago. Once there the pipes were marked up extravagantly. The original purchasers in Sinop professed to realize at *least* a one hundred percent profit on all the pipes they shipped back. Whether there were any implications of customs violations or black market profiteering involved, I really don't know. I didn't personally know the guys involved, but the operation was common knowledge on base. The pipes themselves were quite stunning pieces of craftsmanship. The bowls were usually carved in the shapes of turban-topped bearded heads, with very detailed facial features and hair, and no two were alike. I often wish I had bought one myself, just as a souvenir.

I didn't buy a puzzle ring either, but I should have. Just about everyone else ever stationed at Sinop bought at least one. A puzzle ring consisted of three or four (sometimes more) interlocking pieces which, when properly assembled, formed a very solid and handsome-looking piece of jewelry. The truth is I'm not very patient or good with puzzles, and whenever I would try to assemble one of my friends' puzzle rings, I just couldn't figure it out. It was as mysterious as a Rubik's Cube to me (something I don't think had even been invented yet then). So I figured why buy something I couldn't master. These rings, by the way, were made of stainless steel. The story around Det 4 was that a lot of tableware went missing or "got lost" from the mess hall, and had to be constantly replaced. Odds were fairly good then that your recently purchased whiz-bang Turkish puzzle ring had probably been the knife or fork you ate your ham and cheese omelet with the week or month before.

The tradesmen and artisans of Sinop were in fact quite ingenious in recycling materials in this way. The one major souvenir that I did buy during my tour there was a hand-forged and superbly crafted Bowie knife. A blacksmith shop in town specialized in creating several kinds of knives. The owner had a small book of illustrations which depicted various models, giving their dimensions and other particulars. The smith spoke a little broken English, he was quite easy to deal with, and did a brisk trade with GI's, many of whom are fascinated by knives and weaponry. He made everything from a machete, sword or sabre all the way on down to a small delicate-looking but deadly stiletto, which came with a boot sheath. The Bowie knife that I bought fell closer to the large end of the product list. I don't really know why I wanted such a big knife. Probably one of those sublimated sex things – *my knife's bigger than* your *knife.* It had about a twelve-inch (*see? BIG!)* highly-polished blade, with the Turkish national symbol of a crescent moon and star etched into the top edge. It had a leather-wound brass haft and came with a leather-wrapped wooden scabbard, with a snap-strap to hold the knife in place and a small polished brass knob at the tip. Yeah, it was way cool. The steel used to produce the blade came from old leaf-springs from cars or trucks, more recycled materials, most ingeniously used to produce a truly superior product.

I remember the day I went to go pick up my order, the smithy's assistant, a burly, swarthy-looking guy with a big black moustache, brought out the knife in its scabbard and presented it to me. I took it out of the sheath and was admiring it. Smiling ferociously, he held out his hand, palm up, so I handed him the knife. He laid it gently across one finger of his hand and held it that way for a moment, I suppose to show me the balance point of the heavy blade or something. Then he paced off about thirty feet from the heavy scarred wooden door of the shop, turned quickly back around, and in a single fluid motion he hurled the knife at the door, where the razor-sharp point lodged deep into the weathered wood with a loud

Hand-forged Turkish knife and scabbard

thunk, humming and quivering in place. The man did this, I suppose, for a couple of reasons: to show that the knife was indeed perfectly balanced for use as a kind of short-distance missile, and to show that it was *sharp*. Whatever his reasons for the demonstration, I was suitably impressed. He made me nervous, as a matter of fact. I politely declined his pantomimed suggestion that I try *my* skill at throwing the knife. I had never thrown a knife in my life. Hell, I'd never owned anything bigger than a jackknife. This Bowie knife was a souvenir for me, nothing more, and I preferred to keep it that way. (Besides, I didn't feel any pressing need to humiliate myself in front of this spooky-looking stranger.)

I think the knife only cost me twenty or thirty dollars at the time, and is easily worth several times that amount now. Even at its original price it seemed pretty valuable to me, so I didn't waste any time about registering it as a deadly weapon with the MP's at the post Provost Marshal's Office. This was required by regulations, and the PMO also provided secure storage for such weapons until you were ready to ship it home.

One other purchase I made in Sinop was a more utilitarian one, a pair of custom-made Wellington-style boots (like motorcycle boots without any buckles). I usually wear a size 13 or 14, depending on the type of shoe or boot, so it's always been difficult for me to find footgear I like. I remember when I was in junior high and high school and saddle shoes and white bucks were briefly in vogue. I wanted a pair of those bucks so badly. Both Elvis and Pat Boone were wearing them at the time. Nope, no dice. The local shoe stores just didn't stock 'em that big. It was probably a good thing. Do you have any idea how *huge* a pair of size 14 *white* shoes look? I would have looked like Frankenstein in nurse's shoes. Anyway, when I found this cobbler's shop downtown, with a guy who looked at my feet and indicated "no problem," I was pretty excited. I'd been hankering after a good pair of Wellies for some time by then, so stepped happily into the shoe-guy's back room to get measured. His method of measuring and fitting was very low-tech. He had me take off my shoes and stand on a piece of old cardboard while he traced around my feet with a broken pencil stub. Then he knelt down and laid his face sideways to the ground and briefly eyeballed my feet, probably to check my arches and the thickness of my feet. Then he stood up, dusted himself off, and said, "Come back one week." I did "come back one week," and the boots were ready. They fit perfectly and were most comfortable. I paid twelve dollars for those boots.

Not wanting to get them all dirty or dusty, I carried them back to post with me, where my roomies were quite impressed with the look and feel of them – *and* with the bargain-basement price. I spent nearly an hour putting a good spit-shine on the already shiny black leather, then pulled them on and took them on their maiden walk down the hallway of the barracks. *Shit!* They squeaked. Not just a little, but a *lot*, and with every step. *SKREEK! SKREEK! SKREEK!* You could hear me coming a block away. At first I was pretty upset, but all the guys thought it was so funny, I couldn't manage to stay mad. They were laughing and making comments about my "musical" boots, and how I sure wouldn't be able to sneak up on anyone, and they'd always know when Bazzett was coming. Oh, well ... They *were* nice-*look*ing boots. And they were comfortable. I decided I could live with a little squeak, er, a *loud* squeak, actually. So I did. I had those boots for several years. And yes, you *could* always hear me coming – in my hand-crafted, custom-fitted Turkish boots. So *what*?

In a clothing store downtown I bought my sister Mary a bathrobe made of very heavy absorbent material very much like

Unkown GI with Tim outside a glassware shop downtown Sinop.

terry-cloth. It was kind of a bright rainbow pattern, with stripes of red, gold, orange, yellow and white. Mary used it for several years, and years later somehow my daughter re-discovered it and *she* used it for a few years, so it must have lasted for over thirty years. Long-wearing hardy material, that Turkish terry-cloth. They just don't make clothes like that anymore. (At least it didn't squeak.)

There was a glassware store in town too, and I did admire longingly some of the figurines and other delicate pieces displayed in its windows, but I am of a rather practical bent, and figured anything glass stood only a very slim chance of surviving shipment home, so I didn't buy anything. I probably should have though. There were really some beautiful blown-glass specimens of vases, and figurines of flowers and animals the like of which I've never seen since.

The south end of Sinop was dominated by the massive gray walls of the prison, which were flanked by narrow dingy cobblestone or dirt streets. Apparently Sinop had once been a prison colony, and the prison itself was a relic of those days. There were usually dozens of beggars scattered along these streets, up against the base of the prison walls. Many of them were crippled, disfigured, missing limbs or appendages, or were blind. They leaned, hunkered, or lay up against the wall with a cup or a bowl to collect alms placed near them. Some of the guys from Det 4 had actually "toured" the prison at some time, and, according to what they had learned, most of these mendicants were former prisoners who just had no place to go upon their release. Some of their missing parts were due to an old system of justice, in which a thief or pickpocket was punished by having his right hand cut off. In the old society, where people all ate from a common dish or bowl of food, they could take food only with their right hands, because traditionally the left hand was the one you used to clean yourself with after defecating. So, if your right hand got chopped off, you were just shit-outa-luck come suppertime, unless you could enlist a friend or family member to feed you. Whether any of these customs were still in effect in the twentieth century, I don't know, but it did make a rather interesting, if gruesome story.

I probably only went up the street past the prison once or twice. That was enough. Hearing the pathetic cries of the beggars and seeing their filthy rags and disfigured stumps was an unnerving experience and left you feeling guilty and vaguely ashamed.

The road past the prison though was the only route to the "ruins," the stone walls and crumbling remnants of an ancient fortress that perched atop a cliff on the southwest edge of Sinop. Probably every GI ever stationed at Sinop made the trek to these

Al and Tim at the ruins.

Joe and Tim at the ruins.

ruins at least once, to climb about on the stones, peer over the ancient battlements at the sea below, and, of course, take photographs of one another striking manly and heroic poses atop this centuries-old rockpile.

* * * * *

In some ways, walking through Sinop was like stepping back in time to the previous century. It was true there were a number of automobiles around (most of them a dozen years old or older), but on the same streets you would also see on any given day crude old wooden carts, with solid wooden discs for wheels that screeched horribly as they turned (almost as badly as my spiffy new boots). These carts and wagons were pulled by bullocks, or cattle. Actually I was never quite sure *what* to call these large work animals. I would characterize the wagons as "ox-carts," but the animals pulling them didn't really fit my image of an ox, so I couldn't call them oxen. *Buffalo*, maybe? They were quite tame, but fearsome looking, with their huge span of heavy horns. More than anything else in *my* limited experience, they looked like those African Cape Buffalo I used to see in all those old *Tarzan* films, starring Johnny Weismuller or Lex Barker. The first time I saw one of these buffalo-powered ox-carts I was just astounded. I could not believe that in

1964 these kinds of conveyances still *existed*, much less that they were still in everyday use for hauling goods. But there they were, larger than life, trundling and screeching their way slowly along, wending their laborious way between the people, cars and the occasional U.S. Army jeep or deuce and a half that crowded the streets of Sinop. Very strange, sur*real* even. It made me want to look around to see where I had parked my time-machine.

That summer I had an up-close and personal encounter with one of those scary-looking beasts. It was at the beach. First I need to explain that the GI's of Det 4 enjoyed their own private beach, on the west side of the Sinop peninsula, just south of town. And it was really quite a beautiful beach, as beaches go. The sands were nearly as white as those at Carmel Beach in California (a place I was to visit years later). And the waters of the Black Sea were very clear and pristine in those days. Since I can't recall any local manufacturing or trades that might have polluted the water, perhaps this was not so surprising. Many years later, Sinop's beaches were to become popular tourist attractions, but in 1964 the GI's seemed to be the only ones around who actually went swimming in the sea. The locals seemed to think of it mainly as a place to go to work, to fish and make a living. In fact there was quite a sizeable fleet of small fishing boats moored in Sinop's western harbor. In any case, beer bashes at the GI beach were quite a popular pastime in the summer. We would get to the beach via a deuce and a half shuttle, which also transported the beer and food, and two or three thirty-gallon galvanized garbage cans filled with ice to keep the beer, hamburgers and hot dogs cold. (We would build a fire on the beach to grill the burgers and dogs over.) We would then spend a whole afternoon body-surfing and swimming, eating and drinking, and just generally enjoying ourselves. And maybe, just *maybe,* dreaming of California, Florida or Jersey beaches, or, in my case, the Lake Michigan beach at Ludington, just an hour from home.

One minor thing you had to be careful about at the beach was where you spread your towel when you claimed a spot on the sand, because sometimes those buffalo (Remember? That's what I started to tell you about) would be roaming about free up and down the shoreline, apparently enjoying *their* day off. They may have been big and scary-looking, and maybe they didn't *look* like a cow, but their shit still looked like a cow-pie, the same kind I'd stepped in from time to time in my grandpa's pastures as a kid, and the same kind of cow-patties I'd mined for big white grubs to put in my dad's bait bucket. Anyway, what I'm trying to say here is you didn't want to spread your towel on a half-concealed cow-pattie (or buffalo pie), so you learned to check out the area before setting up camp, so to speak.

On one of those summer beach outings I had a really great time. I threw myself into the surf repeatedly and swam hard. I played a little touch football and just plain wore myself out. Oh yeah – and I drank a *lot* of beer too. Which is probably why, after a few hours, I lay down on my towel to catch my breath, and fell asleep, or maybe I passed out, from all the alcohol, sun and exertion. I mean I was out *cold*, I'm not sure for how long. When I woke up, lying there next to me, not two feet away, was a ferocious Cape Buffalo, looking right at me. I think I did a kind of backward somersault right off my towel, I was so momentarily terrified – and probably more than a bit addled by all that alcohol I'd imbibed earlier. Keeping my eye on the beast, I backpedaled furiously until I'd put a good fifty feet between us. All the guys around me, who had apparently watched the buffalo amble over and settle down next to me while I was unconscious, were laughing their asses off at me, and at my terror-stricken face and rapid reaction. When I finally came to a stop and set about regaining my composure, I could see that the beast, placidly chewing its cud with that familiar sideways motion of the jaws that is common to ungulates and ruminants the world over, presented absolutely no threat to me whatsoever. Embarrassed by my most *un*-Tarzan-like reaction, I muttered something about *rotten bastards* and *dirty tricks*, and went to find myself a beer. Buffalo Bob and Bison Bill would both have been ashamed of me, not to mention Johnny and Lex.

* * * * *

I haven't said much of anything up to this point about the Turks themselves, the natives, the ah-beys who were an integral, if somewhat invisible part of our everyday lives at Det 4. Because these "brothers" were everywhere you looked on post, if you chose to see them. They cooked and cleaned up in the mess hall. They shoveled snow in the winter and looked after lawns and flower beds in the summer. They drove our trucks and tractors, fetching and hauling all manner of supplies and stuff between town and base. They worked on small grading, landscaping and construction projects around the base. They cut our hair, washed our clothes, and cleaned the barracks. Some of them acted as facility engineers, insuring that our boilers, furnaces, waterpipes and other infra-structure stayed in good repair. The impact of their unobtrusive presence was immense. They made themselves useful and needed in every respect.

But did we *know* them? No, not really. As a matter of fact, due, I suppose, to the classified nature of our mission there, we were strongly advised *not* to fraternize or form bonds of any kind with the Turkish laborers or staff. Given that we referred to all of them with the catch-all title of "ah-bey" (brother), this advice seems monstrously hypocritical. It was a very separate and unequal kind of partnership that we enjoyed at TUSLOG Det 4.

There were Turkish soldiers co-garrisoned with us on the hill – *outside* our base perimeter fence. The Turkish regiment's small collection of simple wooden barracks and a couple small admin buildings were situated just on the other side of the fence, very close by, but we had very little contact with our native military counterparts. We would sometimes see them walking guard, guarding our perimeter on *their* side of the fence, while we walked guard on *our* side. One of my friends claimed to have once come upon a Turkish sergeant-of-the-guard savagely beating a private with his fists and a truncheon, presumably because the private had fallen asleep at his post. This was taking place, of course, on the other side of the fence, so there was nothing my friend could do about it. Not that he would have tried to intervene, but he said the poor guy was cowering on the ground, pleading, arms over his head trying to protect himself, and bleeding profusely from his scalp and face. It was apparently a very grisly and disturbing sight, and all my friend could do was stand and stare open-mouthed, until the sergeant, suddenly aware he had a witness, jerked the unfortunate victim to his feet and quick-marched him away toward their barracks.

Those barracks, incidentally, were supposedly nothing at all like our comfortable well-appointed ones. They were little more than empty shells offering only the most minimal shelter from the elements, where the soldiers slept on the floor and covered themselves with their greatcoats. This information I got from one of our admin clerks, who occasionally had to go over to the Turkish regiment on liaison matters.

The only other Turks we had frequent contact with were the facility engineers who kept our boilers and heating plant working, not just in the barracks, chow hall and other buildings around post, but also inside our "inner sanctum," the Operations building where we worked. These particular engineer ah-beys were escorted in and out of the facility by cleared and badged personnel (one of us). They were delivered to the boiler room, where they pulled an eight-hour shift of monitoring the pressure gauges and turning and tweaking various valves and switches to keep the plant running smoothly. They were never allowed into our work areas. They were restricted to the boiler room, where they were "guarded" by one of us, presumably so they wouldn't bust out of the room and run wild, wreaking havoc throughout our sacred classified spaces. Just joking, I think. I'm not sure why we had to stay in there with them. General security precautions, I suppose.

"Ah-bey guard" was actually pretty good duty, one you looked forward to, or at least I did. It was like getting a day (or night) off from work. You simply locked yourself into the boiler room with the engineer ah-bey, and kind of kept one eye on him while he made his endless rounds of all the gauges, valves, toggle switches and levers that controlled the heating plant. There was usually a pot of coffee on, and you sat at a desk with a phone that connected you to other rooms in the Ops Center and to the MP's at the entrance gate. You could read a book or newspaper. Sometimes, when the engineer was between rounds of his readings, you'd play a game of checkers with him. He didn't speak much English and you couldn't speak Turkish, so it made for a pretty quiet game and a relaxing shift. At any rate, that was about as personal as it ever got between us and our so-called "brothers" at Det 4.

* * * * *

That spring, along with Al Trott, I did have one very unsettling encounter with some of the local residents. It was probably in late March or early April, because all the flora of the region seemed to be bursting into bloom and the grass seemed greener than I'd ever seen it, as I gazed off across the point that morning. We were on

Al and Tim off to explore the Cape.

break, and it was a gorgeous sunny day, so I suggested to Al that we hike out to the end of the point, out beyond the wire, and explore the countryside a bit. Our base was located near the middle of the peninsula that was Cape Sinop, and we'd never seen what was out at the extreme end of the point. Al, always an energetic let's-do-it sort of guy, was all for it, so we exited post at the main gate and walked back around the outside edge of the perimeter fence until we could turn north, out toward the headlands of the cape. Upon closer inspection, the grass wasn't as plentiful and lush as it had looked from a distance, but scattered and rather sparse. The landscape was dotted with rocks and boulders and creased by deep gullies choked with a low undergrowth of bushes and small stunted trees. Since I'm not a botanist or geologist I can't be much more specific than that, and anyway, this *was* forty years ago.

The thin grass and rocky terrain hardly looked suitable for grazing, but we hadn't gone far, perhaps a quarter mile or so, when we came over a rise and were confronted with a small flock of sheep, a couple dozen at most. A small undernourished-looking boy, perhaps ten or eleven years old, was tending the sheep, sitting on a rock holding a long stick – not a real shepherd's crook or anything elaborate, just a carefully trimmed tree branch five or six feet long. He seemed surprised when he saw us, which I suppose

Sheep grazing out on the point.

was natural, since I don't think many GI's ever ventured out onto the far reaches of the point. After all, there was nothing out here but whatever nature had allowed, and I don't think Det 4 harbored many naturalists in its ranks. *My* only reason for wanting to explore the countryside a little was that it was a beautiful spring day. And I may have been thinking about similar days in my not-so-distant childhood , when I used to wander back along the creek that ran across the back fields of Grandpa's little farm, where I would climb up into the branches of an enormous old willow tree that overhung the stream, or poke around in the stone piles with a stick, looking for snakes sunning themselves. Walking these fields and hills out beyond the base gave me a similar "school's-out" and footloose kind of feeling.

But now this small shepherd jumped up from his rocky perch and walked quickly over to us, right arm outstretched with palm upturned in that by-now unpleasantly familiar gesture of supplication that we encountered every time we went into Sinop and had to deal with the ever-present groups of ragged street urchins.

"You got gum, Ah-bey? Chic-a-let, cigarette, *mon*ey?"

Had we been in town, we would have undoubtedly ignored this entreaty, since we had learned, through bitter experience, that if you gave one of these beggars anything, they would all hound you for more for the rest of the day. But this time it must have seemed safe to be generous. What the hell, we figured, there was no one else around, just this one little guy. So Al found a pack of Juicy Fruit in his pocket and gave the kid a couple of sticks, the last two sticks in the pack, actually. The boy took the gum and backed off, smiling and bowing in apparent gratitude, then turn and ran off over a nearby rise.

Al and I walked on, feeling better about ourselves for this small act of kindness, and enjoying the bright sunshine and a soft balmy breeze with just a hint of salt air blowing in from further out on the point. We continued to hike in that direction, hoping to reach the headlands and get a look at the sea from a new vantage point. The terrain became steeper, more rugged and uneven, gouged with gullies and rocky brush-choked ravines., but we kept going, skirting as many of these depressions and obstacles as we could.

We had just stopped to rest, and were sitting on some small boulders at the rock-strewn edge of a deep ravine which fell away to a depth of thirty or forty feet at our feet, when we heard young voices, talking excitedly in Turkish, coming up behind us. Our little shepherd was back, and he had brought five others with him, some of them not so little. Two of them were tall thin gangly teenagers with wispy beginnings of beards on their cheeks and chins. As they came over the hill and spied us, the original gum-getter pointed at us and jabbered something excitedly to the older boys, probably telling them what a soft touch we were, or maybe reminding them how rich all Americans were. In any case, the motley group approached us straightaway, with a definite air of purpose and anticipation about them. The tallest and probably the oldest boy was carrying a long heavy stick. Again, it wasn't anything so picturesque or biblical as a shepherd's crook, but it did look as though it may have been sanded and smoothed in some fashion. It was reasonably straight and stout-looking, much like the staff Robin Hood used to knock Little John off that log bridge and into the stream. I mean it was a sub*stan*tial-looking stick. Well, this kid strode right up to Al, and, with no attempts at greetings or opening pleasantries, he thrust out his dirt-encrusted hand, palm up.

"*GUM,* Ah-bey. Cig-ret, *MONEY.*"

This was *not* a request. This character was *not* begging. He was de*man*ding. His eyes were hard and unfriendly, his expression grim and hostile. Al regarded this punk evenly, his hackles beginning to rise as the two faced off like two strange dogs. I know humans don't have hackles, but Al was famous on our trick for his short fuse, and when he got mad the color would rise from his neck up into his cheeks, and I could see the tell-tale flush rising out of his shirt collar.

"Nope," he replied. "No more gum. No money. And no cigarettes." He pointedly did not apologize.

The panhandling punk jabbed his index finger towards Al's pants pocket, then held out his hand again, "*GUM!*"

Looking this creep straight in the eye (actually the kid was probably half a head taller than Al, but that didn't faze him), Al reached deliberately into his pocket, brought out the empty Juicy Fruit pack and slapped it viciously into the outstretched palm.

"There you go, *Ass-hole*. That's all you get."

The Turk turned the pack up and peered into it, then flung it angrily down onto the ground. Moving a threatening millimeter or two closer, he gripped his staff a little tighter, his other hand now at his side curled into a fist, and thrust his face at Al's.

"*MONey, CIG-ret. GIVE!*"

I guess we weren't his ah-beys anymore, because he was no longer using that familiar form of address, and I could tell Al wasn't feeling any too brotherly towards him either. As a matter of fact, I sensed that Al was edging dangerously close to employing that even *more* familiar form of address – *mother.*

Reaching into both pockets, Al slowly turned them out, and replied even more slowly through clenched teeth.

"I got nothin' more to give, you mother-*fucker*! (Yup. See? There it was.) So you *better* back off, and get outa my *face!*"

The menace in Al's voice and the rising color in his face were unmistakable. There was no language barrier in this kind of elemental face-down. The punk blinked, then backed away, his threatening demeanor suddenly gone, replaced by a sulky teenager's pouty look, as he muttered something to his partners-in-crime, probably trying to save some face, but it wasn't working. The smaller boys looked away uneasily, frowning, but the other teenage hoodlum actually sneered at him and said something that sounded sharp and cutting.

You might ask here, what was *I* doing throughout this threatening exchange? Good question; a fair question. But I can't really honestly remember. I was probably doing my best to put up a good front and trying to look fierce like Al was, maybe borrowing a page from Norm and puffing myself up to look as large and threatening as possible. In*side* though, I'm quite sure I was consumed by a welter of conflicting emotions. My fight-or-flee instincts were undoubtedly ramped up to their highest levels, and the adrenaline was pumping, but I was probably *most* glad that it was Al this young hoodlum chose to confront, and not me. If he had known what a pussy pacifist I was, he most certainly would have come after *me*, in which case I honestly don't know what I would have done, but I sincerely doubt that I could have ever come off even nearly as nasty as Al did.

Al was really pissed by now, but he managed to do the diplomatically correct thing. He said, "Come on, Bazzett," and walked briskly away. I hurried quickly after him, hoping fervently that the showdown was over.

Alas, it was not. We hadn't gone twenty feet when we realized that the would-be mugger and his ragged retinue were trailing along behind us. I must have been looking somewhat fearfully over my shoulder, because Al muttered at me out of the side of his mouth, "Ignore the bastards." So we tried to ignore them, and kept walking along the rim of the ravine, although our pleasant morning outing had obviously been spoiled by now. The "spoilers" slowly closed the gap between us until they were directly behind us, and the sulking thug began to swing his staff back and forth in front of him threateningly. I'm not sure if it was on purpose, but the end of his staff grazed the backs of Al's legs as he walked, then dropped down between his feet, nearly tripping him.

Al had had enough. Quickly regaining his balance, he swung around, reached out and snatched the wooden staff viciously away from the kid, moved back a step, and flung the stick in a wide arc out and away over the ravine, where it dropped down into the thick brush and disappeared. Then, his face flushed with barely suppressed rage, Al stepped up to the surprised hooligan, who was still looking down to where his favorite stick had just disappeared.

Pointing down into the gully with his left hand, Al said, "See that, Omar?" Then, stabbing "Omar" twice in the breastbone with a rigid forefinger, he continued, "Well, you're *next*, mother-fucker!" The second finger poke actually knocked the off-balance Omar flat on his ass among the scattered stones. The smaller kids gaped at their leader on the ground, then even braved a titter or two.

Finally perhaps a bit frightened, Omar scrabbled backwards in an impromptu and awkward crab-crawl, trying to get out from under Al's glowering presence. But then, hearing the snickers of his younger gang-members, his face darkened in anger, and his fingers closed over a stone. He scrambled abruptly to his feet and held the stone threateningly, arm cocked to throw. It was a pretty good-sized rock. Al and I both backed off infinitesimally. He threw the stone. We ducked and backed off a bit more. He bent and picked up another rock, a bigger one this time, and suddenly all *six* of them were picking up rocks, and started *throw*ing them – at *us*, for God's sake! We turned and ran, then realized we were running *away* from the base, so we cut in a wide arc, away from the ravine and around our pursuers, and back toward the sanctuary of the base. Their first volley of rocks rained around us. Al took one in the shoulder and I got one in the back, but we kept running.

Holy SHIT! What century was this? We were being STONED*! And by a bunch of fucking* KIDS*, for cripes sake!*

Fortunately, they had to stop to pick up more ammunition, and we kept running, at full tilt by now, our minds filled with visions of our battered bodies being found at the bottom of a washout days later, heads bashed in, eyes gouged out, and worse. We quickly outdistanced our attackers, but could hear their jeering cries and crows of triumph as we continued to run, a little more slowly now, winded by our all-out headlong flight, back towards the gates of the post.

Finally, the gates in sight, we slowed to a walk, gasping and panting, our adrenaline spent. Al was simply *furious*, sputtering and cursing about those "mother-fucking little rag-head bastards." I was mostly just glad to be out of danger and almost back to the safety of the base. It also crossed my mind briefly that we might have just narrowly avoided causing, or provoking, what could have turned into a nasty international incident. Jesus, what if Al had thrown *Omar* over that cliff, instead of his stick?

Feeling vaguely embarrassed and *very* confused about what had just occurred, we avoided each other's eyes as we trudged sweating and exhausted through the main gates and up the road to the barracks. Nothing was said about reporting the incident to our superiors or the MP's. I think we were ashamed to. Certainly we were embarrassed and angry at having been rousted and chased by a handful of malnourished raggedy-ass kids. That was a given. But there was another gnawing, not quite definable subcurrent of something else too, flowing just beneath the surface of our feelings, something we couldn't quite understand and certainly couldn't have put into words. So we kept it to ourselves.

Nevertheless, I still think of that day, and I replay it over and over in my mind, trying to figure out how and why it happened. It's been forty years, and you'd think I would have gained some deep or philosophical insight into that mini-debacle by now, but I can't say that I have. It still bothers me.

* * * * *

A little later that spring, the same unspoken tension raised its head again, this time in a much more public setting. I think it was around the middle of April. There was some kind of national holiday being celebrated, because there were Turkish flags, large and small, on display all over Sinop, where a kind of festival atmosphere prevailed. I was not directly involved, but heard all about it second-hand. The streets of town were apparently more crowded and choked with people and commerce than was usual. The principal players in this imminent debacle were three or four hapless GI's from Det 4 who were on break and in town to have some fun. I didn't know them. They were either assigned to another trick or may have been from Headquarters Company. The story I heard was that they were drunk, but there weren't any bars in Sinop, so if they *were* drunk, they must have gotten that way on base, *before* they went to town. In any case, they had hailed a cab (one of only a few in Sinop, both fifty-something Chevrolets) to take them back to post. As they were climbing into the taxi, one of them fell or lurched against it, losing his balance, and in the process managed to dislodge a small Turkish flag that was fluttering from the cab's radio antenna. The flag ended up on the ground, where the GI stepped on it. I have to believe this was all an unfortunate accident, because I don't think anyone would have been stupid enough to do such a potentially inflammatory thing on purpose. Unhappily for the perpetrator, the incident was witnessed by several Turks in the surrounding throng, who immediately took umbrage at what they saw as flagrant disrespect to their flag and country. Word spread quickly through the crowd, and the small group of Americans was quickly surrounded by an angry shouting mob. Luckily, a Turkish gendarme was nearby and intervened. I doubt if the policeman spoke or understood any English, so he probably only got the Turks' version of what had occurred. He took charge of the American offender and called in additional help to disperse the crowd. It was probably a wise and judicious decision on the policeman's part to quickly hustle the by-now frightened GI culprit off to the local lockup, if only to protect him from the volatile crowd.

The other GI's managed to slip away in the ensuing confusion and quickly beat feet up the hill to base, where they reported, probably in none too coherent a fashion, what had happened, first to the MP's, and then probably also to their bosses. Exactly what kind of political or diplomatic machinations ensued I'm not at all clear on, but our post commander, Colonel Lepke, certainly got involved, and probably conducted some very delicate negotiations with Sinop's mayor, police chief and other local authorities.

Later that afternoon an angry mob of over four hundred angry Turks gathered outside the Sinop jail demanding "justice," meaning, I suppose, *Lynch the bastard!* Or perhaps, judging from my own recent experience, *STONE the bastard!* As far as I know, no one had a rope, but many of the men were "armed" with pitchforks, pikes, shovels, and various other pointed or sharp-edged farm implements. That much became common knowledge, because after the Turkish police chased the mob away from the jail, it surged angrily up the road to Det 4, where the commander had wisely ordered the gates closed and the post locked down. All the men were ordered into the barracks, to stay out of sight. A few very tense hours followed, as the small contingent of MP's guarded the entrance gates and also kept a jeep patrol circling the perimeter pence, while some of our officers did damage control, trying their best to calm down the unruly crowd and listening to the grievances of its ringleaders. Finally, still shouting and grumbling, the mob began to disperse and straggled slowly back down the hill. The flash point had been averted and the worst appeared to be over.

The tense atmosphere continued, however. A couple of days later the MP perimeter patrol discovered a hole cut in the chain link fence near one of our warehouses. The building had been broken into, and, upon taking inventory, it was discovered that a couple cases of blasting caps were missing. (The caps were apparently left over from supplies used the previous year to level the rocky landscape for construction.) Knowing that certain disruptive elements of the local populace were now in possession of potentially lethal explosives, the commander decided to keep the base locked down, and also ordered that additional foot-patrol perimeter guards be deployed. That meant *us*. There weren't enough MP's to do it all, so guard duty rosters were made up which included operations and headquarters troops. The officer of the guard made sure we walked our shifts in pairs. Security was very tight.

What turned all this into high farce, unfortunately, was the usual Det 4 manner of 'arming" its foot patrols. Yup, you guessed it. The same empty M-1 carbines we had been issued when Kennedy was killed. And the operative word here is "empty." It was not a warm and cozy feeling, walking that path along the wire in the dark with a flashlight and an empty weapon. Hell, those big, heavy duty flashlights, with their three or four D-cell batteries, would probably have made better weapons than those damned useless carbines. A lot of nervous guys did try to convince the guard mount chief to issue a clip of ammo, or, lacking that, at least one lousy Barney Fife bullet to button into a shirt pocket. Nope. No dice. What if we shot somebody, went the official reasoning. It could create a sticky "international incident."

What if *we* shot somebody? Hell, what about if somebody shot *us*? Wasn't anyone worried about *that*? *Shee-it!* Like I said, things were pretty tense, and they stayed that way for a week or two. I think Colonel Lepke did the right thing by locking down the base, because if no one went into town, the local merchants lost important needed revenue. The Sinop economy suffered. The Det 4 soldiers, ugly Americans or not, were also *customers*.

So what happened to the poor schnook in the Sinop hoosegow? Again, this is mostly hearsay, but I think the commander managed to get him transferred to our own lockup on base, while the local authorities hemmed and hawed and mumbled and grumbled about a "trial." The final rumor had it that the poor guy was stuffed into a mail bag, then smuggled off post in the back of a truck to the airstrip, where he was flown to Ankara and then back to the states, out of harm's way. I'm sure there was a considerable amount of covert behind-the-scenes diplomacy involved, but we peons were not privy to such details. The tension did gradually dissipate though, and the post was finally opened up again and commerce resumed.

* * * * *

It is not an easy thing for a young man to be isolated in a foreign country, far from home, family , friends, and all the familiar conveniences of American culture that he grew up with. We lived a very narrow repetitive kind of existence at Det 4, which came to feel, finally, like a rude and rowdy kind of cloister. We worked, we ate, we slept, we went to the flicks, we read, we got drunk, we engaged in furtive solitary sex. We even prayed, some of us, occasionally, when we remembered, or when we were depressed or homesick.

Feelings of depression were inevitable after you'd been "on the hill" for several months. The walls, the perimeter fences, the rigid routines – all these things began to close in on you, and you would begin to draw into yourself and think bitterly about all the things you could be doing if you were back home, things you'd taken for granted when you *were* there. Like jumping in the car and going to pick up a couple buddies and cruising the main streets of town and checking out the scene at the A&W Drive-in. Or buying a bag of fifteen-cent hamburgers at the Satellite and heading for the Big Rapids Drive-in movies, not so much for what was playing there, but to see *who* was there, and to hang out with the crowd. Then you'd think about your high school buddies who were still at home, who had decided to go to work or to college, and were getting on with their lives. You started to feel trapped by your constant, never-changing routine, and worried that the world was leaving you behind while you marked time on this endless tedious treadmill that was your life at Det 4. You just got to feeling angry, but you weren't sure why.

We came to call it the *FTA* phenomenon. Well, we probably didn't really call this feeling a "phenomenon." No, what we did was we'd get frustrated and angry and we would blame the army for our predicament and for these dark unnameable feelings. So we brooded, and we said "FTA" a lot, which, of course, as anyone who has ever been in the army knows, means *FUCK THE ARMY!* This rude expression provided us with a feeling of solidarity. We peons understood it intuitively, and took some small comfort in it, although it tended to leave a kind of bitter aftertaste in your mouth. The army, the organization and the authority, became a faceless "enemy," and also a scapegoat for all our pent-up frustrations (not the least of which were probably sexual in nature).

Our supervisors and officers were well aware of the FTA phenomenon, but they needed us to carry out the all-important mission, so they learned not to hear the *FTA*'s that exploded around them every day. They walked softly and cultivated tact and diplomacy to a fine art, and only reacted if an FTA was too openly defiant or rebellious to be ignored.

By June of 1964 I had been at Det 4 for nearly ten months and was feeling hemmed in and fed up, frustrated and angry for no real reason except that I was still there and wished to be elsewhere, just about *any* place but there. True, I was considered a "short-timer" by then. I wore the short-timer's chain, clipping off a link for each day that passed, and I kept a short-timer's calendar, magic-markered in reverse descending numbers onto a roll of toilet paper. But the end of my Sinop tour couldn't get there soon enough to suit me, so it seemed I was continuously doing a slow burn and spoiling for trouble. In my barely suppressed impatience, I was always hovering dangerously close to crossing that line of open defiance of authority.

We had a trick supervisor, an 058 like us, but as an E-5 he was the ranking operator on our trick. His name was John C. Reilly, and he was from Long Island. I remember that place name, because someone there – I don't think it was Reilly; it might have been Joe Capozzi – always pronounced it the New Yorker way, *Lahn-GAI-land.* Reilly was probably no more than a few years older than us, and I'm not sure if he was already on his second enlistment, or just towards the end of his initial one. But he was a Specialist Fifth Class, of Spec 5, which is the pay-grade equivalent of a buck sergeant, or a non-commissioned officer. As an NCO – and as a supervisor – he was set apart from us lowly enlisted "scum" (as we sometimes referred to ourselves). Joe, Al, Norm and I were all still PFC's, a couple steps lower than a Spec 5. Reilly represented authority. He was a first-echelon boss. He was the army personified, in his highly spit-shined boots and crisply starched and pressed fatigues, and a fresh military crew-cut every two weeks. He represented the enemy to our brotherhood of FTA-ers. Behind his back, and sometimes in a joking manner to his face, we called him a "lifer." Lifer is a derogatory term for a career army man. It's derogatory in the sense that it equates an army careerist with a criminal doing a life sentence in prison. It implies that the person is taking refuge in the army because he couldn't make it, couldn't succeed, in the "real world," or "on the outside." It implies, in short, that he's a "loser."

In point of fact, Reilly was anything *but* a loser. He was a very ambitious, highly-organized and efficient soldier and technician, which was probably a major reason he was a Spec 5 and our boss. He was disciplined and dedicated to his work, and, yes, probably to the army too. And he was quite expert at walking that delicate line between pleasing *his* bosses and getting the job done and placating the disgruntled malcontents like me, who did the actual work and were in his charge. *Now* I recognize all this. *Now* I see that John C. Reilly wasn't such a bad guy, that he was just a guy doing his job in the best way he knew how. What I can see *now* is that John C. Reilly was a grown-up, an *adult*, at a time when I was still only fumblingly aspiring to that status. I may have been twenty years old chronologically, but emotionally I was still little more than a confused, lonely and rebellious teenager.

So one night Reilly and I clashed. I can't even remember anymore what we argued about, or what precipitated our blowup. Maybe I was involved in one of those infamous mid-shift office chair choo-choo trains and got caught, or was a little too slow about taking down the masking tape net from an impromptu Ops Center volleyball game. Whatever it was I did (and I have no doubt that I did do *some*thing I shouldn't have), Reilly called me on it, and I got nasty and mouthy back at him, and this in front of other ops – in front of my *friends*. I was unquestionably showing off, being an insufferable jerk, just like I had a few times in high school when I'd gotten myself into trouble for defying teachers or arguing with them. At any rate, Reilly was forced to put me in my place, and reported me to our platoon sergeant, probably for "insubordination," if it were put into official jargon. But it was really all about me being an asshole. And I was.

I had created an untenable and impossible situation for poor Reilly. He needed to be able to command the respect of his men. I had openly defied him, had indeed been insubordinate. Something had to be done. Poor Joe, ever the peacemaker, tried to get me to just apologize to Reilly. Joe was still my friend, but even *he* could see I was in the wrong. I refused to apologize. I was in a state of high dudgeon – translation: I didn't know how to stop being an asshole and salvage my stupid stubborn pride.

Reilly and Staff Sergeant Gnong, our platoon sergeant, put their heads together. Gnong was an easy-going amiable sort of fellow who hated discord, and also hated paperwork. I probably could have been slapped with an Article 15 (a written reprimand with a possible fine attached that would go into my permanent record). But that would have involved a lot of paperwork and meetings. The fact of the matter was, I think neither Reilly nor Gnong had any particular desire to do me any permanent damage, even if I *was* being an asshole. They just wanted to solve the immediate problem with as little fuss as possible.

So they transferred me to another trick. The written reason for my transfer was that there was a shortage of ops on the other trick, which may or may not have been true. I don't know. So nothing negative went into my record. My transfer was effective immediately. In effect I got fired because I had backtalked to my boss. That was fair. It was *more* than fair, considering I was immediately re-hired. I would still be doing the same work, but would be working with a different group of guys.

In a sense then, I got off scott-free for my defiant act of insubordination. I didn't have to apologize to anyone. I wasn't "officially" punished or disciplined. But the truth of the matter was, I was fucked. In attempting to be kind, to go easy on me, Reilly and Gnong had inadvertently come up with the perfect punishment. I may have kept my stupid moronic pride, but I was *so* fucking miserable and unhappy at this sudden change. It proved to be a very hard lesson to me. My FTA attitude had ended up fucking *me*.

I had to move out of the room I'd shared with Joe and Al and Norm for the past several months. I had to leave my best friends and move across the quad to another barracks, where I had to practically start over again. It's true that I knew the guys on my new trick, but they weren't my *friends*. They were just casual acquaintances I knew from the club or from crossing paths in the chow hall or at shift changes in the Ops building. I was absolutely devastated. You know that verse from the bible about how pride cometh before a fall, or something like that? Well my stupid fucking pride had dropped me all the way down to the bottom of the pit. My dad would have simply said I had gotten too big for my britches, and he would have been dead-on right. What an absolute *asshole* I had been. I felt like I had been "cast out into the darkness" – more half-remembered Bible stuff – where there was "weeping and gnashing of teeth." I think I did some of each around that time.

Somehow I managed to get on with things. I went to work with my new shift, got to know a few guys a little better. I made one sort-of-close friend in Roy Hawks, a short rather morose-looking fellow with a big moustache and a wry sense of humor. But I think my "reputation" may have preceded me, because I felt a kind of standoff-ishness in the attitudes of my new co-workers. I didn't blame them. No one wants to be too closely associated with a known troublemaker. So I didn't press anyone too closely. I sought out my old Devens and Meade buddy, Mike Campbell, over in the mail-room, and we hung out together some, playing pool and bowling whenever we could get together. But mostly I kept my mouth shut (*too late*) and did my penance. Because that's what it felt like those last several weeks I spent on the hill, like I was doing penance. I wish I could say that, as part of my penance, I apologized to Reilly for my pig-headedness and for causing him trouble, but I didn't. If you're out there, Reilly, I'm sorry. Mea culpa.

I had been effectively "banished" from my trick and from all my best friends. Oh, it's true I would still see Joe and the other guys here and there, but, because of our different work and break schedules, it was pretty hard to ever do much together anymore. Yup, I was fucked. And I know now that I deserved it. But it was a bitter pill. One perhaps positive effect that my banishment had was that I quit being so angry and rebellious. Instead I felt guilty and repentant. I felt sad. Most of all I felt lonely.

Tim reading mail in his new bunk.

I can't even remember who my roommate was those last several weeks. I think it was just a two-man room though, which space-wise was a step up from the cramped quarters I'd shared with Joe, Al and Norm. But I missed them so much that I barely noticed my "improved circumstances."

I bought a tiny portable record player from a guy who was shipping out. It was a Phillips, not much bigger than a large briefcase, but it had speakers on each end, so technically it was a stereo. I spent more time alone, losing myself in music and books. I discovered Jim Reeves, and took solace in his velvet melodic crooning. I listened to the exotic bird and jungle sounds of Martin Denny's "Quiet Village," and Les Baxter's smooth orchestral interpretations of pop songs like "Running Bear" or "Venus." My musical tastes turned to softer more contemplative sounds, complementing my suddenly more monk-ish lifestyle. I drank and smoked less. I read compulsively. I went to church. I prayed. I think I was praying for my exile to end.

* * * * *

And finally my exile *was* ended. In early August of 1964 my tour in Sinop was over. Joe and I were on our way to Germany.

215

A few months previously we had applied for re-assignment to Germany upon completion of our tours in Turkey, and our requests had been approved, sort of. We had asked to go to Garmisch or Bad Aibling, both plum assignments near the Bavarian Alps – resort country and ski slopes. (I'm not sure exactly *why*, since neither one of us could ski.) We got neither. Instead we both received orders to Field Station Rothwesten, further north in Germany. We didn't know anything about Rothwesten, but at least it was Germany and we were going together.

You might well wonder, I suppose, if I missed home so much and all the stuff that went with it, then why had I requested to go to Germany, instead of taking a normal rotation back to the states, once my Sinop tour was up? It's a fair question, but I'm not sure I remember exactly why. I think part of it was due to that prevalent *FTA* attitude we all tried on in varying degrees of sincerity. We knew that stateside duty still involved things like pulling KP and barracks orderly and casual duty and "all that shit," as we were wont to say in lumping all those unpleasant duties together. In Europe, however, you had local workers who did all those "shit jobs," giving you more free time to have fun. This all sounded logical and manly to us at the time. And, in actuality, once you'd been away from home for a year, the pangs of homesickness tended to subside, and you thought, *What's another year? I might never get another chance to see Europe.* (Because Sinop certainly did not count in fulfilling that recruiter's promise about "seeing the world.") So Joe and I had filled out our Form 1049's and dreamed of Europe and German 'schatzies' once our purgatory time in Turkey was over. And now the time of our deliverance was finally at hand.

The only thing we really regretted was leaving Al and Norm, who had both elected to extend their tours, primarily, I think, because they weren't ready yet to be bothered with all the shit involved in changing duty stations. They hated Sinop, but the routine was at least familiar and comfortable. Of course there was nothing sappy or emotional about our leave-taking. It was one of those macho "see ya" kinds of good-bye, with perhaps an accompanying punch on the shoulder. I think Norm may have added, as a parting shot, "You better write, you fockers!" We promised that we would, but I can't remember that we ever did.

Airline ticket

We departed Det 4 the same way we had arrived, in the back of a deuce and a half, our duffel bags stacked among us. I think there were about a half dozen of us leaving that hot day in August, and we were already sweating through our dress khaki uniforms before we'd even gotten to the bottom of the hill, where we drove slowly through Sinop one last time. The usual rag-tag bunch of kids followed our truck through town, their shrill entreaties ringing on deaf ears. We were all lost in our own thoughts as we made that final run, passing the school, the chai garden and pier, the shops along main street, then around the gray walls of the prison and up the hill past the ruins of the ancient fortress. The only "official" good-bye voiced by any of us to the village came from Fred Beaver, who flipped his cigarette butt out the back of truck and muttered, "Bye, you fuckin' *shit*hole." And on that nostalgic note, we took leave of Sinop forever.

We re-traced our arrival route, traveling the same dusty mountain trails down the coast through Bafra and on to Samsun. There on the afternoon of August 8th we boarded a Turk Hava Yolari (Turkish Airlines) flight bound for Ankara.

* * * * *

Upon landing in Ankara, we learned we would have a four-day layover there. Looking back, I'm not at all sure why there was such a long delay. It seems like with a bit of prior planning the army could have had all the air reservations in place for us well before we left Sinop, and we could have spent just one night in Ankara,

Joe at the entrance of the Hotel Berlin in Ankara

Joe in the main square of downtown Ankara. August, 1964.

218

and then flown on to our new duty station. Or we could have even departed Ankara on the same night we got there, on a red-eye flight to Rome or Frankfurt. Either way the government would have saved a bucket of money. Of course our federal government has probably always been famous for *spending* money, not *saving* it. Probably though, the layover in Ankara was considered an *un*official R&R (rest and recuperation) for the men returning from a hardship tour. We would not be charged any leave for these few days off; instead it would be written off as "travel time." Those four days represented a tacit "wink" from the army, encouraging the men to go have a good time in the city.

We were billeted at the Hotel Berlin, a very adequate, if not a four-star, hotel. Joe and I drew a very comfortable second-floor room with two double beds, a private bath, and a pleasant view of the streets below. The hotel also boasted its own restaurant and bar.

So what do a half dozen soldiers do with themselves for three days in a big city like Ankara? We were, after all, left pretty much to our own devices. As long as we were ready for our flight out on the morning of the 12th, we could do whatever we pleased in the interim. What did we know about Ankara? Very little, actually. We had stopped there only briefly on our way into Turkey, and now we were on our way back out. About the only thing we remembered from our earlier visit was that the taxi drivers were absolutely nuts, and would rather sound their horns and curse than yield or brake. Our first night back, when we took a hair-raising ride to a restaurant that specialized in American cuisine, we quickly found out that *that* sure hadn't changed.

But why beat around the bush here? Let's cut directly to the chase. There was one major attraction in Ankara for GI's, *especially* for those leaving country following a one-year hardship tour – the *kera-hani*. We had been hearing about the kera-hani ever since we had arrived in country. I'm not sure exactly how the term translated literally, but we all knew it was a whore-house. I heard various explanations of how a kera-hani worked, from other more knowledgeable guys on the hill. The one that seemed to be most commonly accepted was that prostitution, under the auspices of a kera-hani, was legal in Turkey, because these houses were actually a kind of debtor's prison. If a woman committed a crime and was fined, or incurred a debt of some sort which she was unable to pay, she was summarily imprisoned in one of these houses, where she could then "work off" her debt to society by selling her "favors." Okay, it's a stupid euphemism, I know, so let's be real. She could literally *fuck* her way out of prison – providing she attracted enough paying customers. These houses were run by the government, which I'm sure took a generous cut of the proceeds, to cover overhead costs.

One of the rumors that circulated freely at Sinop during our tour there was that there was a kera-hani associated with the prison in town. The soldiers of the Turkish regiment garrisoned with us were regular customers there. Well, they weren't *paying* customers. Use of the local kera-hani was considered one of their "benefits." Their pay and living conditions were uniformly lousy, but at least they had this *one* attractive enlistment enticement. Supposedly, the Turkish regimental commander had offered, as a good-will gesture to his American "brothers," free use of the kera-hani to the U.S. troops stationed there. But apparently our chaplain, upon hearing of the offer, immediately objected strongly, so we never even learned exactly where the Sinop kera-hani was located. There was a lot of disgruntled grumbling among our troops while this story was circulating. Like I said, it never got beyond the murky rumor stage.

Prostitution outside of official government-sanctioned kera-hanis was a crime, but it still existed. There are always enterprising, business-minded entrepreneurs, male *and* female, who want to make a living without paying the government its share. Sex will always sell, regardless of the venue. I should add that this imperfect explanation of government-sponsored whore-houses in Turkey in 1964 could well be completely erroneous, but it's the only one I ever got, so it's all I can give you now.

I know you might say I'm still beating around the bush, but I'm really just trying to establish a context here for how I finally lost my virginity. Just be patient, please.

I'm pretty sure I visited the *big* kera-hani in Ankara, the government-run cat-house, but I can't say that I *remember* it. I wasn't drunk, so I can't blame that for not remembering. I only have this very vague image, a kind of hazy mental picture of a vast noisy hall, perhaps two or three stories high, kind of like the inner court of a prison, where you can look up and around you and see metal stairs and rows and tiers of small barred cells, but all the doors are open, and all the occupants are women, in various stages of dress or un-dress. And they're all calling out to you, as you come in the main entrance and stand in the courtyard on the ground level.

We went to the kera-hani in a small group, no more than five or six of us. You didn't have to know where it was. Any taxi driver in town could take you there. Probably at least four of us were first-timers – both as visitors to the kera-hani, and to sex. Well, sex with another *person*. They say there's safety in numbers, and I think we were all glad we hadn't come alone. The place was big and nosiy – and smelly. The scale of the place was quite overwhelming, and, yes, it was actually a bit frightening, especially to us virgins – Joe, Beaver and me. (Well, I'm guessing about Joe and the Beave, but *I* was as virgin as a primo brand of olive oil.)

The cells where the business transactions were carried out provided almost no privacy. The stale smells of sex and sweat, of contraband booze and vomit, pervaded the place. The blatant come-ons shouted out in Turkish, broken English and other foreign languages were anything *but* a turn-on. Joe was startled, and was feeling perhaps a bit paranoid, as we walked down a row of cells on the ground floor peering timidly in, and several different women called out, *Hey, Joe, you want ficky-fick? Joe, you like? Hey, Joe, come bang-bang.*

Eyes big and round, Joe turned to me and asked, "Hey, Bazzett, how do they know my *name*?"

And he was *serious*. He really *did* wonder how all these women knew who he was. And I don't think I was able to help him. Under the circumstances, under the *stress* of the circumstances, it really didn't occur to either one of us that *Joe* was just a whore's euphemism for a GI customer.

In the end, the sheer scale of the operation, the echoing impersonal enormity of it all, scared us away. We left the big kera-hani with our virginities intact.

But that is not the end of the story. One of the guys in our party was *not* a first-timer, in any sense of the word. He had been here before, and had only brought us because we had asked to see the big kera-hani. His name, I think, was Rich. He had been on the Sinop post basketball team, so had been to Ankara a few times before, on team trips. He and Sly and Swede and other team members had all sampled the wares of the kera-hani women.

Swede had even established a certain reputation for his double- and triple-header exploits at the place. Rich, a more private sort of person, had not found the factory-like atmosphere of the prison to his taste, so had sought his pleasures elsewhere. He had discovered that just about any taxi driver in Ankara could also hook you up with a more private liaison at one of the numerous "floating" brothels in the city. Since prostitution as free enterprise was illegal, the whores who plied their trade for profit were forced to keep on the move, one step ahead of the police, so they changed their work locations often, hence the term "floating" brothel.

At any rate, once we'd all "seen the sights" at the big kera-hani, Rich said he was planning to go find a more private place, and asked if anyone else wanted to go along. Joe and a couple other guys politely declined; they'd had enough excitement. But Beaver and I were game. Or maybe we were just determined to carry out our "mission." I think we both figured twenty years was long enough. So we climbed into a taxi with Rich, who did a bit of brusque negotiating with the driver in a mixture of English and pidgin-Turkish. After driving in what seemed like circles for several minutes through the dark streets of Ankara, we were deposited at what looked like a normal apartment building in a semi-residential neighborhood.

We climbed the stairs to a second floor apartment. Rich pressed a buzzer and we were admitted into a semi-darkened foyer by a very attractive, dark-haired woman, possibly in her thirties, who bore a striking resemblance to Lainie Kazan, the singer-actress. She acted as if she knew Rich, greeting him warmly, then ushered us all into a small living room where two other women were sitting on a couch, both wearing wrappers of a shiny, silky-looking fabric. Beaver and I stood self-consciously just inside the room, not knowing where to look or what to do with our hands and feet, while Rich conversed softly in hushed tones with our hostess, who was also dressed in a long silk robe. After a few moments, Rich turned to us and said he needed ten bucks from each of us. We dug out our wallets and handed him the money, which he in turn passed to our hostess. Then he explained that *she* was with *him*, and we could hash out between ourselves who got which of the other two women. He and our hostess then went off down a hall and into another room and closed the door behind them.

An awkward pause would most certainly have followed at this point, except one of the two women, a tall bottle-redhead who looked like she'd been around the block a few times – she could have been forty, but was still very attractive – rose from the couch and came over and took Beaver's hand, and ran her other hand through his red hair. Perhaps she felt a kind of kinship with him as a fellow redhead. She looked into his eyes and said something in Turkish and smiled. Of course Beaver couldn't understand Turkish, but blushed furiously anyway. As the redhead led the Beave past the couch and headed down the hall, she said something sharply to the other girl – and I could see now, even in the dim light, that she *was* just a girl, not a woman. The girl stood up and came over to me and took my hand. Raising her head, she looked up at me, almost shyly it seemed, murmured something, and led me down the narrow hallway to the last of three doors. I couldn't help noticing, as I followed close behind her, our fingers lightly linked, how *tiny* she was, probably no more than five feet tall.

The room she led me into was small, furnished only with a bed and a small table holding a lamp that was turned off and a candle in a jar. The girl bent briefly over the table and I heard a match strike, and when she turned back around the candle was lit, creating a warm glow and emitting a spicy scent I couldn't identify. When she turned to face me, I got my first good look at her face. My breath caught. She was beautiful. I mean, my *God*, she was beautiful!

I know, you're probably thinking, *Sure, this guy is telling about his first time, so he figures he might as well make the girl beautiful, right?* No, that's *not* right. I mean, I understand how you might think that, and it's true that this was my first time, and it seems highly unlikely and improbable that, you know, paying a whore for my first time and all, that she would be beautiful *too*. But she was.

I don't know really how old she was. She could have been anywhere between thirteen and twenty. She had dark shining hair, in one of those pixie-style sort of cuts with points down in front of her small ears, and the top part back-combed and ratted to form a shiny lustrous helmet framing her face. Her eyes were dark too, and her features were small and delicate. She looked half-frightened as she stood there looking at me in the semi-darkness next to the bed.

I was still standing just inside the closed door, suddenly feeling a bit frightened myself, wondering *What in the holy hell is proper etiquette here anyway? What do I do now?*

As though she had decided something for herself, chin suddenly jutting almost defiantly, with a single graceful shrug of her small shoulders, she shed her silken gown, dropping it in a shiny puddle at her feet.

The Turkish word for 'beautiful' sounds like the English word 'gazelle.' This word seems even more fitting when you think of the doe-eyed delicate creature that bears the name, that tiny graceful African antelope. My store of Turkish words was pitifully small, even after nearly a year in country. I knew a few dirty words and rude expressions, none of which seemed suitable here. I knew that *choke ee* meant 'very good," and *choke fi-nah* 'very bad. And I knew that *ga-zel* meant 'beautiful.' And that is what I thought when this girl – this exquisitely beautiful creature – dropped her gown. *Ga-zel.*

My mouth, however, couldn't say the word. It was hanging too far open. I'm sure I must have looked like the classic country rube in the presence of beauty, mouth gaping, standing there in my cheap PX shirt and pants and my black army-issue shoes, absolutely unable to move.

Gisele (I will call her that, because it is the name most closely resembling the word that described her, and because I never learned her name) must have realized how overwhelmed I was feeling, because she smiled, pointed to the bed, then reached out and took me by the arms, turned me half around and gently nudged me down until I was seated on the bed. Then she crouched down before me, naked, and, looking up at me from beneath her dark lashes, she pulled tentatively at one of my shoelaces, untying my shoe.

Suddenly I sprang into action. Kicking off that shoe, I quickly pulled off the other one, not bothering with laces, unbuttoned my shirt and shrugged out of it. I peeled my tee-shirt over my head, jumped to my feet and unbuckled my belt and dropped my trousers and stepped out of them. Throughout my sudden burst of frenzied activity, Gisele remained crouched in front of me, looking up at me, a small smile beginning to flicker across her face.

I stopped, still in my drooping sweat socks and jockey shorts, suddenly embarrassed by my too-evident tumescence, and at a loss as to how to proceed further. Gisele rose from the floor then and lay down on the bed, looking up at me expectantly. Figuring, *what the hell, here goes,* I stripped off my shorts, turned and knelt down on the bed, wishing I had some kind of instructions, so I wouldn't seem like such a *yeni* at this stuff. I just needed something direct and simple, like *insert tab A into slot B, and push all the way in until it locks.* No, wait! Don't *lock!*

Anyway, I'm fumbling around and peering down there into the dark, and the fucking *tab* isn't sliding into the fucking *slot* no matter what I do, and I'm getting more and more frustrated, when Gisele puts out her hand, laying her palm on my chest, and pushes me ever so gently away, and starts to wriggle out from under me. Feeling really stupid, embarrassed, and nearly defeated, I sink slowly back on my heels, my dick beginning to droop dejectedly. Raising herself gracefully off the bed, Giselle places her hands on my shoulders and turns me around and pushes me, still gently, down onto my back.

And this is where everything switches over to slow motion, filtered camera lenses, and soft ambient light.

The girl straddles the boy's thighs, grasping him firmly in her left hand. She slides the three middle fingers of her right hand into her mouth, moistening them thoroughly, then reaches down and lubricates herself, and then, finally, she shows him how well they fit together, how easily – shows him how to do this marvelous wondrous and exquisitely lovely thing that it seems he has been waiting all his life to do.

Looking up at her porcelain skin, at her small perfect pink-tipped breasts, at her white teeth as they bite softly on her lower lip in concentration as she bends to her work, rocking in the candle-light, the boy finally says what he has been thinking since she dropped her robe: "Ga-zel." *He tentatively touches her breast.* "Choke *ga-zel,* so *beautiful."*

Surprised, she pauses in her rocking, and smiles, a young girl's smile, radiant.

He dribbles, stops, sets himself, he goes up, he shoots. He scores! *No-thing-but-net.*

He explodes, shoots up and into her darkness, safety off, full automatic. He fires and fires, and fires again, until his clip is empty, until he is spent.

Watching his face, the girl continues to rock softly for a moment or two, then stops, both hands flat on his nearly hairless sweating chest, feeling his heart as it continues to race. Still smiling, a woman's smile now, she lightly touches his cheek and murmurs something softly. He yearns to understand. Perhaps he does. Cupping her breasts carefully, he tells her once again, "Choke ga-zel" – and it is finished.

Fade to black. Mission accomplished. August 10, 1964, Ankara, Turkey.

On the way back to the hotel afterward, Rich told us that the redhead who had chosen Beaver was actually Gisele's mother, something he had learned from the hostess. Beave was a bit disturbed to learn this, especially when Rich joked gently to him that not only did he finally lose his cherry, he had also become a 'motherfucker' in the process. Beaver chuckled along with us, if a bit ruefully.

I suppose the question might arise as to whether I had "practiced safe sex." The phrasing of that overused, politically correct question makes me smile. Practice, *hell* – there was no time or opportunity to *practice*. It was opening night and I was *on*.

The fact of the matter is I *would* have used protection, but for unforeseen circumstances. I had a condom in my wallet. It was one of those "just-in-case" condoms that a boy usually buys sometime during high school, usually around the age of sixteen or seventeen. I think it's part of the whole rite of passage thing. It doesn't take long for the foil-wrapped package to make an 'o'-shaped impression on the side of your billfold, providing a kind of badge of manhood to flash in the locker room when you empty your pockets and place the wallet on your locker shelf. I had been carrying one of these tin-foil-sealed Trojans since I was about eighteen, and I had taken it out of my wallet that night before leaving the hotel. The truth was I had never really looked closely at a condom. (I won't count the one some joker had blown up like a balloon and hung square in the gym entrance just before a pep rally my junior year of high school.) So I figured I'd better open up the package, just to look at it and figure out how it worked – how it went *on* and stuff, you know? So I carefully peeled open the foil wrapper and tipped it out over my open hand. The familiar 'o'-shaped rim of the rubber dropped out into my palm, along with a small shower of fine, sandy-looking dust. After more than two years of riding around on my bony ass and being sat upon repeatedly, the latex prophylactic had simply disintegrated. So much for my just-in-case safe. *Sure.* Just in case I get a chance to have sex, I'll sprinkle some of this magic dicky dust on my dong. It won't protect anyone, but Tinkerbell's life will be saved, and I will fly away to Neverland.

Anyway, there was no time to go buy a new one, since we were off to the kera-hani for some window-shopping. And afterwards we were prowling the streets of Ankara lookin' for love, and then, finally – like magic – *poof!* my cherry was history. And I never thought once about protecting myself until much later, when the deed was long done. But I'll make a feeble attempt here at putting a politically correct face on all of this by adding, I woulda if I coulda – *may*be.

Otel Berlin
ANKARA OTELCİLİK LTD. ŞTİ.

TEL: 137748 - 116056 - 115158
CABLE AD.: OTEL BERLIN ANKARA

HOTEL BERLIN ANKARA
Seri: E № 5231
ODA - Chambre No.: 206
By. Bn: / Mr. Mme.: CAPOZZI BAZZETT

Mois de / Ay	8	9	10	11	12		
Oda ücreti — Prix de chambre	40 -	40 -	40 -	40 -	//		
Teshin — Chauffage	- -	- -	- -				
Kahvaltı — Petit déjeuner / Kafeteri — Cafétéria							
İçkiler — Consommations — Bar / Otel — Hotel							
Lokanta — Restaurant / Otel — Hotel							
Çamaşır — Lingerie							
Telefon — Phone							
Muhtelif — Divers							
Günlük yekûn — Total de la journée	40 -	40 -	40 -	40 -			
Nakli yekûn — Report		40 -	80 -	120 -			
Umumi yekûn — Total à reporter / Tediyat — Payement		80 -	120 -	160 -			
Baki kalan — Solde à reporter				160 -			
Servis — Service				16 -			
Yekûn — Total				176 -			

Tim and Joe's bill from Hotel Berlin in Ankara

227

Our last night in Ankara we all celebrated by having a big dinner in the hotel restaurant. I won't say we *enjoyed* the cuisine, but we were celebrating, so we sampled a bit of everything. We were finally going to get out of Turkey.

The next morning, August 12th, we boarded a Pan Am flight and departed Ataturk-land for good. Our eleven-month sojourn in the wilderness was over. For some of us the long sexual drought was also over. Off we flew, like the proverbial "big-ass bird," bound for Germany.

PART III

PCS: ROTHWESTEN, GERMANY

Oxtail soup. It was a new taste treat for me, a thick brown gravy-like concoction laced with chopped onions, a rich spicy combination of beef, carrots, and – potatoes, perhaps? It came *mit Brochen*, and was being served up to us in the cafeteria at the *Hauptbahnhof*, in Kassel. Already I was learning some German. I knew how to say *with bread* and *main train station*. And the soup was delicious.

It was late August 1964, and my first time back in Kassel since our initial arrival there by train about a week before. I was in much better shape this time. The morning we flew out of Ankara I had suddenly developed a most inconvenient and unexpected case of traveler's tummy trouble. Shortly after takeoff my belly had begun to rumble and bubble ominously, and I had barely made it to the plane's bathroom when my bowels unloaded with a spectacular splatter. Apparently *some*thing I had ingested at our leaving Turkey celebration dinner the night before was taking its revenge. We hadn't been in Mexico, so I couldn't call it "Montezuma's revenge." Nope, geographically incorrect. But I *had* said many uncomplimentary things about Turkey during the past year, so maybe it was a case of "Ataturk's asshole." Whatever it was, it plagued me the whole journey from Ankara to Rothwesten.

Was it Hannibal that crossed over the Alps on an elephant? Well, I crossed them mounted on the metal toilet seat of an Alitalia Airliner, flying from Rome to Frankfurt. Needless to say, I didn't much enjoy the flight. I spent too much of it closeted in that tiny bathroom, shitting my guts out and throwing up in one of those cute little "airsickness" bags that airlines so politely provide to their passengers. But my distress wasn't because of a bumpy flight. No, in my case it was a result of sampling too many mysterious dishes of Turkish cuisine the night before, and maybe that Turkish beer with the oily sheen floating on top of it had something to do with my problem too.

It's a real pity that I remember so little about that journey from Ankara. I mean we flew into *Rome*, the *Holy City* and the seat of the Catholic *Church*. All those *years* I had spent attending daily Masses at St. Philip's, and then chapel three or four times daily during my year at the seminary. Now here I was in Rome, just a stone's throw from The Vatican, the Holy Father and all those famous cathedrals , and all I could think about was, *Where's the can, forgodsake?* And once I found one, I was afraid to stray too far from it lest I soil myself. To say it was a shitty trip would be accurate, but also an understatement.

By the time we landed in Frankfurt my belly was still burbling, but I had pretty much shit myself out. It was all I could do to drag my duffel aboard the train to Kassel. The train trip would have been a pleasant novelty and an adventure had I been feeling myself, but, again, I stuck close to the toilet and so missed most of the scenery, although I did catch brief glimpses of the railroad ties rushing by when I flushed. But I made it to Kassel, and, with Joe's help, I boarded an army bus that delivered us to our new duty station at Rothwesten, where we were both assigned to the 184th Operations Company.

And now we were out sampling the local cuisine in downtown Kassel, on a weekend pass a week later. My stomach and guts had reconfigured to their original states. I had managed to re-hydrate myself and was feeling good again. You might think I would have learned to be more cautious regarding foreign food, but hey, this stuff was *sooo good!* The thick crusty brochen, when dunked in the soup, just kind of melted in your mouth in a well-seasoned spicy explosion of flavor. Over the next year I was to discover many new and exotic tastes in German fare, but probably the one I loved best and sampled the most was bratwurst, which was served up piping hot from small charcoal braziers set up on street corners and sidewalks throughout downtown Kassel. Unlike our American style hot dogs, brats didn't come with a full-length bun. They were served with a tiny split brochen, just large enough to serve as a "holder" while you ate the sausage, usually liberally smeared with or dipped in *Senf*, a spicy brown mustard.

My sojourn in Germany was so unlike my tour in Sinop that I scarcely know where to begin. I'm not sure I can present an accurate chronological account of my time in Rothwesten and Kassel, primarily because my letters home gradually decreased in direct proportion to all the fun I was having, so I don't have many missives to refer back to and to jog my memory. So I guess I'll just have to wing it.

I'll start with the beer. German beer was a whole different animal from any beer I'd ever had before. Not that I was any great connoisseur of beers – far from it. I mean I'd done a considerable amount of imbibing of brew in the past two years, but it had all been American beer, which all begins to taste pretty much the same once you've downed a few. German beer was stronger. It had a much higher alcohol content and a darker, richer flavor. It could glaze you over in a hurry, especially if you tried to guzzle it the same way you always had your Bud or Blue Ribbon.

But beer was a fact of life in our off-duty fun. It was central to almost all of our nights out, and even sometimes in the barracks. Many of the guys who had already been there for a year or more when Joe and I arrived had even learned to drink their beer warm or at room temperature, which was the way most of the natives preferred it. That was a taste I never did acquire. Fortunately there were a few bars or *Gasthauses* in Kassel that catered almost exclusively to the GI trade, and in these places, thank goodness, the beer was served up cold.

One of these establishments was the Coyote Bar, a place I knew only by hearsay, and it had a lurid reputation as a bad-ass place. It was frequented by *non*-ASA elements of the army. There was a sizeable transportation unit also stationed at Rothwesten garrison – truck drivers and heavy equipment operators, made up mostly of southerners, both black and white. Apparently past conflicts at the Coyote had proven that these types and ASA-ers did not make for a friendly mix. I think the Coyote had been declared permanently off-limits to all ASA personnel, but every now and then some hapless ditty-bopper or linguist would accidentally

Binding Beer coaster (front and back)

wander into the place, inevitably resulting in a brawl that involved an awful ass-kicking, the German police, and sometimes a hospital. Personally, I never set foot in the Coyote and had no desire to. I considered myself a lover, not a fighter.

Happily however, the ASA troops had their own bar to call home. We called it the "Deuce" (or, sometimes, the "Douche"). It's official German name was the *Dusseldorfer Hof*, and it really did become a second home away from the barracks, for me and for countless other ASA soldiers, and not just during my brief stay in Germany, but for many years, throughout the sixties and beyond.

I'll get back to the Deuce. I'll have to, since it figured so prominently in much of our off-duty "playtime." First I should probably tell you something about our *first* home, our barracks on post at Rothwesten.

Rothwesten, by the way, lest there be any confusion, was the site where our field station and garrison was located. The base had been, I think, a German airfield during WWII. The village of Rothwesten often doesn't even show up on maps. It wasn't much more than a wide spot in the road just down the hill outside our main gate. There was a small *Gaststube* there where you could get room temperature beer and other drinks, and perhaps a couple of other small shops, but nothing much worth stopping for, at least from a GI point of view. Kassel and the Deuce was our usual destination whenever we had some time off.

184th Ops. Co. street at Rothwesten. Battalion HQ on left.

Our barracks was an old stone block building, massive and very permanent-looking, three stories high. The ground floor was kind of a half basement, as the building was built into a hillside that sloped down away into a wooded area behind it. The first two floors were filled with private rooms for the men. Well, not private exactly, most of the rooms were two- or three-man rooms, which, for enlisted scum like us, *seemed* private. I suppose living in a half-basement-level room doesn't sound any too classy, but those rooms were just as well-appointed and comfortable as those on the other floors, and had another special advantage. Where the back side of the barracks faced the woods, it was possible to climb out the window, let yourself down to the ground and disappear rather quickly into the trees. More on that "advantage" a bit later.

I never lived on either of the first two floors. Joe and I started out at "the top," and we stayed there. Upon our arrival at the unit, we were assigned to the third floor, up under the tile-topped roof of the barracks. It was a huge open bay area filled with double-tiered bunk beds and the standard government grey metal lockers, the same kind of accommodations we had endured during basic and AIT. It seemed we were experiencing a repeat performance of the billeting conditions as they had been at Sinop when we first arrived there. There was a temporary surplus of personnel at the 184th when we first arrived there in August. However, we'd been there

Our barracks at Rothwesten.

scarcely two months when the old-timers began to leave, to rotate back to the states for re-assignment or discharge, so the third floor bay slowly began to empty out, as the newer guys gradually started moving their gear downstairs into the more private rooms vacated by the departing personnel.

Those first several weeks of communal living were not all bad. When a bunch of guys are thrust together like that in one large crowded room, they can't help getting to know each other in a hurry, and some close bonds of friendship were forged in that cavernous echoing open bay arrangement, and some of them have lasted a lifetime. When Joe and I had stowed our stuff into lockers and staked out a pair of bunks, we almost immediately made friends with the two guys in the bunks next to ours, Tom Gordon and Larry Sanders. Both of these guys had already been in the unit for nearly a year, and had only one more year to go, just like Joe and me.

I quickly learned that Gordon was a Michigander like me. Well, maybe not just like me. He was from Hazel Park. Or was it Ferndale? Anyway, it was one of those Detroit suburbs, which, to my mind anyway, made him a big city boy to my "country mouse" type. He was also a "good Catholic boy" just like Joe and I were. And, like Joe (and Al and Norm, and most of my friends), he was short, probably no more than five six or seven. It seemed I was

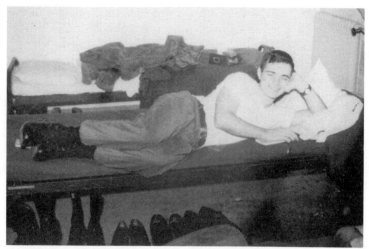

Tom lounging on his bunk and dreaming of his "Sweet Charlotte."

doomed to make short friends and always stick out above the crowd like a towering freak. Actually, I never really though much about this at the time. It was only recently, after I started writing this thing and dug out some old photos to include here, that I noticed this. Most of my closest friends were nearly a foot shorter than me. Hmmm. ... Could this *mean* something? ... *Nah!* Probably not. Who *cares?* We're *still* friends, forty years later.

Tom was short, but very muscular and solidly built. I can't remember if he was a weight lifter or body-builder like Norm and Al had been, but he had the physique. He also had the odor. I mean Gordon was a champion perspirer. ... Is that a word? *Perspire-or,* maybe? Or perhaps *sweater* would be better. No, that's something you wear. What in the hell *is* the correct term for someone who perspires easily and freely – *profusely?*

Let me see. I remember one time when I was a kid, my brother Bob and I were lying on the living room floor playing a board game or something and we'd both taken our shoes off, and I noted loudly and pointedly that Bob's feet really *stank.* My Grandma Bazzett, who was visiting and was sitting nearby knitting, scolded me gently, telling me it wasn't nice to say someone stank. Some people's feet just tended to perspire more than others', she explained. They couldn't help it.

So okay, Gordon. I'm not trying to make a big deal out of this or anything, but I'm mining my memories here, and one of the things I remember about you back then is that, as Grandma would so genteely have put it, you "tended to perspire more than others." I think the reason I remember this is because of a few times when we'd be horsing around in the barracks and you'd put me in a headlock, and by golly, I'd damn near *suffocate*! I mean, *whooo-EY,* it was strong!

But I know you're not like that any more. Nope. It's *Doc-tor* Gordon now, so I'd probably better show some respect.

Okay. ... Well, not just yet. We called Tom "Hurtin'" Gordon. *Hurtin'* was actually a very common slang term at the time, but I don't seem to hear it much anymore, so it's probably dropped completely out of fashion. What did it mean? Well, it sort of implied a lot of things, but mostly a kind of innate defectiveness. It could also imply a weakness of will or indecisiveness – a wishy-washiness, if you will. As a matter of fact, I think "Wishy-Washy" was one of Tom's alternate nicknames.

How else to describe my newfound friend – short, muscular, stocky, stinky – *oops*, I mean possessing an unfortunate tendency to perspire profusely. Dark wavy hair, with an extremely high forehead. You might even call it a "fivehead," it was so high.

Having had my fun, and having said all this, I have to tell you that I love Tom like a brother. He was – and is – a good friend. ... No, wait. There was this one *other* thing he used to do to me, in addition to those horrible headlocks. Because he *could* terrorize and torture me practically at will. He may have been nearly a foot shorter than me, but he was a lot stronger. This other thing he did would just drive me crazy. It was very painful, and, much to my dismay, would render me absolutely helpless, and always caused me to holler uncle. He would sidle casually up to me and engage me in idle chit-chat, and then, just when I was feeling comfortable and relaxed, he would snake a hand out and grab me by that small roll of fat just above my waist that even tall skinny guys have and *twist* it! *JEE-zuz Kee-RIST!* that hurt. It would raise me right up onto my tiptoes as I writhed about in pain trying to escape, but he'd just hang on, pinching and twisting and *hee-hee*-ing evilly until I would literally beg for mercy. Then he would let go and just laugh until he almost cried. You *SADist,* Gordon! How could I have called you my *friend*?! ... Ah, I dunno. But I did, and I still do.

Larry Sanders, Tom and Tim – "dim bulbs all."

Okay, enough about Ol' Hurtin' Gordon. What about my other new pal, Larry Sanders? Totally different story there – except that he was short too. But not thick and muscular like Tom was. No, Larry was just small. Maybe "wiry" would be a good way to describe him, And he was quiet. Larry never said a whole lot, but you could tell he was always considering things carefully behind those GI-issue horn-rimmed glasses he sometimes wore. Yup, I'm pretty sure Larry was definitely a "consider-er." He had a long angular face, often bearing a rather mournful expression, which could be deceiving, because he had a very sharp wit and a dry sense of humor that would surprise you. He sometimes reminded me a bit of Droopy. Remember that cartoon character, Droopy Dawg? That's the one. But his nickname was "Dusty," probably because it went with his last name. I'm not sure who hung the nickname on him. He already had it when I met him.

Larry and Tom had been together since Devens, much like Joe and I had, so they were pretty tight. They were a unit. In any case, within just a day or two of our arrival in the 184th, Joe and I had a couple new pals, valuable ones too, since they'd already been there a while and could show us around and even help ease us into our jobs and the new mission we had to learn at the Ops center.

We met a lot of other guys before long too. But I was telling you about our barracks, wasn't I? It's so easy to get sidetracked when you're trying to remember everything from so long ago. You have to hurry and put things down as you remember them, because ten minutes later you might forget them again. And it's very frustrating too, knowing how much you've already forgotten.

There were probably thirty-five or forty guys living in the open bay of the third floor when we moved in, and many of them were shift workers, who rotated from days to swings to mids. Conditions for this kind of a work schedule were certainly less than ideal, since there were always some guys going to bed when others were just getting up, sometimes just a few feet apart. And in a big cavernous room like that, with metal locker doors and foot locker lids clanging open and slamming shut, and shower shoes flip-flopping up and down the center aisle, and all the normal farting around (not to mention actual *farting*) that goes on in a barracks, it was a pure wonder that anyone ever actually got any sleep. But you did. The things and conditions you can adapt to are really quite amazing. When you're young it's somehow easier to make such adjustments and to adapt easily. I suppose our easy ability to sleep through noise and nearby activity was not unlike the way a baby or small child can fall asleep at a church service where a whole congregation is praying aloud and singing and constantly getting up and down, standing, sitting or kneeling. We adapted.

Probably the main reason we were able to adjust so easily – and this may be hard to believe, especially for older folks who tend to think of teenagers and kids as being rude, loud and annoying – was that everyone showed remarkable consideration for each other. Yes, all these "kids," many of them no more than nineteen or twenty, did their best to be quiet when other guys were trying to sleep. Since most of us *were* shift workers, this phenomenon could probably be at least partially explained by the oft-heard phrase, "Paybacks are hell." But I think there was more to it than just that. We were all in the same boat, so to speak, so we tried to look out for each other, to pull together, and to keep things on an even keel. (Hmmm ... an interesting choice of words. Makes us sound like shipwreck survivors trapped in a lifeboat together. Probably because I recently finished reading the historical bestseller, *In Harm's Way*, a book about the WWII sinking of the *USS Indianapolis*, which was, incidentally, written by another Reed City boy, Doug Stanton. Consciously or not, you sometimes become what you read, and

Tim Bazzett, Joe Capozzi and Bobby Grazioso (Joe's cousin visiting from Berlin) in open bay barracks. September, 1964.

Doug's book does tend to haunt you for quite a while once you've read it. There's your plug, Doug – like you *need* it.)

Probably within a couple weeks of my arrival at Rothwesten, I made a major purchase in downtown Kassel at a music store. I bought a portable stereo, a *Dual*. It had an automatic changer that could accommodate six LP's and twin detachable speakers, probably the nicest record player I had ever owned up to that time. Now I know this purchase may seem to be in direct contradiction to all I've just told you about how considerate we all were to each other about being quiet in the barracks and so on, but actually it's not. In our group of three dozen or so "roommates" in the bay, there were probably at least five or six other stereos and record players, and nearly everyone had a small transistor radio. Guys have to have their tunes after all, and music was always an important element, even in our enforced communal environment. The secret to our generally happy coexistence was, again, consideration. Very rarely were these stereos ever really cranked up. They were played softly and discreetly, usually after a quick look around the room to see who might be sleeping, or trying to. In short, we all did the best we could under difficult circumstances. In fact, I actually have some very pleasant memories of drifting off to sleep in that semi-darkened bay to the faint sounds of The Searchers' "Needles and

Pins" off to my left, and the bouncing beat of The Bobbettes' "Mister Lee" coming from further down the bay. Sound unlikely? Nope. *A-dap-TA-tion.*

I haven't mentioned the other, smaller, room on the top floor of our barracks, but I'd better, since it was there that Tom, Larry, Joe and I finally settled. It was at the top of the stairs, just off the landing. I call it a "smaller" room, but that's only in comparison to the huge cavernous open bay, which I've already described. This room, probably originally intended as a squad leaders' room, was probably fifteen feet wide and maybe thirty feet long, nearly rectangular, but with a small alcove, or "ell," behind the door that opened off the landing. At the opposite end of the room another door opened into the open bay quarters. When Joe and I first arrived, this room, reserved for the senior men, or old-timers, was full.

Although these guys were "senior," they were not unfriendly or unapproachable. Quite the contrary, they were all great guys. I think most of them were senior in rank to us, meaning Spec 4's or Spec 5's. Some of them were linguists and some were electronics technicians and repairmen. The linguists were commonly called "Monterey Marys" – Monterey because they got their training at the Defense Language Institute (DLI) in Monterey, California, and Mary because, um ... Hmm, why in the hell *were* they called *Marys* anyway? I'm not sure, but I think it was originally a pejorative term, meant to indicate that being a linguist, a job that often required a year or more of intense study in a difficult foreign language, was somehow sissy. The tag was probably hung on them by an 058 (*our* MOS) ditty-bopper. Most of us were just high school grads, if *that*, while many of the Marys were college men. If they weren't college grads, most of them had had *some* college, so were generally a few years older. *Our* job, as I've stated earlier, was basically a stimulus-response monkey-work kind of job. Being a linguist required some thought and careful cognitive reasoning, in addition to a good pair of ears.

In any case, I *liked* most of the Marys I met. As a matter of fact, Rich, the guy that got me laid in Ankara, was a Mary. He was also a helluva good basketball player, and exhibited absolutely no signs of sissification.

One of the residents of the smaller squad room was Spec 4 Jim Ross, who was, I believe, a linguist. I remember Jim mostly because he had such a sly, subtle, self-effacing sense of humor. He was an Indian, or, more correctly, I suppose, a "Native American." (Actually, back then I think Jim even called him*self* an Indian.) He was a member of the Wichita Falls tribe, from Oklahoma or Texas, I can't remember which. I was going to say that he rarely smiled, but now that I think about it, that's not strictly true. He did smile, but it was a slow and barely visible kind of transformation that you had to pay close attention to see. He had raven-black straight hair and a smooth, nearly hairless coffee-with-cream colored face. I remember coming into his room one day from the bay – his bed was the first one inside the door – and surprising him sitting on his bunk peering intently into a small shaving mirror he was holding in his left hand up close to his face. I couldn't see what he was holding in his right hand, so I idly inquired, "Whatcha doin', Jim?"

Swiveling his head slowly in my direction, he peered up at me, that slow slight smile beginning to form. Then, holding up his right hand, she showed me a small set of silver tweezers, and solemnly intoned, "Indian Schick," then turned back to his task, painstakingly searching out and then carefully plucking each individual whisker. The pickings were pretty slim, but now I knew why his face always looked so smooth.

Jim was a very quiet but interesting guy who seemed to regard the sometimes crazy shenanigans of us younger guys with a wondering but gentle tolerance. I can't remember him ever going out drinking with the guys. I think he once explained his abstinence by telling me, a slight twinkle in his eye, "Indians and firewater are a bad combination."

He didn't say, *Whiskey heap bad medicine,* but I was thinking it – all those cowboys and Indians movies.

One of the other guys in the squad room was a sleepy-eyed guy named Toby. I think he was an electronics repair tech. Toby was a pop music freak like me and we sometimes sat and talked music. He showed me around some downtown in Kassel and took me to all the best record stores, and we often traded albums. He was a Little Richard fan. I knew of Little Richard, but only from his song, "Long Tall Sally." Toby introduced me to some of his other gospel-influenced music. I especially remember a tune called "Joy, Joy, Joy," a rollicking R&B version of a spiritual that just made "your pants want to get up and dance," if I may borrow a much later musical phrase from Dr. Hook.

Toby suffered from an unusual affliction I had never encountered before. He had "granulated eyelids." When he woke up in the morning his red-rimmed eyes would be stuck shut by a gluey kind of substance that seeped from his tear ducts at night and formed into hard little crystals. Toby kept a small basin of water and a washcloth next to his bed so he could wet and soften this mess and gently wash his eyes open. I felt bad for him, but he just accepted it as just something rather unpleasant he'd been dealt and called it "no big thing."

One other fellow I remember as one of the original residents of the smaller room was Ron Cowens. I think maybe he was a Mary too. He was a voracious reader and we would often talk books. Ron always had a paperback with him, stuffed into a pocket of his field jacket or tucked into his shirt, no matter whether he was on or off duty, in gerbs or civvies. It was a habit I acquired myself later in life, part of the whole "so many books, so little time" lifestyle that serious readers embrace.

Cowens also liked to sleep, and was a very sound and heavy sleeper. One day a bunch of us decided to mess with his mind and carry his bunk, with him sleeping in it, out of the room and onto the landing at the top of the stairs. I think there were four of us involved in this plot, but I'll be damned if I can remember the other guys' names. One of them I can actually picture his face, but no name will come. He was this Polish guy, so I'll call him Kruski. He was notorious in the barracks for his wild craziness while under the influence of strong drink. One time he impulsively head-butted a window in our third-floor bay, shattering it and slashing open both his ears. We wrapped up his bleeding head in a towel and cardboarded up the broken window. The next morning he didn't remember any of it.

I can't remember why we thought moving Cowens and his bed would be so funny, but if Kruski was involved we'd probably been drinking. Stupid ideas seem much funnier when you're drunk. Anyway, we were all whispering and giggling and hee-hee-ing around in the semi-darkened room, getting ourselves situated. On a whispered signal we all gently picked up the sleeping Cowens, bunk and all, but had only gone a couple of steps when Kruski accidentally kicked one of the front legs of the bed and the metal bar that formed the head of the bunk folded abruptly in, crushing his fingers against the frame of the springs. Trying desperately to disengage his hand, Kruski dropped to his knees, face contorted in pain. But even in his distress he tried not to wake Cowens, as a half-whisper, half-scream of "*Mother-FUCK!*" escaped his lips. When I saw how his fingers had been crushed in the hinged bed-frame, I quickly jumped to his side and re-straightened the frame, releasing his fingers, but they were already beginning to swell and turn a ghastly purplish hue, and his middle finger was bent the wrong way at the middle knuckle. It was his right hand and that all-important *fuck-you* finger too. Kruski wouldn't be flipping the bird at anyone for a long time. The other two pranksters, Kruski's buddies, hustled him off down the stairs in search of first aid, leaving the still-snoring Cowens in his bunk, marooned in the middle of the room. I stood there next to it, feeling extremely stupid and vaguely guilty. Looking around, I saw Jim Ross sitting up in his bed looking over at me, shaking his head slowly in amazement, or perhaps disgust. Feeling really ridiculous by now, and perhaps a bit ashamed of myself, I slunk slowly out of the room.

Sometimes I wonder how I still remember these inconsequential things – really stupid shit, after all – some forty years later, and *why*. The gray matter of the brain – memory – apparently follows no logical scheme in the way it files and organizes things. All this crap is just piled up in there like an overstuffed hall closet, and every now and then you open the door a little and some of it falls out. I guess I shouldn't complain. Memories like these have become more important to me in recent years, and I think I'm begining to understand why some older people prefer to live in the past.

I know. I'm rambling. Where was I?

Oh yes, our living arrangements.

After a couple of months, perhaps less, the old-timers in the small room on the third floor had moved out, some of them downstairs to more private accommodations, and some of them back to the states to be discharged, their hitches completed. Tom, Dusty, Joe and I quickly collected our gear and moved into the vacated room. There were other guys in the bay who were probably more senior than us, but they apparently were waiting for the smaller rooms downstairs to become available. Our new room was

Tom Gordon and Joe Capozzi – "young" army buddies.

still a pretty big one, but it seemed a bit more exclusive to us than the enormous and impersonal squad bay where we'd been living, which was, in any case, quickly emptying out as more of the semi-private rooms became available through natural attrition and rotation of the short-timers.

There were just eight single bunks in our new room. I think Toby was still occupying a corner bunk in the ell behind the door, but he left to head back home just a couple weeks after we moved in, and his bunk stayed empty. The other three were soon filled by rather disparate types, but they soon blended smoothly into our small band.

One of these guys was Donnie Center. A bit on the shy side, Donnie claimed to be from Kentucky, and affected a kind of modified southern drawl. However, somehow we managed to find out (probably one of us peeked in his personnel file while pulling CQ) that his "home of record" was actually in Ohio. When we confronted Donnie with this misbegotten information, he hemmed and hawed and grumbled about how it "warn't none o' yer bidness," but then finally allowed as to how he *was* from Ohio, but it was *southern* Ohio, and *almost* in Kentucky, then continued to duck his head and mutter to himself about how "nosey" some folks could be. But his cover was blown, and we continued to torment poor Donnie

Donnie Center

about his Ohio origins every chance we got, not because it mattered to us, but because it mattered to *him* so much. And there were plenty of opportunities to needle him, because every time Donnie introduced himself to someone, he would inevitably add, in his deep-south Ohio drawl, "Ah'm from Kain-tucky."

If any of us were within hearing, particularly Gordon, we would immediately pounce, puncturing Donnie's tale of fake origins. Tom just loved to jump in and say, "Donnie, you *know* you're not from Kentucky. You're from *Ohio*."

Donnie would flush red and hunch his shoulders and glower at Gordon, muttering something down into his chest that sounded like, "Mrrpldrtygrblsnrkr."

Tom, and usually the rest of us too, would laugh until we were red in the face. Well, *Tom* would get red in the face. He *always* grew red-faced while enjoying a good laugh, particularly at someone else's expense.

In spite of all this good-natured ribbing and grumbling, we all got along. Donnie hung out with us and went into town with us often, and generally grew accustomed to our barbed sarcasm and sometimes cruel humor. We were that way with everyone, but particularly so within our own small group. It was a kind of instinctive way of keeping anyone from feeling too self-important or getting too cocky.

Because Donnie wanted so badly to be a southerner, he gravitated naturally towards things southern, country or hillbilly in nature. I think he may have even had some cowboy boots and a Stetson hat he wore on occasion. He also bought himself a pretty nice five-string banjo that he noodled around on, trying to teach himself to play (none too successfully, if I remember correctly). But he did enjoy country music. He had a small record player and a limited collection of records, mostly country stuff. I got my first taste of Bluegrass music listening to Donnie's stuff, most notably Bill Monroe and his Bluegrass Boys. The first time I heard "Blue Moon of Kentucky" (one of Donnie's favorites, naturally), delivered in Monroe's trademark high-lonesome nasal twang, I'm sure I winced. It sounded like the most appalling caterwauling noise I had ever heard. All the other guys in the room shared my reaction, so Donnie learned to play his Bill Monroe records very softly, or else when we were out. (It wasn't until many years later that I finally came to appreciate some of Monroe's music, especially his mandolin picking.) However, we did learn to enjoy a few of Donnie's country artists, especially Hank Snow and what came to be his signature song, "I've Been Everywhere," a tune we could all soon sing along with. But we were quick to remind poor Donnie that Snow wasn't a southerner. Why, he wasn't even an *American.* He was a *Canadian*, for cripesakes, from *Nova Scotia*! Donnie responded with more characteristic muttering into his shirt front.

I know it sounds like we tormented Donnie all the time, but we didn't really. We had lots of good times together. Unfortunately, even when Donnie laughed, it was a source of more mirth for us. His laugh, like his muttering and grumbling, was a kind of muffled, buttoned-down, nearly voiceless sound, also directed down into his shirt collar. Poor Donnie just couldn't seem to cut loose, even when he was laughing. It was such a strange and unusual sound it made the rest of us laugh even harder. Tom used to try to reproduce the sound of Donnie's laugh, and it always came out sounding like *Myurp, myurp, myurp.* This "myurp-myurp" noise quickly caught on in our group and became a kind of subtle catch phrase used to indicate mirth or humor. We all used it. (One more otherwise useless object tumbles from the barely-cracked door of my closet of memories.)

247

Donnie, I hope you knew that underneath all that ribbing, we all loved you and really enjoyed your company. I have only fond memories of the time we spent together.

Leroy Thomas moved into the squad room about the same time we did, or maybe he even beat us in by a day or two. He'd staked out the bunk across from Toby, under a window in the small ell behind the door from the landing. Joe and I hadn't known him before then, but I think Tom and Dusty probably had. Leroy was one of a very small number of black soldiers in the 184th. He was an 058 like the rest of us, which in itself made him even more unique. I'm not sure why, but there just weren't many blacks in the ASA in the early sixties, a time when negro was still a socially acceptable term. Even Leroy's first name was a novelty to me. I think the only time I'd ever heard that name, in my limited experience, was on a radio comedy show (later a TV show too) called *The Great Gildersleeve*. On that show the title character would often call or admonish a teenage boy named Leroy with a special trademark intonation that all the show's listeners came to recognize and learned to imitate. It was kind of a high- to low-pitched drawn-out comical sound – *LEEE-roy!* Hard to explain, really, but if you remember the show then you know exactly what I'm talking about and can probably even still do it yourself. Beyond that association, I also found out some years later that the literal meaning of Leroy is "the king" – an association our friend Leroy probably knew about and preferred.

Leroy never hung out with us much during our breaks. We all got along okay, but he had his own friends, who were from other units, and yes, they were black too. Was there an element of racism or unspoken segregation at work here? I don't think so, at least not on a conscious level. I think it had more to do with establishing and maintaining a certain *comfort* level, both on our part and on the part of Leroy and his friends. Kind of a de facto "birds of a feather" thing perhaps. Leroy had one close buddy who used to come to the room and hang out with him occasionally, and they would go out together too. His friend's name was Jim Barber. They sometimes would talk music with us. I think Barber may have been a jazz afficianado, and seemed to be a very intelligent kind of guy, an intellectual even. Leroy, while he knew his Miles and Trane, was also a Motown fan, and, being from Philadelphia, appreciated the Philly sound too.

Leroy Thomas

The Motown sound was just getting into its groove by the early sixties. The Supremes' first album spawned at least three or four top ten singles, something that rarely happened with albums back then, but the material was all so good and the beat so infectious that you couldn't help loving it. "Where Did Our Love Go" and "Baby Love" were probably two of the most played platters on the jukebox at the Deuce, and of course I had to buy the album, so it was often playing in our room too. It's still one of my all-time favorite LP's.

The Four Tops were a big act then too, and to this day I can't listen to their "I Can't Help Myself" (aka "Sugar Pie Honey Bunch") without remembering Leroy Thomas. I had bought the 45 at the PX when it was brand new, and, from the very first time we played it, we just had to get up and *dance.* Tom and Joe and I were probably doing our modified white boy "slop" step to the tune. Leroy was sitting on his bunk smiling and watching us and finally I guess he just couldn't stand it any more. He got up and joined us, only the step *he* was doing was so much *better – way cooler.* It was so cool we just all gradually stopped and watched him for a moment, then slowly started over, trying to do this thing that Leroy was doing. He was up on his toes and his feet were swiveling from side to side each time they came down, all in perfect time with that big bass backbeat sound. Leroy laughed his big raspy Heathcliffe

Huxtable laugh, but kept encouraging us until we had gotten it *most*ly right, then showed us how to add that all-important "extra touch," by putting loose-fisted hands into your pockets and subtly hoisting the crotch of your pants, thus emphasizing the bulge of your "package."

"Give the ladies a little *pre*-view," he'd say, and then he'd laugh that big laugh again, and we couldn't help joining him.

I can still do that "Mashed Potatoes" swivel step, but only for a minute or so. Otherwise I run the risk of breaking all the small bones in the tops of my feet. I know this because I *did* break a small metatarsal or two several years ago while showing off at a party, and I paid for it, limping around for months afterward. And my wife rolls her eyes and runs for cover whenever she sees my fists slipping into my pockets and my trousers rising, thinking – often out loud – *That is* so *gross! Don't* do *that!*

Hey, it is *not!* My classic rendition of the mashed potatoes is often the hit of the evening, and I have my old pal, Leroy Thomas, to thank for it. Where are you, Leroy? Can you still dance like that?

The last member to join our merry band of pranksters was Bill Wilkes. Bill was a Texan, and, like most Texans, he was *Proud-UVit.* He had a kind of subtle swagger about him. Well, maybe not so subtle. He *was* a Texan, after all. He had dark curly hair and angular features that seemed to be crinkled in a perpetual squint, perhaps in an attempt to emulate that "cowboy look" made famous by John Wayne. Or maybe he just squinted because his face was so often wreathed in the smoke from an ever-present cigarette. In any case, Bill was pretty good at playing the rugged western type. He even had the vocabulary and vernacular down, and his contributions to conversations often consisted of terse *Yup*s, *Nope*s and *Mebbe*s.

Initially, Wilkes was the only one in our group who owned a car, making him an indispensable compadre. His car was a non-descript brown VW Beetle, probably already four or five years old, but reasonably reliable. Since Bill was always unfailingly generous about providing transportation for all of us, the car was usually filled to capacity, which was five – a tight fit, but we got where we were going.

There are a couple of interesting stories to tell about Bill's Bug. One has to do with the "convenience" of a VW. I can't

Bill Wilkes

remember if I had ever even ridden in a Volkswagen before I got to Germany. VW's were pretty rare in western Michigan in the fifties, so probably I hadn't. Probably the smallest car I'd ever ridden in prior to this was Mike Campbell's two-seater T-bird back at Fort Devens. In any case, getting myself into a VW and figuring out which way to fold my legs and when and where to duck my head at first presented me with a problem, with my long six foot five frame, but I soon learned to make the necessary adjustments. A full complement of passengers in Bill's Beetle usually consisted of Bill behind the wheel, of course, me riding shotgun (I took up too much room in the back seat, no matter how I folded myself up), and, in back, Tom and Joe at the windows, and poor Dusty squeezed into the middle, since he was the smallest. During our tour there, this crew made countless runs into Kassel from the base (or, as Ol' Lonesome George Gobel might have said, *Minny, minny trips*).

But I said I had a couple of stories. First a short one about how sometimes it can be handy to have a VW. One night the five of us had been drinking at the small gasthaus in the tiny village of Rothwesten not far from base. This in itself was quite unusual since, as I've already mentioned, Rothwesten was barely a town at all, and we usually went into Kassel to the Deuce to get blitzed. I don't remember how or why we ended up at this teeny bar, but we did, and, after closing the place up around 1 AM, we all trooped happily (read: *loaded*) outside to get in the car and head back to base. After we'd all carefully crammed ourselves into the car, Bill started it up and started to pull out onto the road, but felt the steering pulling sharply to the right. (Bill must have been a little more sober than the rest of us, or he might not have noticed this.) So he stopped the car and got out and walked around the front of it, looked down and discovered his right front tire was flat. Muttering a very Texan-ish, *Well, Shee-it*, he told the rest of us we'd have to get out while he changed the tire, so we all oozed happily back out both doors in that loose fluid style that inebriated soldiers have, to stand around and watch (something else soldiers are good at – a habit born of many work details involving, say, eight men to do a job which requires only one or two).

Well, apparently this was the first time Bill had ever had occasion to change a tire since he'd bought the Bug, because once he'd raised the the front lid and wrestled the spare out of its well, after much banging around and searching and muffled cursing as he bent himself into the dark boot, he finally straightened up and announced, "They ain't no fuckin' jack in here."

Being the resourceful and ingenious bunch that we were, we all stood there staring stupidly back at him, belching and farting and wishing we could go to bed, until, finally, Wilkes suggested that we all simply lift the car up and hold it while he changed the tire. We all immediately agreed that this was a *great* idea, a *wun-nerful* idea, and spent the next couple of minutes milling around the front of the car trying to get situated to find a handhold, bumping into each other and falling down and laughing. Finally we managed to arrange ourselves fore and aft of the Bug's broken foot, with Tom and Joe at the critical lifting points, and Dusty and me on the outside edges (we were obviously the weaker links), and, on the count of three, we easily lifted the little car up, at first with so much drunken enthusiasm that we nearly turned the car on its side. Muttering and *myurp*ing among ourselves, we lowered the vehicle back down to a working level, where Bill quickly pulled off the flat and replaced it with the spare, grimacing and grunting as he tightened down the lug nuts, and also complaining vociferously, "Kee-*RIST!* Who the fuck is cuttin' those rancid *farts?*"

No one owned up to it, but we were all *myurp*ing and shaking with suppressed mirth, I'm not sure *why,* except sometimes when you're schnockered, *every*thing seems funny, and all that room-temperature beer we'd consumed was now taking its revenge, and poor Bill, working as fast as he could, was trapped right in the flight path of all that flatulence. Apparently it was awful enough to nearly bring tears to his eyes. Tightening down the last nut, Bill threw down the tire iron, rose quickly to his feet, and walked several feet away, fanning the air in front of his face with both hands. "Woo-*EE*, you fuckers stink!"

Dropping the car with a muffled *crump*, we all collapsed in a gale of helpless laughter, still pooting and tooting softly, then pulled open the doors and proceeded to fold ourselves back inside. Back behind the wheel, Bill cranked it up and we continued on our redolent merry way back home to the barracks, problem solved, tire changed, no jack necessary – just four drunken gas-powered soldiers. See? Driving a Beetle *can* be convenient sometimes.

But there are other times when maybe it's *not* so convenient. And this story needs a bit more background, I'm afraid, so bear with me, please.

The army had this thing, this *attitude*, where they wanted us to be *soldiers*. I mean they expected us to do really soldierly, military kinds of stuff every now and then. I suppose it was great fun and good training for the officers and career-type NCO's, but for the rank-and-file guys like us who had joined the army to avoid going to work or to college and just wanted to go drinking and have a good time and be left alone, it was really annoying, and sometimes a downright pain in the ass. Don't get me wrong. We didn't mind doing our *jobs*, which in our case was sitting at a rack with a radio and a mill, headsets on, catching dits and dahs to beat the band. As a matter of fact, we took great pride in doing that. We knew it was important to the security of our nation and we worked damn hard at it, often to the actual detriment of our health and well-being. There are a lot of former 058's out there even now, forty years later, who are living with at least a partial hearing loss, some of them deaf in one ear or the other – a direct result of too many hours spent at their jobs, ears blasted by signals, noise, static and interference. I've personally suffered from tinitus for over forty years, and the ringing gets a little more insistent with each passing year.

But it wasn't doing our jobs that we objected to. No, it was that *other* stuff, the *army* kind of stuff, the kind of stuff we referred to as *Mickey-Mouse* or *chicken-shit.*

Inspections were one example. (I'm digressing here, I know, but I'll get back around to where I was going eventually. It's all part of my "new school conversational" style.) Every now and then our commanding officer at the company or battalion level would get a wild hair up his ass about the "filthy conditions" of our barracks and living area. My *ass!* We never allowed our rooms to get "filthy." Homey, perhaps. Comfortable, maybe, but never 'filthy." In any case, every few months the CO would call for a barracks inspection.

What did this mean? Well, I'll tell you. It meant that we had to give up a few hours of our precious free time, our off-duty time. (Although, technically speaking, and the cadre were always quck to remind us of this fact, a soldier is *always* on duty, 24/7, as we say today. So those hours we could have spent in an enjoyable manner, out drinking and carousing, or lying around on our unmade bunks, reading, listening to music, or perhaps just picking our noses and scratching our balls, had to be spent instead in a frenzy of preparations for *the in-SPEC-tion.*

It wasn't like this was anything *new* to us. Nope, it was the same old shit we'd been trained to do way back in BCT, and that we'd been subjected to periodically throughout AIT at Devens. But we figured we should be *past* all that horse manure by now. We *knew* how to shine our boots (although perhaps we didn't actually *do* it all that often anymore). We *knew* how to sweep and mop and wax the floors in our rooms (although it *did* seem a waste of time since they just got dirty again). And we *knew* how to arrange our lockers in a precise and military manner, but when you did that there was no place to keep all your *good* stuff, like your stereo and records, your radio, your stash of food (bread, crackers, peanut butter and jelly, cookies and snacks), your extra civvies, your case of empty German beer bottles (remember those ceramic pop-tops with the wire clamps on them?), and all the other important stuff you surrounded yourself with to make your otherwise stark quarters feel like home.

Yes, we *knew* what we had to do, but we were most reluctant to do it. We grumbled and muttered while we cleaned out our lockers, then hung all our uniforms facing in the same direction in our wall lockers, all in the precise by-the-book order: overcoat, raincoat, dress greens, khakis, fatigues and civvies, sleeves all lined up in a neat row, creases carefully aligned. (We learned early to only bother ironing the sleeve that faced out. The side of the uniform that faced into the locker could be – and often was – a puckered mass of wrinkles. Outward appearance was all.) We dutifully collected all of our aforementioned "good stuff" and carried it down three flights of stairs and outside to stash in someone's car until the inspection was over (after which we'd go back outside to get it all and bring it back up all those stairs and put it back). We shined our brass and spit-shined our shoes and boots. We carefully placed our spare pair of combat boots, our low-quarter dress shoes, our civilian shoes (if we had any), and our flip-flops all in a neat row under the ends of our bunks, lining up all the toes with a ruler or straight-edge. We opened our foot lockers to display our army issue white boxers and tee-shirts, black or olive-drab colored socks, all carefully rolled up in a most precise military manner. (Why not? We never *wore* these items anymore. We kept them purely for show.) The top tray of the foot locker displayed a safety razor and blades, toothbrush and tooth powder, all carefully arranged on a white (well, maybe yellowing a bit from age and disuse) towel. And yes, I did say tooth *powder.* And you *know* nobody used *that.* It too, like that particular razor and blades, was purely for show. And on and on, with all that minute SOP crap required for inspections.

We would gently round up all the little dust bunnies that lived under our bunks and in all the corners and dispose of them. We would mop the floors, then put down wax and buff the floors to a high shine and mince around in our socks so as not to mar the gloss. And these were *cement* floors, painted with a standard GI battleship gray enamel.

After spending hours the night before the scheduled inspection doing all this cleaning and spiffing up, we would often wait for *hours* for the CO's inspection party to arrive. Since our room was on the top floor of the last barracks on the battalion street, it was often the last one inspected. If it were a 9 AM inspection, it was often 11 or later by the time the inspectors got around to us. We would impatiently stand by in our freshly laundered or cleaned and pressed uniform of the day, greens, khakis or gerbs, wishing it would just be *over,* so we could bring all our stuff back in from the cars, jump in our civvies and head for the Deuce to do some serious drinking and *forget* all this shit. We wanted to go *play, dammit!*

The actual inspection itself was always pretty anti-climactic. Our CO, Major Foster, might run a hand along the top of a wall locker and find a bit of dust, which the First Sergeant or some other accompanying lackey would dutifully note on a clipboard alongside the name of the locker's owner – *Sanders: dust on wall locker.* (Well, bloody *hell!* Larry couldn't *reach* the top of his locker! And his nickname *was* Dusty.)

Or the Major might ask, "Capozzi, where is your other pair of boots?"

"At the shoe repair shop, sir, getting new heels." (They were *not.* They were stashed in Wilkes's VW because they needed shining.)

Nevertheless, the discrepancy was duly noted on the clipboard, where, after the inspection was over, all the "gigs" could be toted up for each man, each room, each trick or platoon, *et cetera, et cetera, et* cet*era.*

"Specialist Bazzett, when was the last time you got a haircut?"

"I can't remember, sir."

"I believe *that. Get* one!"

"Yessir." (On the clipboard.)

"Private Wilkes, what is that brown spot on your can of tooth powder?"

Still at attention, but ducking his head slightly to look, Bill peered into his foot locker tray at the offending item, then snapped back to attention. "It looks lahk rust, sir."

"Don't you brush your teeth, Private Wilkes?"

"Yessir, but Ah use toothpaste, sir." (Well, of *course* he used paste. *No* one actually *used* that ridiculous antiquated fucking tooth *powder.* It was for *show.*)

"Better get a new tooth powder, Wilkes."

"Yessir." (Clipboard.)

And on and on. You *see? Chic-ken-fucking-SHIT!*

Here's another example of how the army insisted we be "soldiers." Everyone was issued a weapon upon his assignment to the unit. The M-1, the rifle I had (barely) qualified with and which had busted my balls throughout basic training was by this time officially relegated to the status of antique, at least as far as the

M-14

active-duty army was concerned. It had been replaced by the M-14, a weapon nearly as large and cumbersome as the M-1, but not quite as heavy, since some parts were made of high-impact plastic. I never did actually fire an M-14. Yes, "officially" I had an M-14 assigned to me the whole year I was stationed at Rothwesten, and "officially" I cleaned and inspected the weapon once a month. The fact of the matter was the only time I ever *saw* the rifle was once or twice when we were subjected to a full field gear and equipment inspection. On those rare occasions we went to the battalion arms room and signed out our M-14's to take back to the barracks to put on display on our bunks for the inspection. Supposedly our weapons *were* cleaned and inspected on a monthly basis, but not by us. Instead we each paid a small monthly fee to some anonymous soul who worked in the armory and had nothing better to do than sit and clean and oil rifles all day. And we were all fine with this "unofficial" arrangement. More drinking time for us.

On those rare occasions when we did draw our weapons for inspection purposes, it was such a novelty for us that everyone got out their cameras and snapped photos of each other posing with their rifles in various fierce or foolish ways. We were *bad mo-fo's,* man! We were "the ultimate weapon" personified. Often these poses violated all rules of safety, with someone inevitably pointing his weapon at someone else's head. Luckily, we were never issued any ammunition. Sometimes I wondered if the army high command had sort of tacitly agreed that ASA personnel should never be trusted with live ammo. If so, good thinking, guys.

At any rate, in this particular case, the army's attempt to keep us feeling like soldiers failed miserably because of this unofficial system of paying off the armorer to do our monthly weapons maintenance. Whether he actually *did* what he was paid to do is another question. At the time we couldn't have cared less. Most un-soldierly, I know, but this *was* the ASA.

* * * * *

Rear: Fred Powers, Tom Gordon, Unknown, Joe Capozzi, Bill Wilkes
Front: Tim Bazzett

"The Ultimate Weapon," full field gear – armed and dangerous
Left to right:
Fred Powers, Tom Gordon, Tim Bazzett, Joe Capozzi, Bill Wilkes

Tom Gordon

Tom Gordon
and Leroy Thomas

Joe Capozzi

259

Tim Bazzett

*Bill Wilkes,
Joe Capozzi,
Tim Bazzett,
Tom Gordon
and Leroy Thomas*

*Leroy Thomas,
Bill Wilkes,
and Tom Gordon*

Motor pool duty was yet another military thing we were saddled with on a regular basis. And for some mysterious reason we always pulled this detail after coming off a mid shift. Not a very good idea, because no one *ever* got enough sleep while working mids. I think I used to average four or five hours of sleep a day when I was on mids, simply because it was very hard to sleep during the daytime while other shifts and "day weenies" (straight day workers) went on about their business all around you, sometimes rather noisily.

Here's how motor pool duty worked. Instead of being trucked back to our barracks from the Ops center, we were dropped off at the entrance to the motor pool. Once there, the sergeant in charge assigned vehicles to pairs of us, giving us a plate or tag number to find it. We would trudge wearily up and down the seemingly endless rows of half-tons, three-quarter tons, deuce-and-a-halfs, trailers and generators, and countless other machines, peering at the license plates in the dim early-morning light, until we found the victim vehicle of the day.

I call it a "victim" because I always felt faintly sorry for the truck that depended on *me* for its maintenance. (I should probably explain here that I'm one of those mechanically clueless guys who, when the *check engine* light comes on on the dashboard, dutifully pops the hood and looks under it and says to himself, *Yup, there's the engine all right. Still there. Yup, yup.* You get the idea.) For that is what we were expected to do during the hour or two we spent milling about at the motor pool – "perform first echelon maintenance as needed." We were supposed to check the oil and all other fluid levels – for brakes, batteries, radiator, etc. – and top them off, again, "as needed." Tire pressure and general vehicle condition was also to be checked, among other things. I can't remember if we were actually given a maintenance check list of any kind to follow, but I think it was more of a hit or miss system on our part.

Usually, when we arrived at the vehicle park it was still too dark to see much, which was probably why we always had to stick around at least a couple hours. The first hour it was too dark to find a hoodlatch or dipstick or see much of anything, and flashlights were almost never available. We were all tired and resentful and wanted to go to bed. So what actually happened, once we located our assigned vehicle, usually a deuce and a half, since they were the most plentiful, was we would pop the hood and prop it open, then look for a comfortable place to sit or lie down until it was time to leave. In the winter we would crawl into the cab to take shelter from the wind and cold. In the milder seasons, one or both of us might lie down underneath the truck. I *know*; it's not a very bright thing to do, but if you positioned yourself in a strategic position, it could appear that you were checking something or inspecting the undercarriage. In any case, one of us usually stood lookout while the other person rested or snoozed.

I suppose I should feel guilty telling you all this, but I can't remember feeling guilty about it at the time, and it was a very long time ago, so I can't seem to work up a guilty feeling now. Sorry. I think we all sort of felt the same way about those trucks that we did about about that plane we were so casually ordered to inspect and service during our stopover in Samsun, back in Turkey. What the hell did *we* know about *planes* – and now *trucks?* We had been trained – at no small expense, I might add – to be manual Morse intercept operators, *not* grease monkeys. Let the motor pool guys keep the trucks running, dammit! That was what *they* were trained for! In this way we managed to justify, or at least rationalize to ourselves, our gross dereliction of duty. And be*sides* (we would always think), we had just worked a full shift at our *real* jobs. We should be able to go home and go to bed!

Technically though, we were wrong. The truth was we *needed* to keep those trucks in good operating condition, and we needed to know how to use them. Here's why. periodically our units would be put on alert status. During these times we would "deploy to the field" to do our jobs – theoretically. In actuality there was always a regular work schedule continuing to support the mission at the Ops building while the other tricks loaded up into the mobile units at the motor pool, started up the trucks (with lots of crossed fingers that they *would* start after sitting idle for so long with only slipshod maintenance performed), and formed a convoy. We didn't go far – sometimes only off into a field somewhere else on post where we would "circle up the wagons," so to speak, and set up for field operations – or try to.

I should probably first explain here that many of the aforementioned trucks, particularly the big deuce and a halfs, carried big boxes in their beds which were essentially mobile communications centers, equipped with radios and racks of other electronic equipment – supposedly everything we needed to do our jobs under field conditions. (I think some of these mobile units were called *GLICKs* or *GLI/Cs,* but I'll be damned if I can remember what the acronymn meant.) Other support vehicles in our convoy carried auxiliary comms gear and other field supplies.

Once we arrived at our designated deployment area we had to set up. We would position our comms vans in convenient clusters and unroll tarpaulin-topped shelter areas between the two or three vehicles. We would unload the support trucks and roll out long coils of barbed concertina wire to form a protective perimeter around our campsite. This was delicate work requiring gloves and a great deal of patience. After laying two rows of concertina wire side by side, we would then lay a third row on top, forming a near impenetrable prickly perimeter fence. This job usually left you with several new jagged tears in your clothing no matter how careful you were. Then portable antennae components had to be assembled, erected and tied down with guy wires and stakes. Mobile generators had to be wheeled into position and fired up. Water supplies (hanging Lister bags) and field rations were provided and put in place. I can't remember if we had to dig slit trenches for latrines or if some sort of porta-potties were trucked in, but there must have been *some* place to take a shit. We strung what seemed like miles of commo wire to link up the crank-style field telephones between the command vehicles.

Once everything was set up, connected, and powered up, we would attempt to go to work and do our jobs. "Attempt" is the operative word here, because inevitably things would go wrong. Radios would malfunction, or fail to function at all, due to dampness, cold or general neglect. Antennae connections would have to be re-routed or whole antennae fields moved for better reception, all requiring labor-intensive jerry-rigging, cooperation and experimentation. And lots of yelling back and forth between the vans and the guys rigging the antennae. Imagine a very early and primitive version of those cell phone commercials with the guy walking around with the phone saying, *Can you hear me now?* and you'll get the idea of what went on, only there was no phone, but lots of hollering. It's a good thing we weren't simulating a covert or clandestine operation.

The thing that I remember most about all this was the cramped operating space inside the radio vans. The quarters were extremely close. I think there may have been four operator positions inside one of these "boxes," with all the same essential equipment that we had at our regular work place in the Ops building. But it was all squeezed together into a tiny space in such a way that you felt like an adult at parents' night at school, smushed into a fourth-grader's desk. It was do-able for a normal-sized person, and especially so for people like Joe, Tom and Dusty, who were all, as I've said, barely five and a half feet tall. But for someone like me, with my long legs, it was practically impossible. Even if I could manage to somehow fold myself into the small chair and wedge my knees under the tiny table holding the mill, it was such a cramped claustrophobic feeling, surrounded by the equipment racks and confining walls and low ceiling of the van (I could never stand upright inside the van, as the ceiling was oly about six feet high), that my whole being screamed for release. I felt like a giraffe in a doghouse. Consequently, I spent very little time actually working at a pos. I just couldn't stand it. I invented every possible reason to get out and be somewhere else, *any*where but inside that tiny crowded box. Luckily for me, the other guys understood. They could see my discomfort from the obviously "poor fit" of the van, and they covered for me and sent me on errands, or found other things for me to do.

Here I should probably confess that I *think* I deployed to the field on alert only *once* during my entire year at Rothwesten. But it was enough for me, and probably for the other guys in my group too. These alerts rarely lasted more than forty-eight hours, but the whole deployment thing was such a horrible ordeal and pain in the ass, filled with constant unavoidable foul-ups, vehicle breakdowns, equipment failures and personal discomfort that, once we had experienced it, we would go to almost any lengths to avoid participating again.

Which brings me back around, finally, to where I started to say (go back several pages – you'll find it) that sometimes having a VW Beetle *isn't* so convenient. Well, it is, but it isn't.

Here's what happened. Our trick was on break one morning. I think we'd all been out drinking at the Deuce the night before (a

Clockwise from bottom:
Tom Gordon, Larry Sanders, unknown, Donnie Center, Tim Bazzett

pretty safe guess), so even though it was already 10:00 or so, we were still lying and sitting around in our room in our skivvies or half-dressed, yawning and farting and scratching and wondering what what in the hell had *died* inside our mouths while we were sleeping. Suddenly the siren signalling a general alert began to wail.

It had been a few months or more since we'd been deployed to the field on an alert, but we still remembered how much we'd all hated it and *God-DAMmit!* this was our first day of *break!* They couldn't *do* this to us! Muttering and cursing, we scrambled into our clothes – our *civilian* clothes – and, stuffing things hurriedly and randomly into a laundry bag, we quickly vacated our top floor room and thundered down the stairs to the ground level floor of the barracks. There were five of us making our escape: Tom, Joe, Dusty, myself, and, of course, Bill, our "getaway driver."

Running to the far end of the first floor hallway, we unceremoniously let ourselves into the last room on the left, Jim "Jeeter" Lester's room, I think it was. Lester was one of the most accomplished drinkers in our company, and also one of the best 058's too. But on this particular day Jeeter and his roommate were working days, which meant they would be staying at work in the Ops building and wouldn't be required to deploy to the field. The reason we were going into his room was that the window there

Mess Hall (ground floor) with path leading down the hill, through the trees from the barracks.

opened into the woods behind the barracks. It was only about a four-foot drop down to the ground once we climbed through this window, pushing and shoving and hurrying each other along. The forest floor and the underbrush was still sodden and wet from the early morning rain that occurred nearly every morning that spring. Glancing nervously over our shoulders like escaping convicts, we hurried in a huddle along the path through the dripping trees, finally emerging at the stone steps that led down to the parking lot by the mess hall, where Wilkes had, fortunately, parked his VW the night before. Like a well-choreographed troop of circus clowns, we quickly clambered into our customary configuration in the car, with Tom, Joe and Dusty in the back, me riding shotgun and Bill behind the wheel. Trying our best to look casual and business-as-usual, we cruised carefully down the main street of the base and out the front gate past the MP guard who was busy waving a delivery truck through going the other way. Once around the bend and heading through Rothwesten village, we all heaved a collective sigh of relief. We were *free!* We had made good our escape!

However, soon after we experienced this initial elation and rush of relief, we began to wonder, at first privately, and then collectively and aloud, *What the fuck do we do now?* It was day one of our two-day break. What if the alert lasted a full forty-eight hours, or even *longer?* Where would we *go* and what would we *do* for two days if we couldn't go back to our room? Already we were missing our comfy cluttered top-floor aerie, with its lumpy unmade bunks, homey redolent air of damp musty towels and soiled socks, and the silent skittering dust bunnies that followed us around in a friendly fashion as we went out the door or up and down the stairs to the latrine. The sounding of that siren had pretty much destroyed any sense of peace or control we might have been feeling that morning. We had "escaped," true, but now we were adrift, homeless. As we drove slowly west from the base we pondered our situation. Luckily we all had our break passes in our possession, important documents from a legal or regulations standpoint, but pretty useless when bedtime came around if we couldn't go back to our room without being discovered. Nope. It was pretty clear to all of us that if we wanted to avoid participating in the deployment then we'd have to find somewhere else to sleep that night, and maybe the next one too.

Glumly we continued on into Kassel, where we repaired to the cafeteria at the *Hauptbahnhof* and drowned our sorrows in bowls of delicious oxtail soup, one of the less pricey items on the menu. While we were eating, we opened our wallets and and got out all our Deutschemarks and odd pfennigs of change and counted them all up, considering our collective solvency. It wasn't much. Once

Inside Hauptbahnhof in Kassel.

Looking down the Steppenstrasse in Kassel.

we paid for our lunches and then had our requisite ration of beer at the Deuce that night, there certainly wouldn't be enough money to pay for a room for five people at a local hotel. And of course we couldn't forego the beer. Beer was required. Beer was necessary. Beer was essential. Were we not men?

So we spent the afternoon roaming downtown Kassel, flipping listlessly through record albums at music stores off the Steppenstrasse, knowing full well that we couldn't really buy anything. That evening we spent at the Deuce, which was nearly empty, since most of its regular patrons were either working or else deployed to the field, on alert. Our "escape" from this fate was beginning to leave a rather bitter taste in our mouths as we nursed our strictly rationed beers through the long evening. The Deuce's proprietress, Ilse, must have felt sorry for us, because she fed some coins into the jukebox for us. Unfortunately, one of the tunes we punched in was Bobby Bare's "500 Miles (Away from Home)," which made us feel even worse.

Finally we had to get out. Grumbling and muttering about the "fuckin' army" and "why couldn't they just leave us alone," we climbed back into Wilkes's car and headed north up along the River Weser until Bill found a dirt trail somewhere near Hahn-Munden that led down to an open area along the river bank that may or may not have been a campground. Wasn't the Weser the river that swallowed up all those rats in the story of the Pied Piper of Hamelin? I think it was. Is that relevant here? Probably not, except perhaps in the sense that we were starting to feel rather vermin-like in our unwashed state and self-imposed homelessness.

It was damp and chilly there on the riverbank, and very dark. First we stood in a ragged row along the river, relieving ourselves into the current. Then, re-arranging ourselves as best we could within the cramped confines of the Beetle, we tried to get comfortable, but we remained pretty much jammed up against each other or the hard parts of the car's interior no matter which way we turned or contorted ourselves. It was probably even worse for the three guys in the back seat, and finally Dusty, being the smallest, climbed over the back of the seat and curled himself into a semi-fetal position in the tiny luggage space beneath the oval-shaped back window. He didn't complain, but the pained expression on his long mournful face set Gordon off into a red-faced laughing jag, which quickly spread to the rest of us, as we realized the complete ridiculousness of our situation.

I can't remember if any of us actually slept that night. But we must have dozed off towards dawn, because we were suddenly rudely awakened by a flashlight being shined into the car and a harsh German voice telling us to *Raus!* It was the River Police, who had spied our suspicious-looking group as they cruised by and had come ashore to investigate.

We awkwardly unfolded ourselves and crawled stiffly out of our improvised sleeping place. The *Polizei*'s eyes widened when they saw Dusty emerge from under his coat and climb out of the well behind the back seat. Sleepily we all produced our military ID's and our overnight unit passes which the two officers examined under the light of their flashlight. Then one policeman ducked his head into the car and shone his light around inside, looking behind and under the seats, finally withdrawing, apparently satisfied that we were not gun-runners, drug smugglers or white slavers. Meanwhile we all stood around yawning hugely, stretching and scratching ourselves. Finally the officers returned our ID's and passes and advised us (we *guessed*, since we weren't sure *what* they said) to move on, or go home, or something to that effect, then they stepped back aboard their small riverboat and puttered off upstream.

ARMED FORCES LIBERTY PASS | SERVICE: Army | DATE ISSUED: 7 FEB 1964

LAST NAME—FIRST NAME—MIDDLE INITIAL: Bazzett, Timothy | CARD NO.

SERVICE NO. | GRADE—RATE: Sp/4 E-4

ORGANIZATION—INSTALLATION—BASE: 184th US ASA Company

TIME LIMITS: See Remarks on Reverse Side

SIGNATURE AND GRADE OF ISSUING OFFICER

DD FORM 345 1 Apr 50 REPLACES WD AGO FORMS 7 AND 8, NAV PERS FORM 547 AND CG FORMS 2518 AND 2792 WHICH MAY BE USED.

WEEKDAYS: 25 mile radius of Kassel
WEEKENDS, HOLIDAYS & BREAKS: 125 mile radius of Kassel

..U-TURNS on Autobahn Prohibited"

AUTHORIZED TO WEAR CIVILIAN CLOTHING

Armed Forces Liberty Pass from the 184th.

As soon as their boat had rounded the bend in the river, we all took a quick piss in the bushes and climbed wearily back into the car and headed back down the road into Kassel, all of us sleepily smacking our lips and running furry-feeling tongues over our teeth, trying fruitlessly to rid ourselves of sour morning-mouth and belching up stale beer fumes.

After determining by means of a phone call that the alert was still on, we spent the day wandering the streets and sitting around the train station like vagrants, and later ended up back at the Deuce again. By that evening we were all totally exhausted and wrung out. We knew we couldn't possibly spend another night in the VW, so we pooled all our remaining funds and found a small hotel where a single room didn't cost too much. And it *was* supposed to be a *single.* I think it was Dusty who went in and signed the register and paid the room, probably because he looked the most respectable and honest, even after spending a night tucked behind the back seat. Then later, soon after dark, one at a time, the rest of us slipped in through the lobby, until we were all gathered in the tiny room. Tom and Dusty got the bed, where they arranged themselves head to foot (probably to avoid any semblance of a "special friendship" – myurp, myurp). Bill, Joe and I settled ourselves in the narrow spaces on the floor on both sides and along the foot of the bed. In this way we slept, perhaps not a restful sleep, but certainly a better one than the night before. The next morning, under the startled stare of the elderly inn-keeper, we all filed out together, jumped in the car and quickly got the hell outa Dodge, since the proprietor had followed us out of the lobby and was standing on the steps watching us. We drove back east up the road to Rothwesten and parked in the village, until a few hours later we heard the wail of the siren, signaling the end of the alert.

Heaving huge sighs of relief, we drove back through the front gate and onto base. Back at the barracks we climbed the stairs to our third floor haven where we collapsed onto our bunks for a few blessed hours of sleep, then showered and shaved and went back to work.

Our trick was starting swings. We had managed to avoid the alert, but weren't so sure anymore if it had been worth it. But that night at work we *did* brag about our escape, and *nyah-nyah*-ed all our trickmates about their two days of enforced deployment and "playing army" while *we* had been "enjoying" our break and "living it up" in fancy downtown hotels. Yeah, sure. What a bunch of lying pathetic jerks we were. What the hell did we think we were doing? Well, *now* I know what we were doing. We were making memories – memories that are still with us – about the time we "outsmarted the army." Yeah, sure, Bazzett. Whatever. ... So anyway, that's the *other* story about the convenience – or *lack* thereof – of a VW Beetle. Take my word for it, it's not meant to sleep five.

* * * * *

Train ticket from
Kassel to Kobenhaven

I had another memorable adventure that spring in Germany, one a *little* better than our ill-fated night on the Weser. Tom Gordon and I took a ten-day leave to go to Copenhagen, Denmark. I'm not sure, but I think we picked Copenhagen as our vacation destination because we'd heard stories from some other guys about the Tivoli Gardens amusement park there. This was long before Disney opened any theme parks in Europe, and Tivoli's was touted as a wonderful and fun place for families, and also, supposedly, a great place to meet and pick up girls. It was, naturally, the girls part of this information that intrigued us, so, without doing any further research on Copenhagen or Tivoli's, we put in our leave requests and bought our train tickets and were soon on our way in search of adventure, our dirty little minds filled with vague unformed dreams of finding love – or at least getting laid.

I can't remember why Joe didn't go with us, but it might have been because he had flown home to New York for Christmas and already used up a big chunk of his leave time, and probably his money too.

In any case, Ol' Hurtin' Gordon and (hey, let's face it) equally Ol' Hurtin' Bazzett boarded the train in Kassel one fine spring morning and were off to see the Wizard. And it really *felt* like that kind of an adventure at the time, at least to me, and probably to Tom too. We were both just twenty-one years old and, although we both wanted desperately to be seen and treated as adults, we were still boys, not far removed from the good Catholic boys we'd been brought up to be. Both Michiganders (or "Michi-*gonians,*" as Tom was fond of calling us), our "heart of the heart of the country" origins had provided us with pretty sheltered lives up to this time. True, I had finally lost my cherry in Turkey, but my outlook on life (and probably Tom's too) was still pretty virginal. Tom had a steady girlfriend back home in Hazel Park to whom he wrote faithfully every week, and, true to his Catholic upbringing, he was doing his best to remain faithful to his Charlotte and "save himself" for marriage. (And yes, sweet Charlotte, no matter what you may have suspected, or perhaps even still wonder about from time to time now, some forty years later, Tommy was a *good* boy. So hush, hush. Okay?)

The fact of the matter was, we were both ripe for a little sin – or a *big* sin, or a *lot* of sin. Luckily, that old bugaboo of "Catholic guilt," firmly implanted in our soft and malleable little psyches way back in sixth grade when the Baltimore Catechism lessons dwelt an inordinately long time on the subject of purity and *im*-purity, was still very much with us, no matter how hard we tried to push it to the backs of our minds. It was tough still trying to be the "soldier of Christ" that Confirmation had made you, when all you *really* wanted to be sometimes was a *soldier*, and to indulge freely in all the nasty groaty things that soldiers are supposedly notorious for. I don't mean the *really* bad stuff, like plundering, raping and pillaging (and just what the hell *is* "pillaging" anyway?). No, I just mean a little healthy, sweaty, no-strings, athletic consensual sex with some rosy-cheeked jolly *Fraulein* who just happened to love to fuck. This was, after all, pretty much every GI's fantasy, albeit one that was rarely, if ever, realized.

Anyway, a lot of this kind of shit was floating through our heads as we set off on our journey to *vun*-derful *Kobenhaven.* We wanted to be bad, but not *too* bad, and yet we wanted to be good too – but not *too* good. You see what I mean? Very conflicting feelings. *Damn* that Catholic guilt!

So what kind of adventures did we have? I *call* them adventures, but you have to understand, we were just kids. *Every*thing was still an adventure to us. Our "adventures" weren't the stuff of James Bond or *The Man Who Knew Too Much* kinds of adventures. They were, instead, the *Wow!-I-can't-believe-I'm-here* or the *I-can't-believe-I'm-doing-this* kind of wide-eyed kids' adventures.

We had to switch trains in Hamburg and had a layover of several hours. In 1965 Hamburg was still famous for being a wide-open city with lots of opportunities for sin and sex. But it was also more recently world famous for being the city where The Beatles cut their musical teeth. The Fab Four had spent several months a couple years earlier performing nightly at the Star Club on the *Reeperbahn* strip in downtown Hamburg. These were the youthful, pre-Ringo Beatles, with greaser Pete Best pounding out the rhythms and John Lennon screaming frantically at the top of his lungs on old R&B tunes like "Long Tall Sally," "Twist and Shout," and "Roll Over Beethoven."

By the time Tom and I got to Hamburg, The Beatles had already recorded four albums and were well on their way to becoming the most popular and successful band in the world. I was already a devoted fan just from listening to their music, and my enthusiasm was only increased by the fact that Joe and four other guys had formed a band on base that winter and were putting together an impressive playlist of songs which already included many Beatle tunes. I had become a rabid supporter of *their* band, The Panics (more on them later), and had taken on the interesting role of transcribing song lyrics off records for them, so they could all learn songs more quickly. As our roommate and buddy, Tom was in on a lot of this too, so when we disembarked from our train in Hamburg that late afternoon, we knew exactly where we wanted to go. We headed straight for the *Reeperbahn* and the Star Club, the Mecca of early Beatle fans everywhere.

I wish I had written more letters home during my year in Germany. If I had, perhaps I would have had some record of my time there to refer to now when I'm trying so desperately to remember details of those times. But I guess I was too busy doing and experiencing things to be bothered with writing them down. I would love to be able to tell you the names of some of the bands we heard that night on the *Reeperbahn*, at the Star Club and at a few other clubs we wandered into, but I just don't remember. They were mostly British bands though, looking for their big breaks, hoping against hope to follow in the footsteps of the Beatles. For the so-called British Invasion of the sixties didn't just happen in

America. No, Beatle wannabees were all over Europe performing in clubs too – bands from England, Scotland, Ireland and Wales, all hoping to make their mark on the modern musical scene.

It was all really a rush for Tom and me, as we made our way from one noisy venue to another up and down the glittering neon-lit strip that was the *Reeperbahn,* choked with crowds of young people, many of them from other countries in Europe, all "making the scene" in their grubby punk fashions or Carnaby Street clothes, trying to connect with the music and, of course, with each other.

In those days of long locks and facial hair of all kinds, Tom and I undoubtedly stuck out like sore thumbs with our GI haircuts and PX-purchased pants and shirts and the Gomer-ish expressions of wide-eyed wonder which we tried our best to suppress, but couldn't. It was all just too exhilarating, too *much.* I'm sure I was probably thinking stuff like, *Wow! Here I am on the* Reeperbahn *in* Hamburg*!* or *Here I am in the* Star Club, *where the* Beatles *played!* So if I had a *Gaw-Haw-lee, Sar-gint Carter!* kind of look on my face all evening, it just couldn't be helped.

So we spent our few short hours soaking up the hip atmosphere and ogling all the girls in their fringed vests, see-through blouses and mini-skirts, even though they pretty much ignored us – we were so *obviously* soldiers. Okay, so there were no spies, no dangers, no unexplained disappearances or other mysteries, but it was, nevertheless, an *adventure,* at least to us hurtin' Michigonians. Before we knew it, it was time for us to hustle back to the station and catch our train to Copenhagen.

In some ways, Copenhagen was a bit anti-climactic, especially after the bright lights and youthful excitement of the *Reeperbahn.* I mean we had an okay time there, but it wasn't quite what we had expected. For one thing, we learned soon after our arrival there that Tivoli's wasn't open yet. It was too early in the spring. I think the grand opening for the season was scheduled for the following week. So it was poor planning on our part, I suppose, and bad luck. We should have done a bit more research before rushing off to Denmark, but we hadn't. No big world-famous amusement park for us then, darn it. We'd both grown up around summer fairs and carnivals and knew they were great places to meet girls, so we were pretty disappointed, but we sucked it up and made the best of things.

We had a room at an inexpensive (of *course* cheap, we were poor GI's) youth hostel which had comfortable beds and a clean toilet and bath just down the hall, so that became our base of operations for the week we spent in the city. There was a cafeteria on the same block that featured a sort of all-you-could-eat breakfast buffet where we filled up every morning before beginning our day's wanderings. Since there was no Tivoli Gardens to go hunt girls in, we picked up tourist brochures here and there and walked all over the city, taking in various attractions the brochures directed us to. We gawked at the palace and grounds of the Danish royal family. In the harbor we ogled the statue of *The Little Mermaid*, a fairy tale character made famous by Hans Christian Anderson. I think there was an Anderson museum we meandered through too.

One evening we went to a jazz club, wearing our coats and ties and feeling uncomfortable and out of place. We weren't really into jazz, having been brought up on Top 40 tunes, but we reasoned that maybe we'd meet some babes there. No such luck, not for nerds like us anyway. The evening was a bust. I think I only remember it *because* it was a jazz spot, something completely new and unique to my experience. There were a few couples dancing, but I had no clue as to how one would dance to that kind of music. Not that it mattered. This wasn't exactly the *Reeperbahn,* but the chicks were still pointedly ignoring us.

On the one Sunday morning we spent in Copenhagen (it may have been *Easter* Sunday) we dutifully got dressed up and walked uptown to an enormous ornate cathedral, where we attended a solemn high Mass with lots of Bach-ian organ music and were suitably humbled and impressed. It wasn't until afterwards that we somehow discovered it wasn't even a Catholic cathedral, but we sure were fooled. It was all the same standing, sitting and kneeling we were used to and we *felt* like we'd been to Mass, so decided that was all that mattered. We were covered.

On one afternoon, after walking what seemed like miles, gawking at all the sights, we went to a movie, mostly I think so we could sit down and rest for a while. The film was an American one, *Father Goose*, a WWII comedy-drama starring Cary Grant and Leslie Caron. It was in English with Danish subtitles. We were most thankful it wasn't the reverse, and enjoyed the film and the brief respite from tourist-ing immensely. I still have fond feelings for that film and watch it again from time to time when it shows up on television, and remember the first time I saw it, in a theater in Denmark. A unique memory in itself for a boy from Reed City.

Now I realize that while probably not much of this sounds like an adventure, to *us* every day seemed like one. Unfortunately, after just six or seven days, we began to run out of money. I guess we didn't budget very carefully, not that we had much money to begin with. You might wonder where did our money go. Well, the answer to that is a bit embarrassing. I'd like to be able to tell you that we spent it on *manly* things – you know, wine, women, song. We didn't like wine. The women didn't seem to like *us*. And we weren't much into jazz, which Copenhagen was famous for. Nope. We spent our money mostly on pastry. Yup, *sweets*.

The word "Danish" take on a whole new meaning when you're in Denmark, especially in downtown Copenhagen. You don't have to "order out" for Danish and coffee there. Instead you can wander between bakeries – and there were a *lot* of bakeries – and stand with your nose pressed against the glass of the front windows and examine row upon row of mouth-wateringly decorated and frosted delicacies, filled and topped with all manner of fruits, nuts, honey-sugar glazes and other strange unidentifiable sweet concoctions. It was almost impossible for Tom and me to pass these establishments without going in and picking out something new to try. Even though we knew our funds were rapidly being depleted by these delectable taste treats, we couldn't stop ourselves. We literally sampled ourselves into insolvency. Soon we were flat broke.

So on the seventh day of our ten-day leave we said goodbye to the city, packed our bags and trudged back to the train station where we boarded a train back to Kassel, our wallets empty and with just a few candy bars to see us through the day-long train ride home.

We got back to Hamburg late that afternoon and, again, had a few hours to kill before our connecting train to Kassel left. Flat broke and hungry, we wandered aimlessly up and down the streets near the *Bahnhof*. Quite by accident, we soon blundered upon a mysterious street called simply *Strasse,* or "The Street." The end of this street was semi-walled off by a tall green-painted board fence about eight feet high, a kind of "privacy fence." However, there was a gap at each end of this fence that you could walk through to gain access to the street itself. As Tom and I approached this street from down the block, we could see people, mostly men, going into and coming out of the street through these gaps. Curious, we wandered closer and then went in at one end of the fence.

Here I just have to say, *"And what to our wondering eyes should appear ..."* No, it wasn't a miniature sleigh, or tiny reindeer either. It was *better!* It was a whole streetful of *whores* under glass – or, more accurately I suppose, *behind* glass. How to describe the strangely surreal scene that suddenly confronted us as dusk began to fall in Hamburg? "The Street" was only one block long and was quite narrow, more of an alley really, but, like most streets in Germany (then *and* now), its cobblestone surface was scrupulously clean. There were large picture-window-sized showcase windows in the buildings on both sides of the alley at street level. The second floors above had smaller, dimly-lit curtained windows facing the street. But the street level showcases were the real attractions here.

There were several of these picture windows on each side of the street, all softly lit by small footlights placed strategically along the bottom edge of the window. Each display case window had its own decorative theme of colors and materials, some in red velvet, others in purple silks or pink satins, with draped and hanging curtains as a backdrop or tied with a matching sash at either side of the front of the window. But at the center of each display case, ah, um ... Why do I keep calling it a "display case"? Makes it sound like a meat market, doesn't it? Hmm. ... Maybe that's why.

Where was I? In the center of each, er, window, a prostitute lounged on a divan, a chaise, a bed, or, in one bizarre setting, a woman reclined across what looked like a dentist's chair. These women were in various stages of undress, clad in scanty lingerie combinations in colors that usually matched or tastefully contrasted with their window's particular decorative scheme. The whore in the dental chair wore what looked like an extremely abbreviated nurse's uniform (or maybe a dental hygienist's), complete with a small cap fastened on her garish red-toned mane of hair. The women were all, without exception, quite attractive. Or if they weren't, then the right lighting, setting, and makeup really *can* work wonders.

Tom and I were understandably stunned by this unexpected tableau. Moving slowly with the flow of the crowd of anonymous men who were walking up one side of the alley and then back down the other, we gaped open-mouthed at this lascivious display of feminine pulchritude. We were *window-shopping,* for cripes sake!

And it *was* a deliciously lascivious scene, because these girls were showing off their wares and struttin' their stuff within the confines of their personal meat display cases, and doing everything possible both inside and *out*side the bounds of decency to show that they would "work hard for the money," as the disco chanteuse Donna Summer would put it some years later. I will not elaborate beyond this, but I'm pretty sure that Tom and I were both thinking something to the effect of, *I don't think we're in Michigan anymore, Toto.*

If ever there was a "near occasion of sin," as the nuns and our catechism used to call worldly or fleshly temptations, "den dis wad da place." You just couldn't get much nearer to sin than this without actually rubbing yourself up against it, an idea which certainly did flash across my mind a time or two. It was as if we had fallen through the looking glass and joined a whole bunch of very naughty Alices in Wonder-Land. Except I didn't have to drink from any mysterious potions to feel myself getting larger, then smaller, larger, smaller. Larger, larger! Whew! What a place!

I would like to be able to report that, once we realized what kind of a place this was, we immediately hustled ourselves right out of there with all possible speed, like the good Catholic boys we had been brought up to be. Alas, I am unable to report this. It was simply too *fas*cinating – especially to two unsophisticated un-jaded midwestern goobers like Tom and me. Nope, we didn't run away. Instead we meandered up and down, and up and down that street minny minny times over, at first just staring in wonder and trying to take it all in, and then, finally, snickering and winking back at the whores as they postured and posed on their various furnishings, forming pouty little *moues* with their mouths at us, or sending some not-so-subtle bumps and grinds our way and beckoning us toward the small entrance doors near each window that opened into narrow stairways that led up to the second floor where the real business was apparently transacted. We watched some of the other men on the street as they furtively entered and exited these doors.

It was just our luck – and probably a good thing, for the sake of our immortal souls – that we were broke. I remember Tom, in response to the red-headed dental hygienist's beckoning gestures, turning both his front pockets inside-out and putting out his hands palms up in that universal gesture of *Hey, sorry, I'm broke*, a wry, self-effacing smile on his face. Making a dismissive motion with both hands, the whore laughed and turned her attention to someone else.

I laughed at Tom and said, "Guess you won't be gettin' your teeth cleaned today, eh?"

Tom busted out laughing then too, and together we finally departed this surreal den of iniquity, the Alice's Wonderland, simultaneously shrinking back to our actual sizes. The *Strasse* turned out to be one of the most interesting highlights of our Danish vacation. We may not have made it to Tivoli Gardens in Copenhagen, but we got to walk through the funhouse in Hamburg. Our brief visit to The Street gave window-shopping a whole new meaning we would never forget.

We finally arrived back in Kassel sometime after midnight and were fortunate enough to hitch a ride back to post with some friends. We hadn't eaten for nearly twenty-four hours and were famished. The mess hall had already closed its doors after midnight chow, but we pounded on the doors until one of the cooks let us in, and, hearing our story of woe and hunger, took pity on us and cooked up up some French toast and warmed up a few blackened weenies to go with it. Pouring hot maple syrup over it all, we dug in and chowed down, and nothing had ever tasted so good. We were *home*!

* * * * *

Home is a funny thing, you know? Our top floor seven-man room in that old stone barracks really did come to feel like home the last several months we lived there. Our tightly knit group was like a kind of family, and we were always busy doing something, and the thing that really took control of our lives during that time was music, and, more specifically, The Panics.

Geez, how do I even begin to describe how important The Panics were to me, and to our whole group? Where to start? Probably at the beginning, huh?

As I remember it, we had only been at Rothwesten a couple of months when Joe met another guitarist and fellow rock and roll enthusiast one day at the service club. His name was Gene

Gene Hedgepeth and Joe Capozzi

Hedgepeth. I probably shouldn't just call him "another guitarist." That might be construed as implying that Gene and Joe were equally talented on the guitar, and Gene would be the first to assure you that his musical talents came nowhere near Joe's. While it is true that Joe played mostly by ear, he could read some music, and his "ear" was golden. He was a truly quick study at learning just about any song. Gene had to work a lot harder at it, and Joe was the right person to help him, being infinitely patient and pretty soft-spoken by nature. The most important thing that Gene brought to the mix was his enthusiasm for playing and his driving ambition to form a real band. He wanted to *perform* and be noticed. Joe was a lot shyer and a little leery of the spotlight, but he didn't object to Gene's big plans and dreams.

In any case, Joe and Gene started meeting once or twice a week at the service club, where they would book one of the sound-proof music rooms, and sit down with their guitars and amps and work out a song or two together. Mostly they started out with instrumentals, Ventures stuff like Joe had played with Al Trott and SSG Clark back in Sinop. But the Ventures were not really much of a "dance" kind of band. And Gene wanted to *sing.* He wanted to do stuff that was popular right then, stuff people would get up and dance to. Joe, while a wonderful instrumentalist and musician, was not much of a singer, and wasn't real keen on doing songs like that,

Tim and Gene

but eventually Gene's urging won him over, so they started practicing some songs with vocal tracks too. What was hot right then, of course, was everything Beatles and – at the other end of the pop spectrum – The Rolling Stones.

I like to compare the Beatles and the Stones in the mid-sixties to Pat Boone and Elvis in the fifties. Pat Boone was somebody so clean-cut and white-bread-and-whole-milk wholesome that even his teenage fans' *parents* were comfortable with him. With his pearly personable smile, trimmed and neatly combed hair, cardigan letter sweaters, clean pressed chinos and spotless white bucks, Boone looked like the ideal boyfriend for your teenage daughter. Elvis, on the other hand, with his turned-up collar, greased-back DA, hooded eyes and trademark curled-lip sneer, seemed to radiate an aura of sex and danger. *Hide your daughters!*

The Beatles, once their manager, Brian Epstein, had cleaned them all up and given them prissy little matching narrow-lapeled suits and little boy moppet haircuts which flopped about endearingly when they performed, also presented a non-threatening puppy dog sort of image. (Maybe fathers figured if their *hair* was that soft and floppy then maybe so were all their *other* appendages and body parts.) While perhaps not too many parents could appreciate the Beatles' music, at least they considered them harmless, and, again, no serious threat to the virginity of their prepubescent and teenage daughters who were shrieking themselves silly over "the boys." The Stones, however, were another matter altogether. Mick and Keith were such sleazy-looking scuzz-balls from the very beginning that they were *always* a hide-your-daughters band. And much of their early music was that dark and threatening-sounding R&B-based stuff too.

At any rate, Gene convinced Joe that they just *had* to include some Beatles and Stones stuff in their playlist as soon as possible. I know this because *I* was there too. I couldn't (and don't) play any instruments, but I loved all things pop and I liked to sing, so I agreed with Gene, and pushed for adding some songs with vocals to the duo's slowly growing repertoire. So they started working out tunes like "I Saw Her Standing There" and "Twist and Shout" from the Beatles early albums and "You Better Move On" and "Time Is on My Side" from the Stones. From my standpoint, of course, this was a lot more fun, because I got to sing along with them while they worked out the chord changes, bridges and guitar solos. Joe, of course, played lead guitar from the beginning, while Gene, with his more modest musical skills, was relegated to playing rhythm guitar.

My singing was another matter. I could carry a tune and I had the enthusiasm, but my vocal range was never great, and my voice has always had a rather nasal, country-sounding twang, kind of a hybrid mix of Ricky Nelson and Hank Williams, two singers I greatly admired. As a mater of fact, I kept trying to convince Joe and Gene to include a few songs from Rick's hits in their playlist, songs like "Poor Little Fool" and "Lonesome Town." They could play the songs without too much trouble, and occasionally humored me in the practice sessions and let me sing them, but I don't think they ever used those songs once they started performing. I *did* persuade them, however, to do a modified version of Henry Mancini's "Moon River," which seems an unlikely musical choice for an aspiring rock band, but Joe worked out a very pleasing cha-cha kind of arrangement (unless he stole it from a Ventures' version, I don't know), and that song stayed in their repertoire. (I think the Panics were probably the *only* dance band in the Kassel area that played "Moon River.") I've always loved that song, although I've always wondered what, exactly, is a "huckleberry friend."

Those early days of the not yet complete band were probably some of the most exciting times, at least from my standpoint, since I was never to become a real player or permanent member of the Panics, although I always remained one of their staunchest supporters and an ardent fan. That winter the band began to come together. Gene brought in another Headquarters Company musician, Joe Rindini, who found his niche playing electric bass. Joe was from the Boston area. He and Joe Capozzi immediately hit it off, maybe due in part to their common Italian heritage, and an easy kind of bantering manner quickly sprang up between them. Gene became a natural "foil" and was often the butt of small jokes, a role which he accepted good-naturedly. (I always thought that Gene *looked* as Italian as the two Joes, but I don't think I ever asked him if there were any Italians in his family woodpile.) Not too long ago I was talking with Joe R on the phone about those early days of the Panics, and was surprised when he told me that he had never played the bass before when he joined the Panics. He had played a little guitar, but there were already two guitar players and he wanted into the band in the worst way, so he bought an electric bass (one of those that looked like a big fiddle, just like Paul's) and taught himself to play it as he went along. He must have been pretty good at faking it, because I don't remember him ever getting yelled at for screwing up. Not that there was ever much yelling, but Gene

Joe Rindini

285

did get chided gently by Joe C every now and then when he'd get too busy smiling at the girls and forget to change chords. Joe C was always the "quality control" guy of the group. He was always striving for the best sound and the best possible arrangements.

I can't remember just when or how the final two members of the band got involved, but it was probably by word of mouth. The two Joes and Gene let it be known that they were forming a band and rehearsing, and it wasn't long before they had added a drummer, and, somewhat to *my* disappointment, a vocalist.

Both of the last two members were from the 184th Operations Company, the same unit Joe C and I were assigned to. The drummer was from Pennsylvania. His name was Chris Musser, and his blonde boyish good looks and easy charm were an immediate asset to the group, offering a stark but welcome contrast to the three dark Mediterranean types. Moreover, Chris was extremely talented, both on the drums and as a singer and performer. It was easy to see from the start that he would be a "chick magnet" once the band started performing in public venues – and he *was* too.

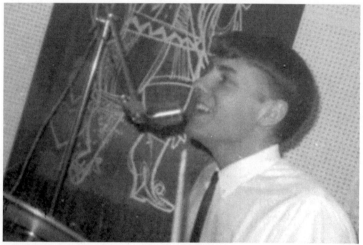

Chris Musser

Mike Chesley was the final addition to the band. He "auditioned" for the other guys for the slot of lead vocalist. It was immediately apparent that Mike could sing. He had a very

Mike Chesley

impressive range of probably at least two octaves, and his breath control, phrasing and very distinct enunciation set him apart from the amateurs – like me. Mike wasn't a very big guy, maybe five seven or eight, kind of skinny and perhaps just a bit geeky-looking, with a receding chin, reddish hair and horn-rimmed glasses. All-in-all he wasn't very impressive *looking*, but when he opened his mouth and that big resonant pitch-perfect voice came booming out, it was a revelation, and I think everybody in the band knew that the vocalist job was his. (Years later, in the late eighties, I think it was, I would think of Mike whenever I heard a Brit pop singer named Rick Astley. Also slender and red-haired, Astley's booming multi-octave voice catapulted him to the top of the charts a couple of times with the songs "Never Gonna Give You Up" and "Together Forever.") I knew I certainly couldn't compete with a voice like Mike's, so I resigned myself with as much grace as possible to a permanent supporting role of go-fer, roadie, lyrics transcriptionist, or whatever the guys needed me to do. I had been there from the beginning and I wasn't just going to fade away completely. And I got along fine with all the guys, or at least I like to think I did.

In case you haven't noticed, this narrative isn't exactly strictly chronological in nature. I mean, give me a *break!* I'm sixty years old, for cripe sake, and memories are *not* naturally chronological. I have to write things down when I *think* of them, before I *forget* them again. If I spent all my time making notes and trying to *organize* my memories, I'd probably never even get started, and after all, once you've turned that corner at sixty, you never know how much time you've got left, so I figure I'd better hurry up and get stuff down, and *screw* the chronology. Okay?

So personnel-wise the Panics were probably already complete by around Christmas of '64. Joe Capozzi took a couple weeks leave and went home for Christmas. I stayed, along with my other roommates, and I don't really remember much about my only Christmas in Germany, except that we worked twelve-hour shifts during that two or three week holiday period in order to compensate for the missing personnel who were on leave with their families. The long hours at work during that time did at least cause time to go quickly. After twelve hours at work, you really only had time to eat and sleep, and very little else. I don't think we even had enough energy to go out drinking at the Deuce at night.

I can't remember if I made it to church for Christmas that year. As a matter of fact, I'm not even sure where the chapel *was* at Rothwesten. It seems like I vaguely remember once racing up an outside stairway one Sunday with Tom or Joe because we were late for Mass, so I *think* the chapel may have been upstairs over the service club, or maybe over the PX snack bar, but I'm really not sure.

So yes, what you're thinking is true. The attractions of drinking and partying and rock and roll just about made a proper pagan out of me that year. Although I may have made it to Mass a couple of times, for the most part my "good Catholic boy" persona was fading fast. It wasn't that I lost my faith or stopped *believing* or anything so radical as that. I was just always too tired or too busy, and I was full of that youthful "ain't-never-gonna-die" sureness that most young people have. I could be good and go to church *later*. Not really acceptable excuses, I know, but there it is nonetheless. I wasn't exactly a *bad* boy, but I guess I wasn't a particularly *good* one either.

I turned twenty-one in late January of 1965. To celebrate this milestone, of course, I went to the Deuce with all my buddies and roommates, who were most generous in providing me with a plentitude of liquid refreshment.

Let's talk about the Deuce a bit. The *Dusseldorfer Hof* was "our" bar. The soldiers of the ASA stationed at Rothwesten were its most faithful and regular patrons. There were almost no German customers at the Deuce, except for the girls who were "regulars," and, like I said earlier, necessary "furnishings" for a successful GI hangout. But the Deuce was so much more than just a *Gasthaus* or bar. It was almost like a second home, a place where you could go and and hang out and just feel comfortable in your own skin.

The Deuce was kind of an advanced version of a teenage hangout that had flourished in Reed City when I was a kid. (Warning: Here comes one of my lengthy digressions.) In the fifties it was called The Newsstand, or Ma Brown's, after its owner. By the early sixties, when I was old enough to go there, it had become Mike's Place, after its new owner, Mike Mayhew. Mike's has been gone for many years now, but I can still picture it in my mind. It had one of those old-fashioned narrow storefront stone facades, and was located right next to the old Post Office on East Upton, on the same side of the street that held Henry's Bar, the pool hall, the Reed Theater, the barber shop (where Bill Slankard, Ken Main and Jerry Sprague kept the town's male population looking presentable), and, on the corner, Floyd Wood's clothing store, Skogmo's. (All these venerable establishments are gone now, replaced by progress, in the form of one of the largest Yoplait yogurt plants in the country. Good for the local economy, of course, but hard on memories.)

When you entered Mike's Place, on your left was a long marble-topped soda fountain, fronted by a row of vinyl cushion-topped stools, the kind you could spin yourself all the way around on if you felt like it. (Of course, two of the drugstores in town, Bonsall's and Dykstra's, boasted the same kind of soda fountain and stools.) Behind the fountain counter were the usual ice-cream bins, the soda spigots, jars of maraschino cherries, pickles, onions and condiments, and, against the wall, a grill and deep-fryer where burgers and fries were prepared. To your right as you came in the door was a long magazine rack, rising from the floor to eye-level, filled with what seemed a wealth of all manner of periodicals. The selections leaned heavily, as I remember, to Hollywood-type stuff like *Photoplay*, *Modern Screen*, and *Teen*. Men's magazines were available too, with titles like *True*, *Argosy* and *Sports Afield*, or *Popular Mechanics* and *Popular Science*. *Playboy* was probably there too, but that wasn't a magazine you wanted to be seen reading in mixed company when you were only sixteen or so. The magazines stretched all the way down the wall to a short row of booths with tables that could hold four people each – or five or six if the occupants really *liked* each other.

Past these booths a short flight of three or four steps led up to the inner sanctum of Mike's, where the store widened out a bit to accommodate a small dance floor flanked on both sides by more booths, but dominated by a brightly-lit hulking jukebox situated against the back wall. As I remember it, not much dancing ever took place up in this area, but, in the darker corners of these upper booths, there was a considerable amount of illicit, furtive "romance" taking place – i.e. "making out" and light and heavy "petting," all of which was usually carried out under an ever-present pall of cigarette smoke. These are things I only glimpsed a few times, as I myself was usually relegated to the outer fringes with the kids who stayed down by the soda fountain and magazines. It was an unspoken rule that only the really "cool" kids penetrated the upper reaches of Mike's.

My parents strongly discouraged my brothers and me from hanging out at Mike's. I think they probably figured that that many teenagers all crammed into one place with little or no adult supervision couldn't be up to much good. (Parents can be pretty darned perceptive sometimes, although such perceptiveness could be a real nuisance to a guy's social life.) But I did manage to sneak into Mike's from time to time after school and breathe in the the scents, sights and sounds. I can still recall the delicious smell of frying hamburgers and the reek of onions and cooking grease, all mixed in with the cigarette smoke and competing mixture of perfume, cologne, hair spray and sweat. And always the *music* – classic songs like "Handy Man" (not the much-later watered down James Taylor version, of course, but the original, by Jimmy Jones and his pleading falsetto), Del Shannon's "Runaway," or Neil Sedaka's "Stairway to Heaven." The jukebox rarely fell silent in a time when it only cost a nickel a tune, or *six* for a quarter.

So of *course* the kids all loved it at Mike's in Reed City all those years ago. They were comfortable there, and could be themselves, or they could work on the "cooler" personae they were trying so desperately to develop. They could usually be just a little larger than life there. They weren't just someone's dutiful son or daughter, or someone else's younger brother brother or sister. They could be unique and *special* at Mike's.

The Deuce

The Deuce, in Kassel, was the same kind of place. (*See?* I'm back.) The GI's who frequented the Deuce were, after all, only a few years older than the kids at Mike's. You could get a Coke at the Deuce, but beer was the drink of choice, and it flowed freely there, in more ways than one.

You entered the Deuce by going up an outside set of concrete steps on the end of the building. When you came in, the bathroom was on your right. I feel compelled to at least briefly describe the john here, because (1) it was a small culture shock the first time you saw it, and (2) because it was one of the places where the beer always flowed freely, once it had been processed through the patrons' systems. There was so *much* beer that got pissed back out in that Deutsche-style latrine that we used to jokingly speculate that it probably drained into holding tanks somewhere in the basement, then was piped back up to the draft spigots behind the bar and back into our glasses to continue a never-ending cycle.

The Deuce's bathroom, or the "pisser," as I came to call it, since the one toilet always seemed to be out of order, plugged up with something or so splattered with vomit or shit that you would never even *consider* actually *sit*ting on it, was, as I started to say, something of a shock for first-timers. It had a sink and the aforementioned toilet, but its main and most used fixture was "the wall." In lieu of a row of urinals, or even a trough-type urinal like we had in basic, there was simply a wall with a shallow gutter running along the floor at the bottom edge. A perforated pipe ran horizontally across the wall at a height of about four feet and water ran continuously down the wall from this pipe into the the gutter, sluicing away the barely processed beer into a floor drain at the lowest end. So, when nature called, you quite literally just pissed on the wall. It was actually a liberating, naughty sort of feeling at first, or at least until you got used to it. Above the pipe the the wall was always covered with graffiti, with *FTA* being one of the most popular and frequent phrases represented.

Here I cannot resist another digression within what I'm afraid may already be a digression, I can't remember anymore. But my narrative continues in an uninterrupted flow, kind of like when you're taking a good healthy piss, and can't just stop in mid-stream. Whatever comes out, comes out. And what's coming out here is a timeless tale about the Deuce, the *pissoir* there, and one Sumner H. Cunningham. And to be honest, I can't even remember if this is actually a true story, but it's become one of those "war stories" that ol' army buddies tell each other when they get together years later and shoot the shit about the "good ol' days." Everyone knows that "war stories" are usually about ninety per cent bullshit, so keep that in mind, okay?

Hmm. ... How can I best describe Cunningham? Where do I start? He was new that winter. I mean he was "new" in so many senses of the word, not simply because he arrived at Rothwesten after we did. No, Sumner had the wide-eyed innocent *new*-ness of a just-hatched baby chick. I don't mean to imply that he bore any actual resemblance to one of those softly fuzzed little yellow peepers that used to show up in children's baskets on Easter Sunday morning. With his round close-cropped head, forward-jutting hard round belly, and rearward-jutting butt, he was more like a real live *Weeble*. Remember those rounded, bottom-heavy little toy characters with their catchy advertising slogan: *Weebles wobble, they don't fall down*? They usually came boxed as a whole little family, with a Poppa Weeble, a Momma Weeble and a Baby

Sumner Cunningham

Weeble. Well, Sumner was Baby Weeble come alive, except for one thing, his voice. At barely more than five feet tall, Sumner had this big booming nearly bass voice that, coming from his small serially spherical shape, took you completely by surprise. And his *laugh.* That laugh was completely unique to me at the time, but nearly twenty years later I heard that laugh again, on *television.* It was coming from a new TV character called *ALF,* short, as you probably remember, for "Alien Life Form." I liked the show well enough, but every time the furry muppet-like title character erupted in that laugh, that bluff and hearty *HAW-HAW-HAW,* I would remember Sumner H. Cunningham, our small, seemingly newly-minted pal, who suddenly appeared in our midst that winter and stayed.

Probably another reason Sumner seemed so new was his age. I think he may have turned eighteen *after* he arrived. He was one of those kids who got his parents to sign for him so he could enlist in the army at seventeen. And his parentage itself was another interesting part of the mystery that was Sumner H. Cunningham. If I remember correctly (and I may *not*), I think Sumner told us that when he was born his father was already over seventy years old, a concept that was a bit difficult for any of us to get our heads around, because when we tried to calculate it out, it always pointed to the unmistakable fact that Sumner's dad was older than most of our *grand*parents. Well, he *was* from West Virginia, I believe, and we'd always heard that family relationships in that remote and mountainous state could be rather contorted and confusing. (Years later I came to know another fellow from West Virginia who often joked about the unnatural closeness of his large extended family that all dwelt in the same mountain "holler." This guy had always been confused by his uncanny resemblance to his father's older brother, whom he jokingly referred to as "Uncle Dad.")

All of us – Joe, Tom, Dusty, Bill and I – were rather intrigued by Sumner from the start, by his short round solid stature, his squinty-eyed grin and his startling big booming laugh. But ultimately we were captured by his innocence, by his new-ness, and we couldn't help but like him. He evoked conflicting feelings in all of us, I think. His extreme youth and raw innocence made you want to look after him and try to protect him on the one hand, but, on the other hand it also made you want to have just a little fun with him too, or perhaps I should say, at his expense.

To explain. Sumner had never imbibed before. I think he was probably the product of a fundamentalist backwoods Baptist sort of upbringing, but I really don't know. Whatever his religious background was, it had molded him into the Protestant equivalent of a "good Catholic boy," albeit without benefit of the teachings of the Baltimore Catechism. Sumner was obviously a good boy. Whenever we invited him to go along with us to the Deuce, he would decline and tell us that drinking was evil and alcohol was an instrument of the devil. To this we would respond with a good-natured, "Okay, Sumner, if you say so. See you later, Sumner." And off we would go for another night of evil carousing and consuming as many quarts of Beelzebub's best as we could manage.

This went on for some weeks after Sumner's arrival. We never pressured him to go out with us. We just continued to invite him, in a friendly, non-retributional fashion. The thing was, we genuinely *liked* Sumner, at first in the way that you might like a cute puppy or a favorite toy, like a little cowboy Weeble or a stuffed ALF doll, but then later, as we got to know him better, we grew to like him just as a friend. And he responded to this, to our proferred friendship, because he *was* a little strange, and some of the other guys in the unit weren't always as kind to him as we were. In spite of our "evil" ways, I think he looked up to us. We were older and we'd been in the army a year or more longer than he had, and most of us were already Spec 4's to his slick-sleeved E-2.

In any case, after three or four weeks of resisting our invitations to go out and party, Sumner finally caved, but not, I think, because of peer pressure. We never really pressured him. No, I think it was more just loneliness, and maybe curiosity. An army barracks *can* be a pretty empty, echoing lonely place when you're all alone in it, especially when you know all your friends are out having a good time. And we always added, in our invitations, "You don't *have* to drink, Sumner. You can just have a Coke. Come *on!* Loosen up a little."

So one night he just said Okay. He was probably just tired of being alone. We were delighted, and we all went trooping down the stairs and out to Wilkes's car, laughing and talking and telling him all about the wonders and oddities that awaited him at the Deuce. Wide-eyed and wondering, Sumner took it all in, nervously *HAW-HAW*-ing in the appropriate places, especially when we told him about pissing on "the wall" there, a concept that seemed especially foreign to him, as indeed it had to all of us initially.

Upon our arrival at the Deuce we showed Sumner around in a cursory fashion, first taking him through the upper level where the bar and several tables and and always-busy *Foosball* table resided. We introduced him to Ilse and her husband, the proprietors, who held court behind the bar, and they drew beers for all of us except Sumner, who ordered a Coke. Then, going down a few steps, we took him into "the Pit."

The Pit was the lower level of the Deuce, the place where you always ended up by evening's end, the place where you did your serious drinking. It was dimly lit. Shit, it was *dark* down there, lit only by the colored flashing lights of the jukebox, which was wedged into the far back corner and was *never* silent. Immediately to the right of the steps was a large round wooden table, its top scarred by cigarette burns and jackknife-carved initials, dates, the ubiquitous *FTA*, of course, and other graffiti. This table was large enough for a dozen or more people to gather around and was usually full to capacity. There were also a few smaller tables with chairs lined along another wall in the darkness. The center of the pit was for dancing. Yes, there were girls at the Deuce too, "regulars" who either aspired to marrying an American and moving to the

U.S., or else just thought that GI's were more fun than young German men. I mean who the hell *knows* why these particular girls showed up at the Deuce night after night. They were like part of the furniture, only softer, and most of them were not averse to a little friendly sweaty groping there in the darkness of the Pit, whether it was while sitting at a table or barely moving together in the center of the room folded together in what passed for slow dancing.

The floor in the Pit was usually slick or sticky (or both) with spilled beer and booze and littered with butts. The air was thick with cigarette smoke, and redolent with the sweet smells of perfume and after-shave and the sour smells of hops and close-packed bodies and the rancid reek of the occasional beer fart. With all these things – the guys, the girls, the beer and booze, the sights, smells and sounds – the Deuce was, in fact, at that place and time in our young lives, the perfect place. It was like Mike's Place, only with alcohol, and much farther away from Mom and Dad – out of their reach, in fact. It wasn't just *like* Mike's Place. It *was* Mike's, with a license to be *baaad*. It was abso*lute*ly perfect.

This was the place to which we brought our little buddy, Sumner H. Cunningham, just-turned, or perhaps not quite eighteen years old, as brand-new and as green as the hills of his native West Virginia. Into this lower circle of hell, this den of iniquity, down into the *Pit*, he descended hesitatingly, gradually enveloped by the overwhelming noise, scents and smoke, by the *dark*ness. (If you think there's any symbolism here, I'm not going to comment on it. This is not, after all, a *literary* narrative, meant to be studied and dissected. It's just a story about a bunch of guys having fun, got it? Okay, good.)

Clutching his Coke, Cunningham did his best to blend in, sticking as close to us as he could, obviously more than a bit awed, and perhaps even fearful, of the all-encompassing "evil" atmosphere that he suddenly found himself plunged into, after only hearing about it for the past several weeks. As the evening progressed and the beer flowed freely, poor Sumner began feeling increasingly outside of things. When we all roared with laughter at coarse inside jokes or gestures, he usually "didn't get it," and so probably began to wonder if there was some kind of magic potion element to the beer we were drinking that didn't come in his Coke. Everyone there continued to offer to buy Sumner a beer, enjoining

Sumner outside the Ratskeller in Kassel

him jollily to loosen up and have some fun. Finally, once again, he caved, allowing as to how maybe "just one beer" probably couldn't hurt. Well, that one beer led to another, of course, and another after that one, and so on, and our small friend did indeed "loosen up," and started to find almost everything hilariously funny, whether he understood it or not. His unmistakable *HAW-HAW-HAW*-ing rang through the Pit, causing everyone else to just break up. You couldn't hear Sumner's laugh without joining in, it was positively contagious.

After consuming a number of these magic potion beers, Sumner's small system had reached its capacity. Bladder distended and crying for relief, Sumner turned to Tom and me, and asked, in his basso-profundo voice, "Where's the can? I gotta piss really *bad*!"

Not wishing to break off our own drunken discourse, we looked blearily around at him, and I reminded him, "There *is* no can, Sumner. Don'cha remember wha' we tol'ja? You jus' piss on the *wall* here."

Looking desperately about, Sumner nodded uncertainly, then shouldered his way quickly through the shuffling dancers back to the wall beside the jukebox, where he unzipped his fly and, back to the crowded room, *PISSED ON THE WALL!*

Tom and I weren't at first aware what had happened until the dancers on the crowded floor suddenly parted like the Red Sea waters as they scrambled back away from Cunningham, trying to avoid being splattered as he obliviously continued to empty his overtaxed bladder with the force of one of those giant "supersoaker" squirt guns you see kids playing with in the street on hot summer days. Girls streamed screaming up the steps to the bar to report this gross breach of Deuce etiquette to the owners, while the guys, incredulous, gathered on the dance floor staring and laughing and even cheering Cunningham on. Although perhaps a bit startled at suddenly finding himself the center of attention, poor Sumner's bladder was so full that he couldn't just stop in mid-stream, so, *HAW-HAW-HAW*-ing in embarrassment and confusion (*Wasn't I supposed to piss on the wall?*), he kept on squirting until his tank was finally emptied. By this time, summoned by the screaming *Frauleins,* Ilse came bustling down the steps from the bar, her long blonde braid bouncing behind her, and hurried red-faced and blustering over to Cunningham. Towering over our flustered little friend and clucking in an angry mix of English and German, she seized him roughly by the belt and shirt collar and hustled him quickly across the sticky floor of the Pit, up the steps and through the barroom to the exit, where she unceremoniously shoved him out the door and down the stone steps onto the sidewalk. It was undoubtedly the angriest any of us had ever seen Ilse, who was normally more like a benevolent and tolerant older sister to her young patrons.

Poor Sumner lay sprawled and dazed on the cement, the seat of his trousers rucked up into a painful-looking wedgie, fly still half undone and shirt-tails askew. He never knew what hit him, and looked as though he were about to cry, but when he looked back up the steps and saw Tom and me in the crowd staring down at him, he attempted a wry smile and even a half-hearted hesitant *haw-haw* or two, but his heart wasn't in it and the laugh died in his throat.

Ilse was still clucking and shouting angrily at him and shaking her fist, and communicated quite well, in her pidgin English, that he was to "No come back here ever again!"

Seeing the devastated, confused and hurt expression on poor Sumner's face, I suddenly felt deeply ashamed and horribly responsible for his plight, and I guess Tom was having the same feelings, because we almost simultaneously touched Ilse's arm to get her attention and distract her from her flaming tirade at Cunningham. As she turned on us, we instinctively jumped back, but then shamefacedly hung our heads and scuffed our feet from side to side in that classic guilty manner, and haltingly confessed our culpability in this dastardly deed that had so fouled her respectable business establishment. We were *really really* sorry, we told her, but we didn't think he'd actually *do* what he had done.

Softening perhaps just the *teen*siest bit, but not much, Ilse then turned her wrath on *us*, and, grabbing our shoulders, she marched us back into the bar where she provided us with a mop, sponge and, after a few moments, a bucket of soapy water. Then she directed us back down the Pit steps to the scene of the crime, where we conscientiously and ashamedly mopped up and eradicated the still-reeking evidence, while Ilse stood glowering at the top of the steps and all the other guys and the girls watched, snickering and muttering softly as the jukebox continued to blare, incidentally but quite appropriately the Ray Charles tune, "Hit the Road, Jack."

This unfortunate episode soon became legend at the Deuce, and bestowed on Cunningham a certain special celebrity – a status that no one else could ever quite match. Because Ilse didn't banish us from the Deuce forever. I guess she recognized that "boys will be boys" or something to that effect. In any case, she relented, and after a few days we came slinking back. Although she gave us some really nasty looks at first, she didn't throw us out, and eventually she got over it and we became "family" once again. I like to think that perhaps we just became the stuff of amusing stories that she told her friends and family years later. Even Sumner was allowed back in. This time though we made sure he knew where the bathroom was, where it was *okay* to piss on the wall.

As I started to say, so many pages ago, I turned twenty-one at the Deuce. Minny minny beers were consumed that night. I have a vague memory of standing in the upper bar area halfway through the evening holding yet another sweating glass of chilled beer while Tom, Joe, Dusty and Bill toasted me again. When I attempted to raise my glass to join them in the toast, only my by-then numb hand went up in the air. The slippery glass went crashing to the floor, beer soaking my shoes and socks. Ilse, by then having long forgiven me for my Cunningham-affair indiscretion, came *tsk-tsk*-ing out from behind the bar with a broom and dustpan and quickly swept up the glass fragments, while Joe got me another beer and thrust it into my offending hand, and even helped me to carefully wrap my fingers around the glass in that painstaking attentive way that drunks often affect.

By the end of the evening – or perhaps I should just say *later* in the evening – we were all gathered around the round table in the Pit, stalwart knights all. By this time I was nearly beyond remembering anything, slumped very tenuously in the seat of honor, unfeeling boneless fingers wrapped around yet another beer, eyes glassy. I think I remember at some point in the evening that we joined in one of those swaying group sing-alongs at the table. You guys that were there know what I'm talking about – that ritual where everyone at the table would throw his arms about the shoulders of the guys on either side and the whole group would sway drunkenly in rhythm (or not) and sing some classic drinking ditty together, like "Show Me the Way to Go Home" or "Roll Me Over in the Clover." We would all bray discordantly at the tops of our lungs as we lunged back and forth, back and forth, spilling beer, belching and scattering cigarette ashes everywhere.

Singing, I should perhaps interject here (*digression* alert), was a time-honored and important part of our regular socialization at the Deuce. Whenever we would finish a set of days swings or mids, it was an unwritten rule that we would all meet that night at the Deuce for a "prayer meeting." Now if I followed my usual pattern of yammering on about my being a "good Catholic boy" here, you would probably expect me to interject something like *See? I didn't totally abandon my religion.* Sorry, but the truth of the matter is there were no prayers at our "prayer meetings." It was just an expression, although we *did* always open the meeting with a "hymn" – sort of.

When we were still new to Rothwesten and the Deuce, these prayer meetings were usually convened and presided over by Jim "Jeeter" Lester, a truly accomplished drinker among drinkers. No matter how much alcohol he consumed – and he could put away prodigious quantities – Lester always kept his cool and maintained an amazing equanimity. I don't know if he composed the opening hymn for these prayer meetings, or if he was only carrying on a tradition begun by an earlier group of ditty-bopper drunks. I think when Jeeter left though, that Mike Chesley, the Panics lead singer, took the torch from him and led the singing of the hymn. It was a simple heartfelt hymn, probably a reaction to six days of chafing under the regimen of rules that governed our work week. It was intoned solemnly in a deep, resonant, and drawn out manner, and went like this:

Himmm,
Himmm,
Fu-uck himmm.

And it was usually repeated several times, or as the spirits moved us.

I know. Nasty, disgusting, sacriligeous, and all that. But at the time it was all very cathartic, like taking a very deep cleansing breath, then letting it slowly out – *AAAAHHH!* All that built-up tension of the just-completed work week would hiss slowly away like a balloon deflating.

At the "round table" in the Deuce. Joe Capozzi, center.

Hmmm. ... Prayer meetings, hymns, lifting our glasses, group sings at the round table. We may not have exactly been knights, but we were certainly "merry men" in those days of yore at the Deuce in downtown Kassel. (Heavy sigh here for days gone by.)

I'm sorry – lost in a reverie. Where the hell was I? ... Oh yes, my twenty-first birthday at the Deuce. The climax of the evening – or perhaps *anti*-climax – came when Ilse came down the steps into the Pit and presented me with a glass (not just a *shot* glass, but a small tumbler, perhaps five or six ounces) of a dark mysterious-looking liquid. Putting the drink down in front of me, she intoned gravely, "Today you are a *man*. You must trink this."

I picked up the glass and sniffed the stuff suspiciously, wondering momentarily if this might perhaps be payback time for the Cunningham episode. But it had a kind of sweet scent, so I took a cautious sip. *Mmmm, good! LI-cor-ish!* Smacking my lips, I started to set the glass back down.

"No," Ilse said, catching my hand with the glass, "You must trink it *all*. Then you will be a *man!*"

No prob-lem-o, I thought, and, raising the glass to my lips, I drank deeply – *glug glug glug* – and then, *nothing*. Darkness and oblivion. After a dozen or more beers, that small sweet glass of *Jaegermeister* did me in. According to later accounts from eyewitnesses, as I emptied the glass (and I *did* empty it, so, technically, I guess I was – *am* – a man), my eyes rolled back in my head, the glass dropped (someone caught it), my head lolled back toward my shoulders, and I slid slowly down my chair and under the table. (Have you ever heard the expression, "to drink someone under the table"? Well, it's a valid turn of phrase. I know. Been there, done that, so to speak.)

The next morning I woke up in my bunk – a man. A miserably sick and hung-over man, but a man nonetheless. There you have it, kids. My twenty-first birthday memory. I know. I'm lucky I didn't die on the spot of acute alcohol poisoning, something you read about now and then in the newspapers today, usually in a story about fraternity parties or initiation ceremonies. And I'm also lucky I had good friends who pulled my pitiful passed-out form from under the table, poured me into the car and took me back to the barracks and tucked me tenderly into bed. Thanks, guys. And thanks for being there to share in my special day too. (Like a Hallmark greeting card sentiment, no?)

Here's one more Deuce memory I have to share. After last call at the bar, usually around one or two in the morning, I think, it was customary for all the hard-core drinkers who were still there to gather around the jukebox in the Pit for a final song. The old-timers knew how to crank up the noise to max by muscling the jukebox away from the wall and reaching behind it to turn the volume control all the way up. Then we would all stand swaying drunkenly, bellowing at the top of our lungs, along with J. Frank Wilson and the Cavaliers –

Oh where o where can my BAY-bee beee?
The Lord took 'er a-WAYY from meee ...

and so on. That song, "The Last Kiss," was a favorite closer at the Deuce that year, 1965.

Although we continued to enjoy our nights out at the Deuce whenever we could, the last several months of our tour were increasingly taken up by activities related to the Panics.

Red, white and blue Panics banner

Once the Christmas holiday season was over, the guys began rehearsing in earnest, and quickly put together a very respectable repertoire of tunes. In March they began performing publicly on post, at first just in the service club, moving out of the small rehearsal rooms and onto the auditorium stage, where they immediately found a most appreciative GI audience. The word got out that a new band – a *good* one – was in town, and soon after that they were booked for engagements at the enlisted men's club (The Hilltop Club) and the slightly mor elite NCO Club.

Talent-wise, the Panics were at first a mixed bag. Joe Capozzi was the musical mentor of the bunch and usually took the lead in working out the arrangements of songs. As the band began to gel though, it became more of a cooperative venture. Mike Chesley was much more than just a singer, he was a fairly talented musician too (he could play a respectable guitar, bass *and* drums) and often made very useful suggestions on how to put a unique spin on a particular number.

Gene Hedgepeth, while not so talented or "natural" a musician as Joe and Mike, was in many ways the real driving force behind the band, at least in the early days. Gene had stars in his eyes. Like the lines from the later hit song by The Byrds, Gene wanted "to be a rock and roll star." It just took him a little longer to get all the details down in his role as rhythm guitarist. He was often too busy winking and grinning at the girls to actually pay attention to anything so mundane as a chord change. This did not go unnoticed by Joe C, who would turn and glower across the stage at the obliviously smiling Gene every time a chord was muffed. Joe took the music itself and the finished sound very seriously.

Joe also bestowed a nickname on Gene early in their friendship. He called him "Mooch," because it seemed like Gene was always bumming change, gum, food. Like Wimpy, it seemed he was always hungry and forever short of funds, so he borrowed, or "mooched," although (also like Wimpy) he always promised to pay the borrowee back.

The other three band members, Joe R, Chris and Mike, I never really got to know quite as well as I did Joe C and Gene. This was not surprising though. The band itself became a fairly tight entity as the their act began to come together. They were all intent on their music and getting it right. I wasn't a member. I was part of a fringe group of hangers-on and friends who followed the band from club to club or wherever they could get a gig. But I tried to be just a little more than that. I even hung out with them while they were rehearsing, trying not to get in the way, but often unable to restrain myself from recommending new songs or making suggestions as they worked out arrangements. Perhaps my most important contribution was my tendency to stay on top of what was popular or just emerging in the Top 40, a natural part of my lifelong love affair with music. I was a compulsive listener of pop, and was enthralled and fascinated by all the new British music at the time. I prowled the record racks in the PX and the downtown music stores whenever I had a few bucks to spare, and my record collection continued to grow during my year in Germany.

One of the first albums I bought in Germany was the debut effort of The Searchers, with their smash hit, "Needles and Pins" (written, interestingly enough, for you trivia buffs, by Sonny Bono). The song became, just a few months later, part of the Panics

The Panics

first playlist, and one of their fans' favorite dance tunes. It was with "Needles and Pins" that I first found my nearly indispensable function with the Panics, as lyric transcriptionist. I would sit next to my stereo, pad and pen in hand, and play the song. listening intently to the words for a few bars, then I would lift the needle from the grooves while I quickly scribbled down all the words I could remember. I would repeat this painstaking process until I was satisfied I had all the words down correctly. Then I would carefully re-copy the lyrics in a legible manner so all the guys in the band could refer to them as they were learning the song. It probably would have been a lot easier to just go to a newsstand and buy a copy of *Hit Parade* magazine, which carried all the words to the latest hits, but it wouldn't have been nearly as much fun, and what I was doing was, after all, a labor of love – *and,* by the time I was finished writing down the lyrics in this manner, *I* would have them memorized myself. I also payed close attention to the vocal harmonies too, and occasionally I would demonstrate the high and low parts to Gene and Chris and the other guys, who usually worked out background harmonies to Mike's lead vocal. The two Joes were no great shakes as singers, but they often lent their voices to choruses.

Besides doing the transcription, I also brought the records themselves along to the practice sessions at the service club, where

305

I would check out a small record player (*my* instrument) and bring it to the rehearsal room so the guys could hear exactly how the original sounded. I usually only had to do this once for each new song, but in this way I was able to get many of the new songs I liked (and a few *old* ones) onto the Panics playlist. Sometimes it wasn't even a hit, but just a tune I felt had great potential, both in terms of general audience appeal and as a dance number. One engaging tune I convinced the guys to learn was a filler from an album by The Newbeats, whose one and only hit was, of course "(I Like) Bread and Butter." The group's lead vocalist sang everything in a high-pitched falsetto a la Frankie Valli. The Panics never did do "Bread and Butter," but at my suggestion they did their own rendition (with*out* the falsetto) of "Pink Dally Rue," an R&B-flavored tune with largely nonsense lyrics and a driving bouncy beat that just forced you up out of your seat and onto the dance floor. In a time when all of the aspiring local dance bands covered many of the same pop tunes, only the Panics did "Pink Dally Rue." It was obscure enough that I think many of their German fans thought it was original with the Panics.

Yes, *German* fans, because it wasn't long before the Panics outgrew the clubs on post and were ready to *really* go public. But before they could do that, they needed transportation, not just for the guys themselves, but for all the equipment that they had accumulated by this time – the guitars, drum set, bass, amps and speakers, cables, mike stands, mixers and reverb units, etc.

I think it was Gene who took the initiative in this matter, and went out and found a used van. Well, it wasn't really a van. It was a station wagon, and not a real big one either, but it was all the guys could afford. It was a pale blue rust-streaked Opel, with probably a few hundred thousand kilometers already on the odometer when Gene found it. This vehicle wasn't just old and worn out. It even *looked* tired. You remember the show *Let's Make a Deal,* where Monty Hall would give the contestants a choice of the three doors and *maybe,* if they picked the right door, they would *WIN A* NEW *CAR!* But sometimes, if they picked the *wrong* door, there might be, behind door number two, two or three goats – or, behind door number three, a *junk* car. Well, this tired old Opel looked a lot like door number three. But, like I said, the price was right, so Gene and the guys pooled their funds and came up with the money. I'm not

Tim and the Panic Wagon

sure if Gene actually *touched* the car before he bought it. Well, I'm sure he touched it, but I mean he obviously didn't, like run his hands over the body checking for soundness or anything. Because the first time the guys took it out for a spin down the *Autobahn*, an odd thing happened. The Opel tried to fly. And I don't mean it went really fast either. What I mean is, it started to flap its "wings." I know, I know. Cars don't have *wings*, not even cool German cars. The thing was though, both front fenders of the Opel were rusted completely through in a pitted brown line that ran from the windshield level all the way down to the rocker panels just behind the wheel wells. So, when the car began to pick up speed going down the highway, the wind would blow into the wheel wells and

The Panics and the Panic Wagon (Tim Green, roadie on far left)

the fenders would begin to "flap," like a large ungainly bird trying clumsily to take off. This happened at any speed over, say, thirty miles an hour, and seriously compromised the handling of the car. Gene and the rest of the band were pretty upset about this, and I'm pretty sure Gene took a lot of flak about the car he'd picked out. He went to a few junkyards to see about getting new (used) fenders, but the price was too steep, especially since they'd already used all their "disposable" (*hah!*) funds in buying the car. So here's what they finally ended up doing. They fixed the problem with duct tape.

You've probably read and heard about all the things you can fix or cure with duct tape, until it's become kind of a universal joke. But it's true. Gene and Joe and I each "liberated" a roll or two of what was called "army green tape" from our supply room. This tape, if it wasn't actually *duct* tape, was the next best thing, or it may have even been *better* than what we later came to know as duct (or 'duck') tape. It was a heavy cloth-like tape, reinforced with nylon or plastic or maybe even "Kryptonite," since I don't think even Superman could destroy this tape. Anyway, we took these rolls of tape and a couple pairs of scissors and spent part of an afternoon "fixing" that Opel. We patched it crossways and we patched it up and down, and not just on the outside. We even crawled underneath the car and reached up inside the fenders and wire-brushed them out some, and then taped and taped and taped some more. The final result looked like the car had undergone a serious operation and was heavily bandaged. And the bright green "bandages" didn't really complement the pale blue color of the car either. But the operation was a success. Not only did the "patient" survive, but it could now tool down the highway at nearly *fifty* mph before it would start trying to unsheathe its now heavily-bound wings. So the guys adapted. They learned to leave early and drive slowly. They christened it "The Panic Wagon" and had a sign lettered to stick in its back window. The Panics had wheels and were ready to roll.

Larry Migliore
and his Panics business card

I think it was probably, again, Gene, who arranged their first gig at a small dance club in Kassel. Later on, at least for a brief time, the Panics had a manager, who dealt with the clubs and set up engagements. This manager was another east coast Italian, from Long Island, named Larry Migliore. He did a pretty good job for the guys too, and they were probably glad to be freed of the business side of their musical endeavors for a while.

Left to right: Joe Rindini, Mike Chesley, Joe Capozzi,Gene Hedgepeth

There were a number of small venues for dance bands in and around Kassel, but I can't remember the names of most of them, even though I'm pretty sure the Panics made the rounds of most of them. One mid-sized club which engaged the Panics quite early on was the Atlantic Club. I remember that the guys were very excited about being booked there, because it meant that they had jumped almost immediately into the second-tier group of bands in the area. In other words, they took off very quickly and gained nearly instant recognition as one of *the* bands to see. I'm absolutely certain that if the band had not been hampered by the constraints of the army and their shift work schedules that they could have become not just one of the top bands in the Kassel area, but one of the top bands in Germany. They worked hard and they had the talent. They were that good.

One of the other important things the Panics had going for them though was their nationality. They were the only American band around, and their obvious talent was icing on the cake. There were several German rock and roll bands in the Kassel area, and some of them were very good too. Unfortunately for many of them, the most popular music of the time was almost exclusively either British or American in origin, and, although these German bands did their best to duplicate these Top 40 hits, because of their accents and unfamiliarity with British and American idioms, their versions were often wooden-sounding and inferior, if not downright laughable. It was painfully obvious that some of their vocals were no more than phonetic parrotings and the singers hadn't a clue as to what they were singing about.

The guys in the Panics quickly noticed this weakness in their competition. They did a lot of "scouting" of other bands in their early days. They capitalized on their American-ness in a couple of ways. They incorporated more songs by American artists into their playlist, whereas the German bands pretty much stuck to tunes by British artists. The Panics added some Beach Boys numbers, songs like "Help Me Rhonda" and the hauntingly beautiful tone poem, "In My Room," with Chris singing high harmony. They did some old tunes too, like Chuck Berry's "Roll Over Beethoven" and "Nadine," along with other oldies like "Hully Gully" and "Way Down Yonder in New Orleans," the latter a standout double-threat performance by Chris, as he sang lead *and* played the drums. They worked out a driving, letter-perfect killer copy of Roy Orbison's "Pretty Woman," one of the most popular dance tunes of the day, with Joe R thumbing that heavy bass line and Mike's voice soaring and swooping just like Roy's did. And Mike and Chris put together their own powerhouse vocal arrangement of "You've Lost that Lovin' Feeling" that would have made Phil Spector himself sit up and take notice.

Two of Mike's favorite American offerings were "Louie Louie" and "Wooly Bully." I think he had a special affinity for the former song, because it was originally recorded by a band called The Wailers out of the Seattle area, where Mike was from. It became a monster hit, however, by the Kingsmen in 1963, and that was the recorded version that I had. I did my best to transcribe the lyrics from "Louie Louie," but without much success. The inside word was that the famously garbled lyrics were incredibly obscene, and, for a time, the record was even banned on many radio stations while the FCC "investigated" its content. Unfortunately – or perhaps fortunately, depending on your point of view – even the FCC couldn't figure out what the actual words were. I didn't have much luck with Doug Sahm's "Wooly Bully" lyrics either, but it was a wondrously rollicking dance tune, and Mike did a marvelously inventive job of faking the words – on *both* songs, which were always audience favorites.

So, yeah, the Panics capitalized on their American-ness and padded their playlist heavily with U.S. tunes. The other thing they did, and this was purely to have fun, was to fake or add bogus lyrics to recognized tunes. I remember particularly an extra bridge they added to the Kinks tune, "You Really Got Me," in which Chris crooned out an old advertising slogan:

"A-*JAAX*, the *FOAM*-ing detergent,
It's *STRONger* than *DIRT,*
It's *STRONger* than *DIRT!*"

And there was another purely nonsense ditty they put together which had the tender refrain of "I hate your *GUTS,*" which Chris would sing while writhing about on the floor (Mike on drums), apparently wracked by the agonies of unrequited love.

Chris on the floor doing "I Hate Your Guts."

I should probably note again here that, while Mike was the front man and lead vocalist for the Panics, he would often yield the spotlight to someone else. This usually worked fairly smoothly because of the fact that Mike could play "a little" of all the instruments. Playing guitar or bass might have presented a bit of a problem, since Mike was left-handed, but, obviously having run into this before, he already knew how to play them "upside-down." Wherever he filled in though, he did it well.

Everyone in the band did get their turn at being the "star," although some – the two Joes – were a bit shy of the spotlight. Joe R did, I think, a pretty respectable rendition of "Walkin' the Dog," and even Joe C had one number which he sang in a kind of stylized monotone:

"Mah bay-bee drew up
In a bi-ig bla-ack Ca-dil-lac."

Sometimes he would vary "drew up" with "*threw* up" to try to make the other guys smile, a completely unnecessary gesture, since they were all already smiling anyway, just at Joe's singing. The Mooch specialized in singing harmony and adding his voice to the chorus. I can't remember if he sang lead on anything, but he was almost *al*ways singing – and grinning that engaging *I-can't-believe-I'm-a-rock-and-roll-star* grin.

Although American hits were a popular and unique staple in the band's repertoire, they also learned many of the British Invasion hits too. Some of Mike's best performances were taken from Brit hits, including "Doo Wah Diddy," "Game of Love" and "House of the Rising Sun," popularized at the time by Manfred Mann, Wayne Fontana and the Mindbenders, and The Animals, respectively. All things Beatle were also carefully and painstakingly worked out and duplicated. The public demanded it. The Panics didn't just learn the Beatles a-side hits though, tunes like "8 Days a Week," "Can't Buy Me Love," "I Should Have Known Better," "And I Love Her," or "A Hard Day's Night" (which became their closing song for every performance). They learned all those and also a few b-sides and the more musically complex Beatle tunes too, songs like "Yes It Is," "She's a Woman," "I Feel Fine" and "Ticket to Ride." I dutifully transcribed the lyrics to all these tunes, and felt privileged to sit in on their practice sessions as they worked out the arrangements and Joe and Gene deciphered the unusual chord patterns with the weird minors and sevenths that the Beatles often employed in these later compositions. It was a rush for me. I wasn't quite *in* the group, but I was *of* the group. I couldn't play an instrument, but I knew all the words and was learning the arrangements right along with the band, and it felt good.

It didn't take long at all for the Panics to form a regular fan base. Their American-ness was an immediate draw, of course, but their hard work and obvious talent kept the fans coming back

The Panics in stripes.

wherever and whenever they played.

Their "image," or packaging, probably didn't hurt either. The Beatles, with their pre-packaged commercial look (Brian Epstein's work) of neat narrow dark suits and ties and pointy-toed boots had set a certain style that most of the bands of the day tried to duplicate. The Panics look was quite different, primarily due to economic restraints. None of the guys could really afford to go out and buy a tailor-made, or even off-the-rack Carnaby Street-style suit and boots. And Army regulations did not permit shaggy over-the-collar hair styles either (although Chris sometimes pushed the limits a bit, with his long shiny blonde hair). So, striving for *some* kind of uniformity, the guys simply opted for *nearly* identical striped button shirts (or sometimes matching Henley pullovers), dark slacks and shoes, and, of course, standard militarily-correct haircuts (i.e. visible whitewalls around the ears). In this way, with no ties and no long floppy locks or narrow lapels, they managed to project a unique casual *American* image. They looked a *little* like the Beach Boys, but probably a lot more like the Kingston Trio.

In any case, the Panics were *hot* in Kassel in very short order, and very much in demand. I am convinced that they could have been a major act in Germany, and maybe throughout Europe, if it hadn't been for the constraints of their "day jobs." But the army wasn't exactly a job you could just quit in order to concentrate on your "art." So the guys had to schedule their gigs in conjunction with their days off. Since they didn't always work the same schedule, this wasn't always a simple matter, and often involved switching shifts with someone else or wheedling favors from a supervisor or platoon sergeant. But somehow they managed, and perhaps the relative infrequency of their appearances actually served to whet their fans' appetites and intensify the enthusiasm when the band finally did take the stage again.

Program for the Tenne Club, April, 1965

By the spring of 1965, the Panics were probably one of the top three bands in the greater Kassel area. The top band at the time was, unquestionably, John O'Hara and the Playboys, a group from Scotland that was touring constantly throughout West Germany, not just around Kassel. They had even headlined at the Star Club in Hamburg several times. Not only were the Playboys an extremely talented and tight-knit musical group, but O'Hara himself was a consumate showman, with a fantastic Tom Jones kind of voice. Like Jones, John O'Hara knew instinctively how to work the crowd, that is, he made all the ladies' hearts go pitty-pat, and made all the men envious. Also like Jones, he often began his performance in a full tux, then gradually dressed down, losing the tie, coat and vest as the evening progressed, perspiring copiously and always emoting effectively to the girls gathered at the stage apron, and he never *ever* muffed a lyric or missed hitting a note. Moreover, his performances could often be really over-the-top scenery-chewing *crazy,* as he swung across the stage or out over the screaming fans on a rope, or climbed the heavy curtains at the sides of the stage. O'Hara also played the saxophone, and would join forces with the band's regular sax man, a black West Indian, in rocking instrumentals like "Watermelon Man" or their signature break tune, "Jumpin' with Symphony Sid." In short, John O'Hara and his Playboys put on one *hell* of a show, and their fans adored them. Their British-ness certainly didn't hurt, but those guys were just plain *GOOD!* Even the Panics – and the Panics' fans – *loved* the Playboys.

The other group that completed the top band triumvirate in Kassel was *Die Kettels*, a home-grown German combo. Instrumentally, the group was very tight and talented, but their vocal renditions of the current English-language hits (which were absolute *musts* on any dance band's playlist) were often a bit stiff and not quite on the mark, since English was not their first language. Most of the guys in the Kettels did speak passable English, but not quite well enough to do real justice to the phrasing, slang catch phrases and other nuances found regularly in many pop song lyrics. Because of this, the Panics had a certain edge on them. And we didn't quite understand the significance of their *name* either. The Kettels, to us, conjured up visions of *Ma and Pa Kettle On the Farm* and other films of that series that starred Marjorie Main and Percy Kilbride. It just didn't *work* as the name of a rock and roll band. The Panics' name, on the other hand, at least brought to mind a sense of frantic excitement that the band tried to live up to in their performances. (The actual origin of the name came from an obscure instrumental called "Panic Button," which the guys tried to work into every gig they played as their signature tune.)

As one of the recognized top bands in the area, the Panics played the top venue in town, the Tenne Club, a huge hall with a high ornate stage and an enormous dance floor that was always full.

Battle of the Bands notice

Panics
playing the
Lumpenball

It was an enormously popular night spot, perhaps *the* place for young people to congregate and dance in 1965. That spring the spirits flowed freely there and love – or at least *lust* – was in the air

Springtime in Germany was – *is* – a special time, particularly for the young. There is a long season observed there called *Fasching*, which actually begins shortly after New Year's, but gets really crazy the last few weeks and days before Ash Wednesday. It's probably the Deutsche equivalent of Mardi Gras, with many of the same customs, like electing a king and queen based on ugliness rather than beauty. There are parades and festivals, and dances with masks and costumes, like the *Lumpenball,* where the men dress in toga-like sheeted costumes and the women wear masks. The Panics were part of all this madness one night when they were part of the musical entertainment at a kind of "Battle of the Bands" at the *Stadthalle,* and they even donned the costumes and got into the spirit of it all.

There is a traditional song that is often heard during the last few frantic days of *Fasching* that goes like this:

Du darst mich lieben fuer drei Tage,
Du musst mich kuessen, das ist deine Pflicht.
Du kannst mir alles lieb uns shoene sagen,
Doch nach dem Namen frag' mich bitte bitte nicht.

It doesn't translate well into English, but essentially it is an ode that glorifies wild and joyous no-strings anonymous sex. It's just one more indication that during *Fasching* there is an unofficial recognition and acceptance of a certain loosening of morals. In other words, the guys get goosey and the girls get loosey, and they all use the same excuse – *It's* Fasching*!* Lust is indeed in the air. And I was there.

When you're only twenty or twenty-one years old, it's great to be alive in Germany in *Fasching* time. I'm not sure I ever heard exactly how the word *Fasching* translates, but it looks and sounds a lot like *fucking*, so maybe that's close enough, at least as a GI translation. The girls were there, out in force, and they were willing, no questions asked. Moral standards were, at least temporarily, suspended.

So, Yes, Virginia, there was sex in Germany. And unlike sex in Sinop, there were often *two* people involved, and an actual *exchange* of bodily fluids, not the just the voiding and disposal of one's own built-up juices. Does this mean I became "sexually active" during this time? No, that would probably be overstating the case, implying an on-going regularity of sexual activity. All it really means is that I did get laid a few times that spring, thanks to *Fasching*. And those few isolated experiences did serve to change forever the way I perceived girls and women. That proverbial pedestal was toppled when I realized that a girl could be just as sexually "hungry" as I was, that she had "needs" too, and that with a small *Fasching*-fueled push, she wouldn't hesitate to satisfy those needs. I learned a lot that spring, including the fact that it *is* possible, with a little mutual cooperation, for two people to have sex in the back seat of a VW Beetle, even if the guy is six foot five. Where there's a will there's a way, and where there's lust there's a lay. The *Fasching* atmosphere was heavy with musk. Everyone was a predator, and not just the men either. It was an eye-opening and educational time for this former altar boy from Reed City.

It certainly didn't hurt either, that I was seen as being "with the band," if not actually *in* the band, because the "groupies" began to gather quickly once the Panics started to attain prominence on the Kassel music scene. There was always a delectable-looking group of regulars – Karens and Ingas, Ursulas, Helgas and Elsas – who followed the band from place to place, wherever they played. Some of these girls were also regulars at the Deuce, or became regulars

Gene

319

Mike with 2 admirers

there after attaching themselves to the band. Luckily for me, there were more girls than there were band members, so I guess you could say I took advantage of the "overflow," because I don't think any of the guys in the band were exactly living like monks during those flush and fleshy times. Mike always seemed to have a girl on each arm, Chris was usually surrounded by blonde *Frauleins*, Gene's loopy grin drew girls like flies to honey, and even the two normally shy Joes got their fair share of feminine attention. It was, in short, a heady and glorious time for all of us.

It was also about this same time that a near calamity almost scuttled the band's quickly-rising star. At a time when the Panics had a full calendar of playdates stretching several weeks into the future, they suddenly lost their front man. Mike Chesley was riding in the front seat of a Mercedes taxi cab one night in downtown Kassel when the car broadsided another taxi. Seatbelts were practically unheard of in those times, and the impact threw Mike into the windshield, leaving him with a concussion, a fractured jaw and some broken and loosened teeth. Although he recovered fairly quickly from the concussion, his broken jaw was wired shut and he was forced to stand down from his bandstand duties for at least a couple of weeks while his jaw and teeth mended.

The Panics were, quite literally, in a panic. This could be the end of them. How could they meet their obligations and play the already-scheduled dates over the next few weeks? None of the other band members actually knew *all* the song lyrics across their now extensive repertoire. What the hell were they going to *do*?

Yup, you guessed it. Enter the hero. It was *TRANSCRIPTION MAN* to the rescue! The Beach Boys had an instrumental tune on an album back then called "Carl's Big Chance." Well this was "Bazzett's Big Break." The circumstances were crappy, true, but, because I had been there from the very beginning, had actually written out all the lyrics and practically taught them to the band, and had been there for virtually every performance, singing along in the crowd, I was it. I was the solution. This is the story then, kids, of how your daddy became – albeit only briefly – a bona fide *rock and roll star*.

I think I maybe got to rehearse with the band just once before the next scheduled performance, which was at the Atlantic Club. Because it was the Panics performing that night, the place was absolutely packed. The band's star was burning brightly and the fans were anxious to see and hear them again, but there was also, I think, an element of curiosity at work that night. Word had apparently leaked out about Mike's accident and temporary incapacitation, so the crowd was hovering about the bandstand early, waiting to see how the band would handle the situation.

I had always thought I could do this, had thought I was ready, but when I saw that capacity crowd gathering round, I was suddenly scared *shitless*! I couldn't *do this*! What in the *hell* had I been *think*ing? My knees were actually shaking and my throat was dry. And yet this was my moment.

The band opened the set with their signature instrumental, "Panic Button," giving me a few minutes to get myself together. Then I was on. We segued into the mid-tempo Terry Stafford tune, "Suspicion," and I started singing – *sort* of. My throat was constricted and my voice came out sounding tiny and distant, even though I upped the mic volume and strained desperately to project my voice the way Mike always did so effortlessly. Sensing my panic, Gene and Chris chimed in and joined me in singing the song, which helped. Finally my throat began to relax and air rushed into my lungs. I began to calm down. By the time that song was over, I was able to sing normally, and, a bit more confidently now, we launched quickly into "I Should Have Known Better" (hmm ...

appropriate, no?), one of my favorite Beatle tunes. I could hear myself now, and decided I didn't sound *too* bad. I was no John O'Hara or Mike Chesley, but at least I was hitting the notes – and I knew the words. My *memory* didn't fail me. I still had that slightly nasal country-western-tinged Ricky-Hank flavor to everything I sang, but it would have to do. No one was *boo*-ing me and the dance floor was full of gyrating happy couples. The liquor and beer were flowing, so the club management was happy. The band seemed visibly relieved and relaxed now, and I was suddenly suffused with such a rush of happiness and pure *joy,* that I could barely contain myself. I knew now just how Little Richard felt when he sang: "I got that *JOY JOY JOY JOY* down in my heart!" This was just so much *fuck-ing FUN!*

And by God, there were the *girls*, the groupies, gathered around the bandstand like they always were, only this time they were looking up at *me!* This time I wasn't just *with* the band. I was *in* the band. I was *part* of it. At *this* time, in *this* place, I was suddenly a *star*, and I was flat *loving* it! The dance floor was still full when we roared next into "Roll Over Beethoven," and it stayed full throughout the evening until we finally closed with a hoarse but heartfelt "It's Been a Hard Day's Night." Mike was momentarily down, but the Panics were still here, still on top of things. We could get through this minor setback.

Tim's big break.

Ticket stub to Tenne. April 29, 1965.

And we did. I fronted the band one more time the following week, at a smaller club, packed again, so I guessed my vocals hadn't damaged the band's reputation too badly. I had been hoping to sing at the *Tenne* the following week, but by then Mike was champing at the bit, wired-up jaw be damned, to get back onstage, and the *Tenne* was considered the pinnacle venue of the region, so I couldn't really blame him. I had had my turn in the spotlight and had helped the band to survive. After that I held an unofficial honorary membership in the band. I was like the "fifth Beatle" for the Panics. By now it's possible that some of the guys may have even forgotten this tiny chapter in the Panics' story, but I will never forget it. As kids today say, *It was totally awe-some!*

I got one more short turn onstage a couple months later. I had written a song. Or rather I wrote a few verses of simple lyrics and had a vague notion of a melody to put with them, so Joe Capozzi sat down with me one day and added some chords, a bridge, and even a brief guitar solo. It was called "Please Love Me Again." The melody, I realized later, was very close to that of the then-popular "Don't Let the Sun Catch You Crying," by Gerry and the Pacemakers. The song itself has been long since lost, but I can still remember a few lines –

"Please love me again
Like you did before
If you'll just ease this pain
Oh I'll never ask more ..."

Once we'd gotten it all down and practiced it a few times, Joe and I played a rough cut for the band, and the other guys liked it enough to work out a full band treatment. The next time the band played the *Tenne* I made my final appearance as a Panic, just to do that song (which was, I might add, the *only* original composition the Panics ever did). Mike graciously yielded me the microphone so I could croon my pitiful paean of lost love.

Was my song simple, copycat, insipid? Sure it was. But did it get me girls? You bet your sweet ass it did! My semi-inclusion in the group upped my stock considerably and that last summer in Germany was a good one for me, as it undoubtedly was for all the boys in the band. I didn't exactly become a predator, but I did leave myself open to new and pleasurable experiences, and enjoyed them whenever they presented themselves. Life was good.

* * * * *

In spite of all these pleasant distractions, however, I did have other, larger and more far-reaching things on my mind too. Back in January my brother Bob had gotten married. He and Maureen had been going together for a few years by then, so it came as no big surprise. My best friend, Keith Eichenberg, had married his high school sweetheart, Dianne Lindsey, the previous fall and was holding down a well-paying job at the Reed City Tool & Die. In June Bob graduated from the Pharmacy program at Ferris State and he and Maureen moved to Illinois, where he'd gotten a job with Walgreen. My brother Bill had finally finished college at Michigan Tech and was back home sending out resumes and looking for a job. Other high school chums were already juniors in college and some were also already engaged or married. I heard about all these things in letters from home, from my folks and friends. So, although I *was* having a good time, I also began to feel a kind of creeping vague anxiety that I was somehow being left behind in the larger scheme of things.

All these people were engaged in what seemed to me to be more important, life-changing endeavors, getting ahead and "getting on" with their lives, while I simply seemed to be doing the same things over and over, marking time. I didn't know if other people in circumstances similar to mine felt the same way, but the feeling persisted, and it gradually became more and more disturbing to me, until I finally decided I had to do something about it. Probably sometime around May or June then, I initiated official paperwork at the personnel office to secure an "early out" from the army in order to attend college.

I was due to be separated from the service in late September of 1965, so I applied for a thirty-day early out, which would get me home in late August, so I could get enrolled at Ferris for the fall semester. While it was true that I still wasn't sure what I wanted to do with my life, I continued to chafe under the unpleasant yoke of military rules and regulations. I knew that I wanted out and wanted to get on with my life, whatever that meant. At the time I think I was filled with that typical youthful sense of limitless opportunity and the naive certainty that whatever I did would be important and would "make a difference."

In the meantime, there were other unforeseen developments happening back home. My dad sold his grain elevator and feed business in June and "retired." He was only 55, but he'd apparently done all right financially over the years and had had enough of the daily grind (no mill-type pun intended). None of his sons seemed even remotely interested in carrying on in the family business he had spent twenty years building, a fact which I'm sure was very disappointing to him, although I never heard him complain about it. At any rate, Dad sold both the Kent Elevator and the Evart Milling Company to his younger business partner, Loren Gerber. Then he bought plane tickets for himself and Mom, and, after arranging for Keith and Dianne Eichenberg to stay at the house and look after Mary and Chris, off they flew to see the sights of Europe and to visit two of their sons, Rich and me.

Rich Bazzett washing his jeep at St. Andreasburg. 1964

Rich was stationed at St. Andreasburg, a small outstation in the Hartz Mountains not far from Kassel and Rothwesten, but we didn't really see much of each other during the year I spent there. He had his life and friends and routine, and I had mine. But when Mom and Dad flew into Amsterdam on KLM, Rich arranged to pick them up there and took some time off to show them around the area a bit, being the ever-dutiful son, and maybe still feeling a bit guilty about abandoning the ship of Dad's business.

When Dad decided to do something like touring Europe, he didn't do it halfway. He planned to see as much of the continent as possible, and, with Rich's assistance, he purchased a car near Kassel, a brand-new red VW 1500 stationwagon, a model that wasn't even available in the U.S. Driving their new car, he and Mom traveled all over Europe over the next six weeks, making stops in France, Switzerland, Austria, Italy and Scandinavia before shipping the car back to the states. Then they flew to London and on to Dublin, where they rented a car and spent another week rambling through the narrow lanes and across the green hills of the land of their ancestors, staying at rustic B&B's throughout Ireland and spending their evenings swapping stories with the natives at local pubs. Of all the places they visited on this, their first European tour (because they did go back again), Ireland was the place that most remained in their hearts.

Mom and Dad with Rich

Rothwesten Mess Hall

I got to spend a couple of days with Mom and Dad around Rothwesten and Kassel before they set off on their grand tour. I hadn't seen them in nearly two years, so it was a welcome reunion, but it also served to increase that anxious sense of time passing me by. I began to feel, for the first time since my arrival in Germany, a vague feeling of homesickness, even though Mom and Dad were both right there with me at the time. I showed them through our barracks and where I lived, and even took them for a meal in the mess hall to assure them that I was being well fed.

They also came and visited me one afternoon over at the service club where the band was practicing, up on the stage in the auditorium for a change. Mom says she still remembers coming up the stairs and hearing my voice, singing. For some reason Mike wasn't there that day, so I was filling in on a few vocals while the band rehearsed. I was singing our up-tempo rendition of "Moon River" (a favorite song of Mom's, who is a big Andy Williams fan), when Mom and Dad came in. They stayed a while to listen, so I managed to coax the guys to do a Rick Nelson song with me, "Poor Little Fool." Then we did "Stagger Lee" and Sam Cooke's "Bring It On Home to Me" and even my original song. (I was taping that day and got several of the songs recorded on a recent purchase, a small portable reel-to-reel *Uher*. I brought the recorder and tapes home with me, but somehow, somewhere it all got lost, so none of my short-lived musical career survives.) Mom was thrilled at seeing her "boy" on stage and singing, and has ever since retained a mistaken impression that I was *in* the band and was *the* lead singer, a notion I confess I've never tried very hard to correct.

Then Dad and Mom were gone again, off to tour the continent. I fell back into my regular routine of work and play, but it never felt quite the same. I had set certain bureaucratic wheels in motion that seemed to speed up the very tempo of my life. June soon turned to July, and although I tried frantically to stuff all the pleasure and enjoyment I could into those final weeks, there just never seemed to be enough time to do all that I wanted to do.

In July I was promoted to Spec 5 and I sleepwalked through the necessary motions of getting the new rank patches sewn on my uniforms, but it hardly seemed important anymore. In spirit I was already gone and rank seemed laughably unimportant by then. Joe and Tom and Dusty all got their promotions too and we did the requisite celebrating, but at the same time we also poo-pooh-ed the importance of this so-called military milestone. Promotions were only important to "lifers," and soon we would all be civilians again. *FTA* forever, and all that.

By the end of July my early-out request came back stamped *APPROVED*. I wasn't sure anymore that it was really what I wanted, but it was too late. The administrative wheels continued to grind inexorably forward as I alternately eagerly anticipated and then dreaded my day of departure.

Other forces were also at work in the world during this time, forces that could well have changed my life. Almost a year before, on August 1, 1964, torpedo boats of North Viet Nam had attacked an American destroyer, the *USS Maddox*, in the Gulf of Tonkin, prompting the U.S. Congress to immediately draft a resolution which was to lead to a massive buildup of American troops in Southeast Asia. By the summer of 1965 that buildup was picking up steam as the Pentagon poured tens of thousands of additional troops into the quagmire of Viet Nam. The Gulf of Tonkin Resolution taken by Congress in 1964 had barely been a blip on our personal radars in Sinop and then Rothwesten, where we continued to go about our daily duties and have fun in our off-duty time. But then in August of 1965 persistent rumors began to circulate that all active duty military personnel might be involuntarily extended due to the troop buildup in Viet Nam. *That* registered, not just with me, but with all my friends, who were due to separate from the service in the next two months.

Within our small circle, we had never paid much attention to what was going on in Viet Nam, or even thought much about it at all. Sheltered by our own ignorance, we figured, hey, war was grunt work. They didn't need guys like us ASA types in Viet Nam. That was all for the infantry and the Marines. Boy, were we wrong. Ignorance really *is* bliss some times, I guess.

Years later I found out that the very first American casualty in Viet Nam was an ASA soldier. He was Spec 4 James T. Davis. Like us, he had received his AIT at Fort Devens, but as a DF (direction finding) specialist. After that he was posted to Viet Nam as part of the U.S. advisory force there and assigned to the 3rd Radio Research Unit at Tan Son Nhut Air Base. Davis was acting as an advisor for a nine-man DF squad of South Vietnamese troops when their truck was ambushed by Viet Cong. All ten men were killed. It was December 22, 1961. I was still in high school. I had never heard of Viet Nam.

In any case, the extension rumor proved to be mostly false. (Only a small number of Marines were actually involuntarily extended.) By mid-August I was officially ROD ("relieved of duty) and spent the usual requisite few days trudging from door-to-door all over the base carrying a clipboard full of clearing-post forms to be signed and/or initialed by every major, minor and petty official imaginable. I packed everything I couldn't fit into my duffel bag into plywood and cardboard boxes and schlepped them over to the transportation office to be shipped home. I spent long daytime hours sitting in our empty room while my roommates were at work, feeling torn and confused and more than a bit superfluous.

I spent one miserable night saying good-bye to a sweet girl who had attached herself to me over the past few weeks, listening to her cry, and trying half-heartedly to comfort her with false words of love and empty promises that we both knew I would never keep. She was a Deuce girl. I was pretty sure I was only one in a long line of GI boyfriends. I had even known the guy before me, who had rotated back to the states a few months before. I figured there would be someone else as soon as I was gone, so I didn't feel too guilty about taking what I could get while I could.

The last few days were, in many ways, truly awful. I wanted to go home, but I also wanted to stay. Most of my friends would all be getting out of the service within the next month or two, but I was the only one of our group that was leaving in August. I hated the thought of leaving all by myself. But the paperwork was done. My separation was non-negotiable by this point, and I was due on campus at Ferris in just a matter of days to get registered for classes. There was no going back now.

So finally, on a grey rainy morning (it *fig*ured) in the waning days of August, I said good-bye to all my roomies – Joe, Tom, Dusty, Bill, Leroy and Donnie. They left for work and I caught a shuttle bus into Kassel and boarded a train to Frankfurt. Most of that day is now forgotten, but I know I got onto a trembling old prop-job aircraft of Saturn Airlines a few hours later and took off into the lowering skies over Germany.

My flight made one stop, at Shannon Field in Dublin, where we had a three- or four-hour layover. I wandered into the airport souvenir shop and, on an impulse, I bought a carved wooden crucifix for my Grandma Bazzett. I knew she would appreciate it all the more because it came from Ireland. And maybe, just *may*be, this purchase was a subconscious attempt on my part to start getting back to being the "good Catholic boy" I had once been not so very long ago. I was, at any rate, suddenly painfully aware, as I stood there in the gift shop holding that crucifix, that I had probably not attended Mass or received Holy Communion more than half a dozen times in the past year. Shocked and vaguely ashamed at this realization, I made a silent vow to myself to try to do better, and to get my sinful ass back to church.

The flight back to the states was long, but uneventful. We landed at McGuire Air Force Base in New Jersey. It was late on a Friday afternoon by the time I dragged my duffel tiredly into the personnel section, where a bored-looking sergeant glanced over my orders and told me I'd have to come back on Monday morning, and sent me over to a nearby supply room where I was issued some bedding and directed to the transient barracks. I slept there for the next three nights, experiencing an unsettling feeling of *deja vu,* as my stay there reminded me of the first night I slept on an army bunk in the transient barracks at Fort Wayne in Detroit nearly three years before. This unsettled rather creepy feeling only increased when I learned, quite by accident, from overheard snatches of conversations between my bunkmates, that several of them were "Section 8's," that is they were receiving bad conduct, undesirable or dishonorable discharges for various offenses ranging from insubordination and striking a superior officer to rape and murder. A few of them had just been released from the U.S. military prison in Mannheim. Boy, was I in good company. My last night there I slept with one eye open and my watch and wallet stuffed into my pillowcase.

I filled the empty hours that weekend wandering the base, browsing through the big PX and going to the movies, and somehow survived until Monday morning. The personnel section quickly processed our orders and loaded several of us into a van that transported us to to Fort Hamilton in Brooklyn, where I received plane tickets and was also given a final pay, which included payment for nearly two months of unused leave. With a few hundred bucks in my pocket I felt rich. I was then quickly and summarily debriefed and officially separated from the army. I was a civilian again. Well, not completely, since I was technically *re-assigned* to the inactive reserves. I was still dressed in my wrinkled summer khaki uniform.

The army gave me a ride to Idlewild Airport (or was it JFK by then?) where I was to catch a flight to Detroit. Of course I had to wait a couple hours, but I stayed put in the airport. There was no way I was gonna miss *this* flight. Later that afternoon I landed at Detroit Metro. After making a few inquiries, I learned that I could fly right into Reed City if I first flew to Grand Rapids. So I took a limo ride from Metro to Willow Run Airport over near Ypsilanti. From there I took a short hop across to Grand Rapids. A few more hours of waiting ensued, since the the next North Central Airlines "Blue Goose" flight to Reed City wasn't until nearly 9 PM. The flight was actually to Traverse City with a stop at Miller Airport in Reed City. I think there were only about six or seven passengers on the flight, and when we touched down in Reed City I was the only one who got off.

It was already pretty dark as I trudged tiredly across the the tarmac dragging my duffel bag behind me. I hadn't phoned ahead or told anyone I was coming home that day, so I expected I would have to call my folks to come and get me. But as I approached the terminal a big middle-aged guy in a sport shirt and slacks came out to greet me.

He shook my hand with a friendly, "Welcome home, soldier. What's your name and where are you headed?"

Exhausted, I told him my name.

"Why, you must be one of Ellis's boys," he responded. "Come on. I'll give you a ride home."

He led me out to the parking lot, empty except for a brand-new-looking shiny Cadillac sedan. He took me over to it, opened the trunk, took my bag from me and threw it in.

"Let's go," he said. So I opened the passenger-side door and eased my tired body down into the soft leather seat, and we were off.

The car headed south down the familiar route of 131 and across the bridge where the highway turned into Chestnut Street. We cruised slowly through town, past the darkened storefronts, then Dobben's Chevrolet, the Dairy Queen, Delbert Stanton's Shell station. We turned right on West Church. Two blocks up the street the long sleek car nosed left into the bottom of our sloping driveway, tucked between Gordon's and Peterson's houses, and purred softly up the grade until it stopped in the circle in front of our garage.

The driver got out and popped open the trunk and handed me my bag. I thanked him sleepily and turned to go in, but Dad and Mom were already coming out the door, their faces wreathed in smiles of surprise and delight. Mom caught me up in a hug while Dad went over and shook my Good Samaritan driver's hand and exchanged a few quiet words with him, then the Caddy drove quietly away.

Dad turned and shook my hand, and said excitedly, "Do you know who that was?"

I suddenly realized that I hadn't even asked the man's name, so I shook my head stupidly. "No. Who was it?"

"That was Jim Miller. He owns the airport and Miller Industries too. That was some chauffeur you had!" Dad exclaimed, chuckling and beaming at me.

I nodded my head in agreement and, stretching, looked up at the star-filled summer sky. It was August 25, 1965. I had been gone for two years. Upon my return I was politely chauffeured directly to my door by the town's wealthiest and most respected citizen, who shook my hand, helped me with my bag, and welcomed me back. This could only happen in Reed City.

I was home.

AFTERWORD

I spent a lot of time on the telephone and the internet while I was writing this book trying to locate as many of the guys as I could. But it has been forty years or more, so I couldn't find everyone. Below is a listing of the guys I did find which I offer as a kind of "Where Are They Now" addendum. I'm still looking for some of the other guys, but if I don't find them I'm hoping maybe someday they'll run across this book, read it, and call me.

Mike Campbell is retired from the Kellogg Company and lives in East Leroy, Michigan. He is married with three children.

Donnie Center is retired from the U.S. Forest Service and lives on a small farm near Campton, Kentucky. He is married and has three children.

Jim Claunch is a warehouse and shipping supervisor for Dayton Tire in Oklahoma City. He lives in Newcastle, Oklahoma, is married and has three children.

Bill Couture has his own business as a real estate appraiser and lives in Petoskey, Michigan. He is married and has four children.

Jim Farra is in a business partnership with his brother in the Atlanta area. He is a widower and lives in Tucker, Georgia.

Tom Gordon has been a police officer and is a clinical psychologist. He is currently the Director of the Department of Human Services for Oakland County and lives in Rochester, Michigan. He is married and has two children.

Doug Hura is retired from a career in management and lives in Grosse Ile, Michigan. He is married and has three children.

Dick Kuhn is the mayor of Gibraltar, Michigan. He is married and has three children.

Larry Migliore is a senior business analyst for Information Services for Madison Square Garden and Radio City Music Hall. He is married with four children and lives on Long Island in Wantagh, New York.

Lynn Pontz is a realtor and partner in a property management company in Ludington, Michigan. He is married and has two children.

Larry Sanders worked as a building engineer for the public schools in Marysville, Michigan, where he is now retired. He is married and has three children.

Al Trott is a hydraulics firm technician and lives in Hudson, Ohio. He is married with three children.

Norm Yurong is retired from the Hawaii Metropolitan Police and lives in Kaneohe, Hawaii. He is married and has two children.

THE PANICS

Joe Capozzi is retired from a career in the electronics industry (IBM and Fujitsu). He lives in Las Vegas, is married and has three children.

Mike Chesley is a retired computer systems engineer and lives in Port Hadlock, Washington. He is married and has two children.

Gene Hedgepeth has his own business servicing high-end appliances and lives in Mountaintop, Pennsylvania. He is married with three children.

Joe Rindini is the general manager of a retail automotive store and lives in Buzzards Bay, Massachusetts. He is married with two children.

Chris Musser is the used car manager for a large auto dealership in State College, Pennsylvania. He is married with three children.

ACKNOWLEDGEMENTS

Once again, I am especially grateful to my son, Scott, for his sterling and professional efforts in putting this book all together for me. Layout, design, cover, dealing with the printers – he does it all. I am also most grateful to my wife, Terri, for giving me room to write and for her continued love, understanding and patience. I couldn't do any of this without her. Thanks too to my mother, Daisy Bazzett, for her careful proof-reading of the text and for her generous, from-the-heart introduction.

The photos and other memorabilia in thebook were drawn from my own collection and also from those of Daisy Bazzett, Mike Campbell, Joe Capozzi, Mike Chesley, and Larry Migliore. Thanks to everyone for sharing.

I would also like to thank the following people for their help and support in the preparation, promotion and distribution of both this book and my first book: Lynn Anderson, Carol Andres, Graden Benzing, Elizabeth Kane Buzzelli, Jim Crees, Maury Dean, Jeannette Fleury, Tom and Char Gordon, Ronald Jager, Elizabeth Marek, Jim and Mary Murnik, Ron Neal, B.J. Northon, Phyllis Obermeier, Neil A. Patten, Tom Rademacher, Amy Reynolds, Bill Smith, Derald and Bonnie Stanton, Doug and Anne Stanton, Amy Van Ooyen, and Mary Jo Zazueta.

A heartfelt thanks also goes out to the people of Reed City for their continued generous and wholehearted support of my first efforts at writing.

And finally I offer special thanks and greetings to all the guys I served with, both those that are in the book and those that are not. I hope this little book finds its way to you somehow and that you enjoy reading it as much as I did writing it. Thanks for the memories, guys.

"ASA all the way!"

ABOUT THE AUTHOR

Timothy James Bazzett has worked as a mill hand, a tree trimmer, a grocery stockboy and bagger, a drugstore clerk, a dishwasher, a school custodian, a natural gasline maintenance worker, and a teamster dockworker. He taught English for five years at Monroe County Community College and spent eight years in the U.S. Army. He is now retired from the Department of Defense and lives with his wife and two dogs in Michigan, where he continues to try to reinvent himself as a writer.

Reed City Boy

Take a trip back in time to the way things were fifty years ago. Tim Bazzett's rambling memoir of his boyhood in Reed City will most certainly make you laugh, and might make you cry. It's all here – the work, the play, the frustrations and joys of growing up working-class and Catholic in the heart of small-town America. Anyone who has ever been there will chuckle, remember and relate to *Reed City Boy.*

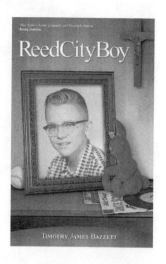

"For anyone who has ever thought about living in a small town– where most people, it's true, do know your name–Tim Bazzett has written the perfect book. For those who grew up in small towns, in places like Reed City (where I was born), this tale is a reminder of those lost spring afternoons when the redwing blackbirds called down by the river, and the smell of the creosote bridge was in the air, with your whole life ahead of you. This book is funny, poignant, and blazingly honest."

Doug Stanton
Best Selling Author of *In Harm's Way*

"Bazzett tells all with a witty, sometimes hilarious, style so often missing from memoir writing. ... A very American boy's life [in] whimsical essays written with a sense of joy and pride. ... This is the kind of book I wish my dad or grandfather had written. I would know them better now."

Elizabeth Kane Buzzelli
Traverse City Record-Eagle

"Bazzett manages to capture the magic and mystery as well as all the quirks and foibles of growing up in Small Town U.S.A. ... This is a fun book! Well worth the read."

Jim Crees
Pioneer News Network

"The best autobiography I have read in years. ... Paints a picture with a fine artist's brush. ... *Reed City Boy* has universal appeal [and] could easily become a best-seller."

Dr. Maury Dean
Pop Musicologist and author of
Rock and Roll Gold Rush and *The Rock Revolution*

"It ought to be required reading for every self-absorbed, video game-addicted, non-chore performing youngster ... *Reed City Boy* captures a certain bygone warmth. ... It honors growing up in small-town America [and depicts] a life that might be defined as a melding of Opie, Beaver and Dobie."

Tom Rademacher
Grand Rapids Press

"A wonderful, touching and honest memoir that will make many smile in empathy as they remember the tortured rites of adolescence. ... A terrific read. I can't wait for the sequel!"

Dr. Neil A. Patten
Ferris State University , Professor of Communications

"Delightful! ... Touching, funny, and infused with a love of family, friends and, certainly, Reed City. ... Refreshingly devoid of the usual anger and angst associated with memories of one's youth. ... Write on!"

Dr. Thomas Gordon
Director of Human Services for Oakland County, Michigan

"Bazzett shares his memories of growing up in Reed City, attending Catholic boarding school in Grand Rapids in the 1950s and working at the local A&P grocery store."
Lansing State Journal

"Pays tribute to small town life."
Cadillac News

"A good, honest, and straightforward portrait. ... A touching story."
Ronald Jager
Author of *Eighty Acres*

"'Don't tell Mom, OK?' In *Reed City Boy* Tim Bazzett tells all, making his parents proud and leaving his readers anxiously awaiting his next book, which we certainly hope will not be his last."
Amy J. Van Ooyen
Author of *Transplants* and Michigan's U.P. Writer of the Year

ReedCityBoy

Part 1

To order send check or money order for $14.95 made payable to TJ Bazzett to:

PO Box 282
Reed City, MI 49677-0282

(Michigan residents add 6% sales tax)

For more information, visit us online at:
www.rathole.com/ReedCityBoy

SoldierBoy

Part 2

To order send check or money order for $16.00 made payable to TJ Bazzett to:

PO Box 282
Reed City, MI 49677-0282

(Michigan residents add 6% sales tax)

For more information, visit us online at:
www.rathole.com/SoldierBoy

Pinhead

Part 3

To order send check or money order for $16.00 made payable to TJ Bazzett to:

PO Box 282
Reed City, MI 49677-0282

(Michigan residents add 6% sales tax)

For more information, visit us online at:
www.rathole.com/Pinhead

3749661R00215

Made in the USA
San Bernardino, CA
22 August 2013